Completion

Stitching Together Life's Journey

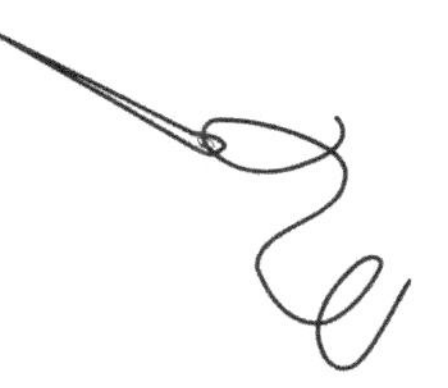

by

Sheila R. Burns-Owens

Watersprings PUBLISHING

Completion: Stitching Together Life's Journey
Published by Watersprings Publishing,
a division of Watersprings Media House, LLC.
P.O. Box 1284 Olive Branch, MS 38654
www.waterspringspublishing.com

Contact the publisher for bulk orders and permission requests.

Printed in the United States of America.

ISBN-13: 979-8-9894494-3-9

Dedication

This book Completion is first dedicated to my Lord and Savior, Jesus Christ, who created me and allowed me to be me.

Secondly, to my husband, Willie Curlee Owens, who continues to love me and put up with me through it all. He also did just about all the driving during our road trips. Traveling has been physically demanding, but he has flown, cruised, and driven through it all.

To my parents for the blueprints that they have laid out and their unconditional love.

To my two offsprings, grandchildren, family, and friends who have been taking this journey with me for the last 65 years, wherever you jumped on in my timeline of life,

I thank God that you did not jump off.

May God Continue to Bless You All!

Table of Contents

Introduction

Completion. What is Completion? My mother often started sentences with, "If I can help someone…" because helping was a big part of her nature. I want this book to help many somebodies. This book is about life after retirement. It's not a book for only retirees or those close to retirement. Just like twenty, thirty, and forty-somethings should be investing in their retirement plans, this book should encourage, prayerfully, everyone to invest toward their retirement dreams. This book should even inspire new 'what I will do after I stop working' imaginings, as well as what I can do now while I am still part of the workforce. *Completion* is written to incite living your best life no matter what stage of life you are in. Your ideas do not have to begin at retirement, but your dreams will most likely expand when you have more freedom to live life on your own terms.

The most significant influence in my family is my mother, Alonzetta C. Moten Burns, whom we call Ma-ee. She has greatly impacted her children, grandchildren, great-grandchildren, and every family member and everyone connected to the family. Therefore, I will refer to my mother's contributions to my journey throughout this book.

In this book, I take you along my journey of Completion with my prayer that it will aid you on whatever your journey might be.

Completion started as a book on my travels after retiring, but it morphed into including the fragments of things that came together to make what is now my life:

- My journey goes from working in New York as an educator to my retirement.
- My weight loss struggles and how it counteracts no matter how I try with my love of food.
- My introduction and purpose of my hobby and how it keeps me, with my short attention span, focused.
- Witnessing my spur-of-the-moment adventures and my ever-growing future travel plans.
- The reveal of the unexpected launch of my small business.
- The uncovering of me and what I consider my unusual makeup whom God called into ministry.
- My no-holds-barred glimpse at my 42 years of marriage.
- How I dabble a little in societal stigmas and the need for self-awareness and self-love
- My perspectives as I delve into aging and death.
- The ups and downs of my physical, emotional, spiritual, and mental health resulted in this book *Completion*.

As my journey came together, it seemed more and more universal. It is an experience many can relate to and prayerfully be helped and inspired by. I pray that my journey can help you on your path to completion.

I started this book in October 2021. I probably should have started this book in 2018 when planning my travels. If not in 2018, maybe in 2019 when I went to my first state, Indiana. I invited myself to join my daughter in Indianapolis as she attended a conference that began my 50-state journey. Starting this book at the beginning of my journey would have allowed me to articulate fully on paper the wow factor that each day of my expedition delivered. I unexpectedly completed an unimaginable feat of leisurely travel. I know people who can check off states because of their business travels. My projection in finishing this book was when I completed all 50 states in North America, with Alaska being my last state. Even though I have been to all 50 states, I went to 49 states between 2019 and 2022. As of October 2022, with New Jersey being my home base, I can proclaim that this book and my 50 state visits are completed.

My friend Rosemarie Dunham asked me on October 1, 2021, "If my husband and I ever thought of writing about the wonderful trips you two have been on?" I believe God sends people into my life to plant seeds, and Rosemarie planted the seed in me for this book. Some chapters may be repetitive because of the overlapping parts of my life. I also digress into parts of my past. Hopefully, reminiscing about my past will evoke memories of your good old days. There is a quote by the author Cara Black that "our past informs the present." It says, "Memory makes the map we carry, no matter how hard we try to erase it." Throughout this book, Completion, you will see that God has a way of working unexpectedly (for me) in my life.

My daughter asked if this book would be written in my voice. The answer is, of course. This book is written in my voice: how I talk, teach, preach, and give advice to anyone who will listen. With the assistance of spell check, I must also include the thesaurus, Grammarly, Literary Consultant extraordinaire Marita Golden, Athena C. Shack, and Watersprings Publishing.

I am overly thankful to God for all of my blessings throughout my life and this book. I worked hard for many years, sometimes two jobs, so retiring at age 58 is truly a blessing. Receiving an additional income to provide the extras in my life at age 62 through social security is part of God's overflow of blessings.

In *Completion*, like in my life, I am open and honest about things many people do not freely discuss. I will tell you my age, and I thank God for each year that God allows me to be on this earth. I confess my actual weight without fudging and what works for me today in my weight loss battle. I will admit that I am a different type of clergyperson. My physical health and this thing we call aging are discussed. I am also open about the fact that I have issues. I am transparent about my mental health and my work with my therapist because there are things that I still struggle with.

What does all this have to do with *Completion* or being complete? To be complete, you must know yourself. You have to self-reflect and examine and reexamine yourself daily. I am a big advocate for journaling, and I suggest journaling throughout your life and looking back upon how God has blessed you even through those difficult times. I look at myself deeply and often. Even though my changes might be what I consider to be gradual, I see myself. I pray daily, asking God to help me be what God has for me to be. I look in the mirror, even imaginary ones, and reexamine Sheila from the inside out, front to back, and from top to bottom. Because I know myself so well, I am constantly asking God to give me a clean heart and renew in me a right spirit (Psalm 51).

Completion is doing everything that I want to do and doing it to its completion and doing it entirely to Completion without cutting corners or compromises. I do not want any wouldofs, shouldofs, or couldofs in these next chapters of my life's journeys. The need to complete things could be an advantage as well as a disadvantage because of my obsessive personality. We are all good for making excuses such as I cannot, I do not know how; I cannot afford it, I am too old, I am not old enough, I need a man/husband or a woman/wife, or someone to do it or do it with. . . the excuses go on and on, and they limit us. I pray that this book, *Completion,* will spark something in you, retired or not, that will make you say I want to do it, I can do it, and I am going to do it... Whatever your "it" may be… There are no limits!

I am always encouraging people to 'do it!' What is your "it," and what is stopping it?

When my grandnephew, Szymon, was eight years old, he said, "I was ready, but I was not prepared." It is so easy to be ready for your plan, but more importantly, you need to be prepared for that plan. Let Completion help prepare you for your next… and do it!

"

Because of who I was created
to be, I strive for completion in
every aspect of my life.

"

Completion

What is my completion? Because of who I was created to be, I strive for completion in every aspect of my life. I am self-diagnosed with OCD - Obsessive-Compulsive Disorder and recently confirmed ADHD - Attention Deficit Hyperactivity Disorder. Top that off with being anal-retentive. Yes, I have accepted the fact that I have some issues. I'm not saying that my conditions are bad, but they are recognized aspects of my life that make me, me!

My OCD causes me to be overly observant, detail-oriented, and extremely obsessed with order. What I see and do must be what I consider right, organized, straight, and balanced. With the number of items, I look for symmetry. I avoid all odd numbers (except for the number 5 because my brain recognizes it as half). I avoid an odd number of things; I find it taxing to my inner being to buy three things; it has to be two or four, even if I only need three. Through my mind's eye, everything has to be what I regard as precise or perfect. Everything I do now, no matter what or where, is strategically, meticulously planned, and scheduled well in advance. I often feel like my brain will not slow down. I have a heightened sense of structure and correctness. I often try to dismiss perfection, but I still consistently double and triple-check everything. I often question myself after leaving the house: if I used deodorant, did I turn off things like the lights or the stove? Did I close and lock the door? Is everything in order? Even as a child, rooms, not only my bedroom but every room, had to be neat and clean;

drawers and closets had to be organized and shut completely. My sisters, Sharon first and then Shelley, were not fans of sharing a room with me because I was obsessed with things being in what I considered in order and I was (I take that back) I am a tattle tale, they call it a snitch now. Even the food cans that my younger sister Shelley played with, like toys and food boxes in the pantry or cabinet for me, had to be in size order, with matching brands and items lined up neatly. All these obsessions have continued throughout my life.

My ADHD makes it difficult for my mind and body to be still, resulting in my mind rarely being at rest. Paying attention and relaxing is next to impossible, and so is focusing on one thing, idea, or issue at a time.

Being anal-retentive has me paying so much attention to detail that it becomes an obsession and an annoyance to others most of the time. I have learned or am learning to stifle a lot of my idiosyncrasies.

I do not allow myself to look at what I call my "issues" as a bad thing. I see it as understanding who I am and my workings. I am very much aware that because of the combination of OCD, ADHD, and being anal-retentive, this trio does not allow my brain to stop, and I often feel overwhelmed. Because of these tendencies, I am also very impulsive, always preoccupied, and extremely impatient.

I always have new bright ideas or something else to do while being fixated on setting my next objective before finishing whatever I started but yet I cannot leave things unfinished.

I have the tendency to jump into things because of my bright ideas, and then I try to figure out whatever I jump into and how it should work. Two recent examples of this are my string quilting business #Her2ndStitch and this book Completion. I plunged feet first into my business, thinking it was all about making and prayerfully selling pillows without considering the business and marketing aspects until #Her2ndStitch was launched. This impulsiveness to blindly enter this business probably causes my accountant, Lonnie, angst yearly. Secondly, writing this book without a clue about the steps to authorship. I just did it, with much prayer, without doing my due diligence to discover the intricacies involved in writing a book and having it published and sold, as well as the patience needed for the required timeline. No, I am definitely not endorsing this method for anyone because it comes with a lot of backtracking and unnecessary stress. I stepped out on faith, and the success of my business and this book are in my daily prayers.

In saying all that, I am determined to have completion. I want completion, but I have no idea what that will look like. Once I set and complete a plan (correction even before finishing a plan), I begin planning another one. As OCD/ADHD as I am, it is okay because that is how I function. I now wonder if I truly want complete completion on this side of the Jordan. I also wonder if God will allow my planning to continue while in heaven with my Heavenly Father.

I am a person who cannot rest until I finish what I started, and I am always preparing for my next (which is one of the reasons that it is so necessary that I have a therapist to help me navigate this sometimes overwhelming task).

People would ask me, "What will I do now that I am retired?" My response was always a big fat NOTHING! I have been "doing" for so long; now I want to just "be." My prayer is that this book will help others to "just be" and "be you."

So, what is my completion? Why am I writing a book on completion?

Let me start with why I am writing this book. I am not only writing this book because of a suggestion made for me to write a book. I created this book about completion because

I feel so many people of color (including those of us who are aging) are finding excuses not to do the things they enjoy. In Completion - if I can help someone during my journey, then I too will be complete.

It amazes me that we think certain things are for "them" and not us. Dr. Darius Daniels, in his book 'Your Purpose Is Calling,' would define how I feel about us as a people not always being comfortable stepping into any arena "unique discontent." I truly believe that we are all able to do exceedingly abundantly above all that we ask or think, according to the power that worketh within us (Ephesians 3:20). We should not put limits on ourselves.

My parents made it their mission to expose us to everything they could, from museums to Sunday Road trips, to August vacations. My parents would take us to Patricia Murphy's Restaurant in Yonkers to teach us how to eat in a "fancy" restaurant. Our exposure included, for a short while, piano lessons. My mother did not believe us when we told her that the supposedly sweet lady would hit us on our knuckles when we made mistakes and chastised us for not sitting up straight enough. We were enrolled in ballet and modern dance on the Grand Concourse near Fordham Road in the Bronx, wearing black leotards and pink tights; Shelley also took tap dance lessons.

As children, my sister Sharon and I were enrolled in Charm School at the Harlem YWCA on 125th Street in the Village of Harlem (the building is now the 125th Street Post Office). It seems like my parents wanted to put our learned etiquette to the test because Sharon was presented into society as a Debutant wearing a long white gown with long white gloves and her hair pinned up with a hairpiece on top, entering this Black societal world of womanly potential. While Shelley and I were Junior Debs with matching satin baby blue gowns, short gloves, and pressed hair with curls, we felt grown and looked like black princesses waiting for our turns to be the next two presented into society. My mother looked gorgeous in her gold embroidered trim black velvet gown, filled with pride in this accomplishment for her firstborn. My mother was accompanied by her two handsome gentlemen: my father, Julius Sr., in his black tuxedo, and my brother, Julius Jr., in his black suit, white shirt, and a tie. We stood proudly as a family, taking a picture in front of a red velvety wallpapered wall. I remember going from The Bronx to Brooklyn on weekends for instructions on proper etiquette and rehearsals of our presentation. My sister, other prospective debutants, and their partners practiced entrances and ballroom dance. I also remember being in awe of the elegance not only of the décor but of this room filled with Black people of all ages dressed in long gowns with gloves and black suits and tuxedos, with quiet conversations, exquisite place settings with multiple glasses and cutlery. The music playing was tailor-made for ballroom dancing. I think that Shelley and I decided this high society route was fine for Sharon, but we chose other roads to travel.

I continued that exposure that I learned from my parents of exploring new things and places with my children and now my grandchildren; there are no 'us and them' opportunities. Our forever president, Barack Obama, said, "There is no room that you do not belong in." I want us all to be prepared, comfortable, and ready to walk through any doors, sit

Debutant Picture

at any table, break many glass ceilings, and move past being designated the first.

A perfect example of what I am referring to was on a January 2022 Holland American Panama Canal cruise, and we were greeted immediately and enthusiastically by an older African American woman named Rose, who basically lived on cruise ships; she was counting the number of people who looked like her on each voyage. In comparison, my son searched for people under 40 who did not work on the ship. It is like our cultural nod that the father Dre on ABC's Blackish tried to explain to his perplexed son Junior. We either give a nod or a smile in recognition that I see you and you are not alone. People of color and young adults traveling should not be uncommon no matter what Cruise line and/or destination. I am saying no matter what Cruise line or destination because to me, it seems as though young people tend to gravitate towards Carnival, Norwegian, and Royal Caribbean Cruise lines and their less expensive beach destinations. I understand the draw of fun ships and entertaining destinations, but I want them to know that they can be open to widening their scope with cruises. I must admit that I do hear more and more from both people of color and young people venturing out further than Florida, Mexico, and the Caribbean and vacationing in other countries all over the world. Believe me, I understand that finances can sometimes be a concern when it comes to extensive traveling, but there are many inexpensive ways to enjoy life and explore the world if that's your desire. I discovered many tour groups exist for whatever you identify as your walk of life to travel with. There are singles, seniors, LGBTQIA2S+ community groups, and more specified groups. If you have the flexibility, airlines always have special flight offers. Also, I recommend using the expertise of a travel agent to help with your travels and keeping an eye out for special deals.

I need to digress more into finances. Budgeting is also important. I do not want anyone to rack up debts to enjoy their lives. I am just learning how to be fiscally responsible at the ripe age of 65 because I decided, what my mother has been advising for many years, that I will not pay interest on my credit cards anymore. First, by paying off my existing credit cards and only using them for their perks, I am starting to purchase only what I can pay off on time without paying any interest. In other words, I am finally learning to spend what I can afford. I have spent many years in debt, scrounging from paycheck to paycheck, and at one time almost on the brink of bankruptcy from trying to live beyond my means.

I recently heard about the Joy Fund on ABC's GMA (Good Morning America). A young lady named Parween Mander explained how to save and pay down your debt. She said you can "break the cycle of living paycheck to paycheck." She further explains that you must look at your psychology about money. It was suggested that you either adopt a 50-30-20 plan or a 50-10-50 plan; 50 goes to your needs (paying bills), 30 or 10 goes to wants (joy fund), and 20 or 40 goes to savings (including paying down debts). If I incorporate this Joy Fund philosophy, I know that most of my pension goes for paying household bills, personal items, and groceries, as well as 10 percent to my tithes and about 10 percent to savings. With my additional income through social security, another 10 percent of my gross income is also tithed. An additional 10 percent is for my needs, 20 percent is for savings, and 60 percent is now going into the Joy of Traveling. The Joy Fund is what gives you joy. If traveling gives you joy, then budget for your adventures and enjoyment!

After listening to the Audible book by Sarah Jakes Roberts, 'Woman Evolve,' I must add what she called a generational goal. I need to include a generational plan in my future planning. I must reflect on what I will pass on to my future generation. When I read my devotional, "Daily Devotional The Word For You Today The Village Of Hope a Bob Gass Ministry," there was a reminder about savings. It said you need to tithe ten percent to God and ten percent to savings. In addition to traveling and exposure to my future generations, one of my generational plans will be the importance of passing on a mindset of developing generational wealth. The wealth part might be a little late for my daughter, who seems to spend like me, but it is never too late to change your mindset. Prayerfully, she will become more fiscally conscientious before age 65. My son should be fine because he is diligent about saving as long as he passes on his practicality with saving and investing to his three children.

In budgeting, you would be amazed how coins in a jar add up. My children and I would collect change when we started cruising and going to Caribbean islands when they were young. They would exchange the change for paper currency and calculate how much they could spend each day on the cruise. This was before all cruise expenses were placed on your designated credit card. Having a vacation club or Christmas club plan through a credit union or bank, with funds coming directly out of your direct deposit and no easy access, helps to make your travel plans a reality. Extra designated saving accounts also help. My children and I were fashionistas when they were growing up because of the layaway plans at the Marshalls Department Store. I use that same installment mentality in planning and saving for my next adventure.

It is so important for me to expose young people to the world and a multitude of cultures. We even moved to Teaneck, New Jersey, to live in a multicultural community and further expose our children to other cultures.

As an elementary school teacher and a former youth leader at my church, I have always included trips and introductions to new things as part of my curriculum. I remember as a third-grade through fifth-grade teacher doing a study of China and taking my class to downtown New York City to explore Chinatown and eat dim sum at a Chinese restaurant. When the study of New York City was part of the curriculum, I took my classes to the Empire State Building, also on the top of the World Trade Center, and on the Circle Liner to reinforce and expand their learning and exposure to their city outside of their village of Harlem neighborhoods. However, I also took them to places like the Apollo Theatre and the Schomburg Museum to reinforce an appreciation of their culture. Also, being a youth leader with my husband, in addition to amusement parks, we took the church youth to the Poconos Mountains in Pennsylvania for many adventures, including camping in tents, skiing, snowboarding, ice-skating, and we also had a youth retreat. We went on a bus trip overnight to the Rocking Horse Ranch in Upstate New York for horseback riding. All outings were part of my plan to expand these young people's horizons while having fun.

I am a plan-setter. Set your plan (I prefer plan over goal because not meeting a goal seems disappointing). I plan out my year. I also have a five-year plan. I completed my plan to visit all 50 states in August 2022. I have an every-five-years cruise plan. Creating a vision board and a visible timeline works for me. You can also make an (I am not going to say a wish list) I'm going to make it happen list.

God willing, I plan to visit the six other continents by age 70 (which is less than five years from now). I try not to say that I want to – I say I will. I believe in speaking things into existence as I trust that God will do as God has always done in my life. . . make it happen. Romans 4:17b says, *"Calleth those things which be not as though they were."*

I keep my eyes open, and I am learning to accept the people that God is sending to plant a seed of (I used to say possibilities); now I am saying opportunities into my life.

For some reason, I had the desire to go to Panama. I do not know if this desire stemmed from two people from Panama: Mother Eutrene Woods from church and Myrna Harrison from the hair salon talking about their country. But when my niece Ashley went for her birthday in January a few years ago, I knew it was a doable January milestone birthday trip.

When preparing for a trip to Canada, I met a lady in the locker room at the gym who lived in Canada, which was more of a confirmation than an inspiration. We discussed the providences that I was going to visit, and she shared with me her knowledge and some of her experiences of her Canadian life, as well as the expectations of unpredictable climate changes. This was the first time I saw this lady at the gym, and I have not seen her since. Yes, I believe that God will send angels our way.

As I prepared for this last state, an August Alaskan cruise, ironically, both my friend Dulcie went on an Alaskan cruise in April, and Howard from the gym went on that same cruise in July that we would be going on in August. I also met people from Alaska on the Panama Canal cruise. All these encounters helped with packing and also picking and choosing excursions for Alaska.

These unexpected encounters before my trips prove that there are no coincidences with God. People are coming to me from everywhere, telling me about parts of various countries I will visit.

My travel to-do list is constantly expanding. My daughter Shené mentioned visiting every HBCU - Historically Black

College and Universities. When she is ready, I am ready, too. She also decided that we would have a new Mother's Day tradition and meet up somewhere and spend it together sometime in May, based on her availability. She always reminds me that "some people have to work, you know!" I am typing right now on Mother's Day Eve at the Bethany Beach Ocean Suites Residence Inn in Delaware. Shené is on the bed next to me as she is doing her schoolwork for her doctorate on our first mother/daughter Mother's Day weekend. I also recently read Ebony's online magazine article about 10 Domestic Black-Owned Hotels and Resorts around the country that I have added to my vision board. My cousin Bryan opened my eyes through his travels to places I never considered visiting, like the Seychelles Islands, Iceland, Bali, the Czech Republic, and Dubai. I could go on and on, but I am encouraging him to write his book. He has visited 42 countries so far, inspiring me to expand my travel pallet. We discussed going to India together for fabrics for my company, #Her2ndStitch. I also want to visit and buy authentic African fabrics from Ghana and Mali.

My prayer is that my journey will bless your journey. Amen!

I want you to dream outside of
the box that society, tradition,
and generations before you,
your haters, or even the box
you have placed yourself in.

2

The Completion Begins

The Completion begins. My completion begins. My daughter Shené gifted me with a coloring book, "Travel-ish – Black Women Around the World - Adult Coloring Book for Stress Relief & Travel Inspiration" by Ashley N. Company. Tileah (my daughter from another mother) just gifted me with the book Catch Me If You Can by Jessica Nabongo, a young lady who traveled to every country. Jessica Nabongo attended St. John's University in New York like Tileah and just so happens to be a friend of my cousin, Bryan. My cousin met up with Jessica Nabongo and other friends in the Seychelles Islands, Jessica's last country. Tileah also gifted me with a travel journal. I am a journal-type person, so having a separate journal for travel is perfect. I found coloring and journaling to be very relaxing. Using colors in the coloring books and in my journals helps express, enhance, or suppress my mood, which is why I also travel with sharpened colored pencils.

I just heard a commercial with the title "See Her." "If you can see her, you can be her!" In this book, I want you to see my life in retirement and all the behind-the-scenes parts or people that make events in my life happen. Not that I want you to want to be me, but I want you to know that you can be and do! Remember, "With God, all things are possible" (Matthew 19:26).

I want you to dream outside of the box that society, tradition, and generations before you, your haters, or even the box you have placed yourself in.

I had an aha moment after what I consider a unique baby dedication; I told my daughter that I admire how her generation, those in their thirties and forties, are thinking outside the box and forming and creating their own customs and traditions. An example is Friendsgiving, which is now a popular annual November event. This generation has extraordinary gender reveal celebrations. They are doing what is best for their babies, such as home births with midwives and doulas. Unlike my generation, this group of young adults does not allow themselves to be consumed by what other people think about them and their choices aside from their obsession with selfies and social media. They are discovering who they are as a person and not rushing into marriage or creating a family. This group of young people will bravely fly to exotic places worldwide by themselves if necessary. They have adopted a healthier lifestyle. This generation keeps in touch with long-time friends through social media, and they encourage and celebrate each other. Also, through COVID-19 isolation, they continued to have get-togethers, brunches, lunches, dinners, and celebrations virtually. This generation has also broken the identity boxes and made decisions about their own identity. It is a generation that has taken ownership and takes pride in who they are, no matter their size, shape, shade, race, ethnicity, gender, or sexuality.

I am ecstatic about this generation of men, of fathers, and the time they spend with their children. The elimination of gender roles and the roles that this generation of men take on, which I know that men in the past would never consider their responsibilities, is commendable now, as it prayerfully will become the norm.

Using my son J. as an example, my son taking his son Dasaiah to basketball and football practices and games is the expectation of a father-and-son relationship. But it is not unusual to see my son at the grocery store shopping for his family meals, preparing "real" nutritious gourmet meals, and cleaning the house (not often enough - as his mother, I can say that he can be a slob), washing his daughters' hair or taking out their braids, taking them to school or picking them up from school, helping with homework, attending school events, are all common occurrences for my son. J. joined the school board at his daughter's school to ensure equity in their education and for the children who look like them. Going on bike rides together, working out in his home gym with them, and even including yoga. Taking Darby, his youngest daughter, to gymnastics weekly and Jayla, his oldest daughter, to golf practices and matches, as well as school dances and activities. His taking on the shared responsibility for taking his daughters to Girl Scout meetings and clothes shopping, including being man enough to shop the Bra Patch with his teenage daughter, has become part of his norm. With both parents working, shared responsibility these days is a must. I appreciate my firstborn's intentionality, exploration, and involvement in his children's education placements from preschool to college.

I heard on my car radio about DADication - fatherhood. gov has a series of new PSAs. I love that it encourages fathers to show their "#DADication" by making time for their children, even when parenting isn't easy.

I am a daddy's girl, and I applaud all fathers who are fathering. My father worked hard six days a week from early morning to late at night because he owned his business, Reliable Cleaners, aka "the Shop," at 620 Lenox Avenue in the Village of Harlem. My husband worked two jobs as our children grew up working both day and night. However, both men and fathers always prioritized their children and always found time to spend quality time with them.

As a daddy's girl who has cherished memories of spending time with my father and being with him at "The Shop," eavesdropping on grown folk's conversations. Listening to the numerous life-changing stories that his customers had to tell. Seeing the regulars hanging around day in and day out playing numbers straight, box, or combination and waiting for each number to come out with the hopes they hit, or my father would say, "when their ship comes in." The Shop was my first job, at age 13, and the only job I got fired from. I got fired because I decided to go on strike because of what I considered unfair labor practices. I was the only employee at the time.

Because my father worked late each night, I made it my mission to stay up on non-school nights and sit at the dining room table while he ate his dinner after work, talking his ear off. Even as I grew older, I still cherished our moments together. I strongly feel that daughters need a special relationship with their fathers because fathers are the first men in their lives. Fathers are their daughters' first love. Being present and involved, fathers should prepare their daughters for the other men that will enter their lives and hearts. They say that daughters marry their fathers. My husband Willie has that same soft, quiet, easy-going, encouraging nature, just like my father.

My husband Willie has also created a daddy's girl in his daughter Shené. He not only coached football and basketball for his son's teams, but he also coached his daughter's basketball teams and took her to cheerleading practices. He also sat with her and it seemed to be almost daily with vocabulary practices and homework. I tell my husband to this day that Shené has pinky power over him because he cannot say no to her. But now it is mutual because they both would do anything humanly possible for the other one. I know that even though I did not have that longevity with my father, I miss that relationship with my father now that he is gone.

My first memories of traveling were from my father, who introduced me to the adventures of family road trips. I loved our family road trips even though my place was always in the middle, in the back seat, with my legs elevated or split from side to side because of the hump, with my brother Julius and sister Sharon on either side of me. Being older, they could have window seats and look out of the windows during our car rides. My brother often annoyed me with the "I'm not touching you" with his finger close to my face. My parents and my younger sister Shelley were seated in the front (this was before bucket seats) during our family adventures. Looking back, taking car rides with my family has always been my happy place. Even though we were four loud and rumbustious children cooped up six in a car together, there was always a sense of love and joy being together. My father's only day off was Sundays, but he always believed in spending time with family on Sundays. Our Sunday adventures often resulted in a local road trip to places like Bear Mountain and Lake Sebago in Harriman State Park; both are upstate New York. These parks allowed us to get out of the city and see grass and trees because, at that time, we were living in the housing projects in the Village of Harlem. We were surrounded by greenery during these outings, with no sidewalk pavements or buildings in sight. We went swimming and experienced nature with picnics on the grass and paddle boating in the lakes. We, as children, always had so much fun because it seemed we were free and had no restrictions as we had in New York City. I was always tagging along after my brother. I remember following my brother as we gingerly walked close to the edge of the lake on the rocks, but I suddenly slipped into the lake. I think that might be why I fear water going over my head. I sank into what seemed like the bottom of the cold, dark water until I felt my brother's hand pull me out. As always, I got in so much trouble with my brother. Because of me, we had to cut our outing short, and I had to take my wet clothes off and ride home wrapped in a blanket. Our car rides to the Whitestone Drive-In Movies were the best! It was always an exciting adventure because we would get in the car with our pajamas on. Then, we would stop at White Castle's drive-through for a bag full of White Castles, aka tiny hamburgers, to eat during the movie. We always fell asleep on the way home, if not during the movie. My sister reminded me that our father also introduced us to exotic or extraordinary fruits like persimmons, pomegranates, and nectarines. Little things excited us. We would beg our father to drive fast over a huge bump in the road at the Bronx Terminal Market. My father would say, "Are you ready…" We did not wear seatbelts back then, and our mission was to have our heads hit the roof of the car when he drove fast and went over the bump. Thinking back, what was this little happiness doing to my father's car's alignment? I know that he lived to please his family.

Road trips and family road trips have been passed down from my parents to the next generation, and I have passed them on to my children and grandchildren. Just as I practically grew up on what is now Route 95, traveling from New York to South Carolina every summer in August. My children and grandchildren have now grown up experiencing the trek back and forth from New Jersey to Washington, D.C., Virginia, and North Carolina during holidays and summer vacations.

With my travels, I thank God for those who encourage my journeys—those who travel with me: Willie, Shelley, Shené, and Willie J. My sister-in-law Soqui, Szymon, my daughter-in-law Denetra, and my grands, Dasaiah, Jayla, and Darby, are also my travel buddies. My niece Shavon and her son Jabari also met up with me for a trip to Nova Scotia in July 2022.

Since my mother's passing in 2018, my sisters and I have been trying to do more sisterly things, including communicating, starting with morning sister's texts. We are being intentional about spending more time together. Sharing, and sometimes over-sharing, as we become more open and accountable to each other regarding our health, weight, and senior ailments. My mother has always been the nucleus of our relationship. Now that all my sisters are retired, we are trying to spend more time together and arrange some sisters' trips.

For Sharon's 60th birthday, Shelley and I arranged a sister's trip through a mutual co-worker friend, Debra of Sharon, and mine. She let us stay in her beautiful house in upstate New York. This house was Debra's home away from home, and it was cozy and homey, with inspirational signs and knick-knacks that made our sister's weekend even more intimate and special. We also topped the weekend with sisters' massages while celebrating her milestone birthday. Sharon also joined Shelley and me for a weekend sisters' trip to the Poconos. We are trying to set up a double-sisters' trip with our sister Louise and her sisters. Originally, it was supposed to be a trip to Washington, D.C., to The National Museum of African American History and Culture in 2020, but that could not happen because of the COVID-19 pandemic. Now, we are discussing rescheduling that trip to the museum and taking a double-sisters' trip to Texas since one of Louise's two sisters, Yvonne, lives in Dallas. I would love to revisit and spend more time in Texas. Sharon, Shelley, and I recently booked a European cruise to Italy, Greece, and Turkey for 2023.

I thank God and my parents for the many experiences, not only with travel but with exposure to new things and cultures. My mother must have taken us to every museum in New York City. My favorite may have been the Met, the Metropolitan Museum of Art, where I saw paintings and sculptures whose history captivated me from childhood through high school. Another favorite was the Guggenheim Museum. The Guggenheim Museum's round structure was fascinating in itself, and its colorful sculptures and modern pieces of art had me awestruck. I thought maybe I could paint the more modern pieces. I think these early museum visits cultivated my desire to become an artist. I majored in art at John F. Kennedy High School in the Bronx, New York. I continued my love of art and art history throughout high school and in my first two years of college at Howard University in Washington, D.C., before getting more involved in my second love, my major in Elementary Education and a double minor in Psychology and Spanish.

My son's favorite museum was the Museum of Natural History because of the dinosaurs, which he would have gone to weekly if it were up to him. My mother continued her various exposures to the world and activities with her grandchildren, with tennis lessons for her and her first grand, Shavon. My older sister and brother also took tennis lessons. My lack of coordination was probably evident early because I never had tennis lessons like my siblings and Shavon. A sidebar comment: As a grandmother, doing so many things with your grandchildren that you did not get to do with your children is much easier. I realized that I spent so much time trying to raise my children "right" that I missed out on opportunities for the joy of parenthood. There is never a manual for raising each unique child. I heard that you raise your children and love your grandchildren. I love my children too, but with my hectic schedule while raising my two children, I wish I had spent more time appreciating the journey that now seems like a short time together.

My children now always comment on how strict we were with them and that they do not recognize their parents regarding the grandchildren. They often ask Willie and me, "Who are you?" when our grandchildren are around. I let them know that I am not the one raising these children, especially since they live in North Carolina and their father and I are in New Jersey, so the visits are few and far between, which makes each visit special.

I can't say that it is true for everyone, but I am glad to see that young adult parents today are taking the time to enjoy their offspring.

My mother always took her grands to many places. My niece Shequé remembers her grandmother taking them to the Radio City Music Hall Christmas Show. Like my maternal grandmother, Sissie, aka Georgetta Moten, my mother also took her grands to Coney Island in Brooklyn. My mother took her grandchildren to the Brooklyn Aquarium, The Bronx Botanical Gardens, The Bronx Zoo, and Central Park Zoo. My mother loved walking, so she would gather whatever grand was around her when we lived in the Bronx. She walked from Andrews Avenue down Burnside Avenue to the Jerome Avenue Post Office, to the Grand Concourse, or Fordham Road to stores like Alexander's Department Store. I do not think any of her grandchildren objected to these long walking adventures because they always returned with something purchased for them.

Every grandchild knew when it was senior citizen day because that meant a trip to Caldor until 1999, Bradlees until 2001, and then Kohls probably until my mother's grandchildren became college-age.

I, too, take my grandchildren on long walks whenever we are together. Their incentive for these walks in New Jersey is usually to go to Bischoff's in Teaneck for their homemade ice cream and Zai in Bergenfield for macaroons. I am spoiling another generation with shopping trips. Back-to-school shopping for my mother with her grands was always in the Poconos in Pennsylvania during the third week of August during our week at the Shawnee Resort. My daughter once asked my mother when she took them to The Brooklyn Aquariums and not to Coney Island right next door 'What is the Purpose?". My mother never forgot that question. I found it impossible to follow my mother's grandmothering style because she had unbelievable energy, but she taught me a lot about being a wife, mother, and grandmother. But I can proudly say I did not make that one mistake with my grands. I made sure that when I took them to the Brooklyn Aquarium to see the marine life, I took them to Coney Island for a couple of rides, a walk on the beach, and then food from Nathans. I did not want to get my feelings hurt. One time, when my mother took her grands to the Bronx Botanical Gardens, Radio Station KISS FM was having an invite-only Barbeque, and my mother casually joined them. Her granddaughters came home excited, not about the beautiful gardens with exotic flowers but about them "crashing the party." I admire the relationship that my mother had with each of her grandchildren. They each have their own grandma story. Her great-grandchildren also have their special adventures with her.

When I was older, my mother and I worked as educators and had the summers off. My mother and I would set a Wednesday date to stand in line to get tickets at TKTS booths at Times Square to see a Broadway Matinee. I have taken my children to both Broadway and Off-Broadway plays throughout the years. I still love Broadway Shows. I had the opportunity to join a school group to see The Lion King on Broadway. My husband and I loved Motown's "Ain't Too Proud" on Broadway. Recently, I took my daughter to see Tina on Broadway, which was spectacular. I also took my granddaughters this summer to see MJ the Musical on Broadway; amazing is an understatement for this theatre sensation.

I am truly thankful for my parents saying yes and allowing me to leave the country twice for high school educational trips, first to Spain and then to Mexico. My parents also allowed my brother to drive down in their car to Washington, D.C., to Howard University to take my friends (who became my college apartment mates and later my bridesmaids) Gwen, Ronda, and me on a road trip to Tallahassee, Florida, for a Fam-U vs. Howard-U football game.

Gwen reminded me that my parents used to meet the three of us when we lived together at what we considered the halfway point between the Bronx, New York, and Tacoma Park, Maryland, at the Maryland House to bring us groceries and a gas fill-up. Ronda recently reminded me that my father would also give us spending money. She said that she and Gwen would always leave with an extra twenty dollars in their pockets. The trip was a little less than three hours for my parents and a little more than one hour from our apartment. The math does not work, but that is love!

I cannot forget when my mother began driving and got her first car, a Chevy Nova. She took us (my cousin Donnajean, my sisters Sharon and Shelley, and I) with her sister Auntie, aka Thelma Moten (six people in a Nova), to Paradise Farm Resort, upstate New York, for a fun day. With my mouth, I complained about my mother driving so slowly on the way home; she put me out of the car and drove a few feet, and I had to run to catch up. My mouth always got me in trouble, and it still does. Now, both my granddaughters have inherited my feisty mouth trait. My oldest granddaughter Jayla now talks about my 'keeping within the speed limit,' a.k.a. slow driving. They say what goes around comes around.

I mentioned shopping in the Poconos in Pennsylvania. The Pocono Mountains are known for skiing and resorts, including timeshare properties. My mother purchased a timeshare at Shawnee Resort when we got older and started having our children. We had an annual one-week family (the whole family and sometimes even friends too. Although there were only two bedrooms in the villa, we filled every possible space) trip to Shawnee - Ridgetop 190 in the Poconos through her timeshare. That was usually our last outing for the summer before returning to work as teachers, and our children had to go back for a new school year. During school breaks, my mother often used her timeshare for a week in Williamsburg, Virginia, and off-season trips to Ocean City, Maryland. I have inherited that timeshare, but we have not been going to Shawnee because you have a designated week each year, and ours is the third week in August. The third week in August is prime time for the school children in the north, but my grands live in North Carolina, and school starts the second week in August for them. So, Willie and I have been doing what they call an exchange through RCI - Resorts Condominiums International for other vacation spots at different times of the summer. Through these RCI exchanges, we have taken our three grandchildren to Smugglers' Notch Resort in Jefferson, Vermont, in August 2019, and our two granddaughters to South Shore Lake Resort in Hot Springs, Arkansas, in June 2021. We booked the Wish Natal Resort in Natal RN Brazil for Willie and me for August 2023.

My mother and her friends inspired me with their travels to various states for Delta Sigma Theta, Inc. conventions and regionals or just-because trips. They also went on repeated trips to Aruba and St. Maarten with their timeshares. There was also an educational trip to London when my mother and friends got their master's degrees from Bank Street College. I remember "the group" members taking a road trip to North Carolina, "America's Home Furnishing Capital," to look at furniture. My mother ordered a desk, which is now in my sister Shelley's house." The Group" is a group of retired teachers who were friends for probably about sixty years from P.S. 90 and then P.S. 200 in the Village of Harlem. "The Group" met on a regular basis for dining and outings. They also supported each other during good times, such as birthdays and children's weddings (yes, they were all at my wedding), and not-so-good times, such as illnesses and bereavement. There was always a card with collected money from "The Group." Good friends are so necessary.

Many thanks to those who encouraged my travel and those who modeled traveling before me, like my mother and her friends and sorors. My mother and friends also inspired me to stay connected with lifelong friends. Thanks also to my church family, who traveled while working and even more once they retired. Your adventures incentivize my determination to travel and explore what is outside of my North American East Coast bubble.

"

Some people are skirmish about aging, but I proudly look forward to the senior citizen perks.

"

3

Retirement

Retirado/Retirement

Gifted By Carmen (Soqui) Burns-Torres
Estoy jubilada!!! Sin Jefe (no boss),
Sin Preocupaciones (without worries).

God has truly blessed me and continues to bless me. Retiring at age 58 after thirty-one years in education, being healthy and of sound mind is truly a blessing. Being blessed with a pension that increases my monthly salary because of fewer deductions could only be from God. The ability to tap into my TDA - tax-deferred annuity, at 58½, helped to pay off my car and make home improvements. I know my fellow assistant principal and union leader recommended that I not retire until I paid off my car (do not tell him that he was right), but it was time to go. I also know that financial advisors would frown on how I spent the money I saved throughout my teaching career for retirement. While working, sometimes working two jobs, oftentimes work and school, always work and children's activities, we did not have the time or money to make the needed home improvements until we retired.

Crossing the George Washington Bridge to go back and forth from New Jersey to New York daily became exhausting. After living, rather than just sleeping in our Teaneck, New Jersey house (because that is all we had time to do) for 28 years (from our August 1987 purchase to our 2015 retirement), we finally have time to enjoy our house. Because of retirement, we are finally home. I say we because my husband and I both retired the same year.

The icing on the cake is getting social security at 62. I waited, unfortunately, a while before collecting my social security because I originally wanted to hold out for more but then I reminded myself (with the help of my husband Willie and my sister Shelley) once again that not even tomorrow is promised. My social security checks provide for the extras. Some people are skirmish about aging, but I proudly look forward to the senior citizen perks. I am now enjoying the benefits of officially being a retired senior citizen or a seasoned saint at age 65. I thank God for those things that I take for granted. I am painfully aware that everyone is not blessed with a good pension and such things as health insurance, affordable co-pays, and affordable prescription medication. I now at 65, have a lower health insurance premium, a lower co-pay, and free generic prescription medications because I am now at an age where I am eligible for Medicare supplemental insurance. I also know firsthand the struggle of paying for those monthly non-generic medications. My prayer is that this wealthy country of ours would provide free universal health care for all, including mental health treatments. I will digress a little bit more; my prayers include affordable housing, no homelessness or hunger, and quality, healthy, fresh food choices for all. I also must include, after Detroit's clean drinking water issues and the possibility of tainted water in the New York City Jacob Riis Housing Authority complex in the East Village, clean, drinkable water. I also must include equality with the education of all children and equality in health care; the disparities in education and healthcare were evident during the 2020 pandemic. My prayer also includes understanding and acknowledging that we are all our brother's keepers and are responsible for each other no matter who or what they are.

I do not think I purchased books on retirement when I retired. Even though I used to read books on everything, I remember reading every book I could get my hands on about parenting before having my first child. I remember people like my sister, Sharon, who gifted me with at least one retirement book. I think that one of the books was titled Second Act. I really do not know or remember because I gave them all away. I was so ready for my second act, which could not come from a book. But what will that second act look like? My retirement plan was, and still is, to be intentional and do everything I always wanted to do but did not have the time, money, or freedom to do. This was one time that I did not want a book to carve out my path for me.

I retired in 2015 after 31 years in education, and now every day is like heaven. Heaven surely must be like this! I wake up each day thanking God for this blessing of freedom and living my life on my own terms. The million-dollar question that seems to be asked of new retirees is, "What will you do now that you are retired?" "Do" being the operative word. I do not want to "do" anymore! I've known people who died while planning their retirement. I know of people who retired, are bored, and cannot figure out what to do next. I just heard about someone who was upset because she was forced to retire before she was ready at age 75, and she remained active, especially in her immaculate garden, until she left this side of Jordan after age 90.

As for me, I went to the New York State Teacher's Retirement in 2012 when I finally turned 55, and I was told that I could not retire until 2015. I went again in 2013 and was told I had to wait until 2015. I went again in 2014, and guess what? I was told that I had to wait another year. I prayed for a 25-year/age 55 incentive, but it did not happen. I was so ready!

My last day at work was the last day of June 2015, but I decided I wanted a memorable retirement date, so I officially retired on July 15, 2015, my father's birthday. Willie and I went to Calverton Cemetery in Long Island on that day to share my good news with my father at his gravesite. We both went for relaxing massages and a delicious celebratory dinner. We spent the night on Long Island at a hotel with a rooftop pool. I wish I could remember the name of the hotel where we stayed or the name of the spa I found through Groupon. Now, in retirement, I am determined to make all events in my life memorable.

Willie and I have taken many 'need-to-get-away' or "run-away" quick trips to various places. Locally we went to rooftop hotels and quaint inns in Connecticut, as well as to Caesars Poconos Palace and Brookdale Resorts in the Poconos of Pennsylvania, in addition to booking overnight stays at the Sheraton in Parsippany New Jersey (we call the castle) with their extremely comfortable beds, just the two of us for a necessary change of pace throughout the years after having children. Before having our two blessed children, when we lived in Maryland, we used to rent a house initially through Ronda, my apartment-mate's connections, with other couples' friends in Ocean Pine, Maryland, near Ocean City, Maryland (this was way before there were Airbnb's). Willie and I also did two out-of-the-country getaways without our children. The first trip was to Cancun, Mexico during a winter break, we were looking forward to this beach vacation, but it was unexpectedly cold in Cancun, and we did not have anything warm to wear so we basically stayed indoors. The second trip was to the Dominican Republic for an anniversary getaway at an all-inclusive beautiful resort. I remember I recently injured my back at work and could not go horseback riding on the beach, and I love horseback riding. But the property was beautiful, they had vendor displays of island jewelry, and island music with romantic lighting throughout the resort in the evenings. There were several types of restaurants to choose from for dinner and I remember the delicious fresh exotic fruits on display for breakfasts. I also remember having a couples massage under canopies on the beach during their amazing sunset. I mention these outings because it is so important to get away or run away every now and then, even if it is local, to center yourself, refresh yourself, or rejuvenate your relationship.

Speaking of retirement, I remember looking at retirees side-eyed when I was working, and they would talk about how busy they were each day. But now, with my schedule each day, each week, and each month, I understand the busyness. I am working hard on being intentional not to overpack my daily agenda. I try to keep my daily schedule to no more than one or two, possibly three activities per day when I have physical therapy or an appointment (doctors, hair, nails, therapist) while being mindful of my Saturdays being free with Bible Study only because Sundays are the day that I have an early rise. On Sundays, I wear real, presentable clothes, face, hair, and nails; no sweats, no T-shirts, and most of the time, no sneakers. Most of my Sundays are church only and fixing breakfast and dinner for Willie and me. Also, my Wednesdays, like my mother's "Be Good To to Loni" Wednesdays, I keep my Wednesdays, besides the 12 noon prayer call, free and relaxing until 7 p.m. Bible Study. However, my mother always did something special for herself on Wednesdays, hence "Be Good To Loni."

My gym, senior center, and everything else, including grocery shopping, are done on Mondays, Tuesdays, Thursdays, or Fridays. I have four early rise days for church and gym, which I balance off with three get-ups when I want to days.

I am aware that this new season of my life is a blessing from God. God has allowed me to do all the things that I want to do. But what do I want to do? What do they say, "The world is your oyster"? This means I can achieve anything I want in life or go anywhere because God has blessed me with the opportunity as well as the ability to do so. I thank God for my health, strength, mental capacity, will, and finances to do and to be.

Being a bi-vocational associate minister, now that I have retired, my plan was to be more available for my church, First Baptist Church of Teaneck in Teaneck, New Jersey. I have been a member of this church since 1990, Licensed as a minister in 2002, and ordained in 2009. I figured that I would have more time for ministry and study. Although that is all true. For the most part, I am available, and I have increased my platforms for study. But I also realized that there is so much "me" that I have been missing out on. It might sound selfish, but I do not know how to make this sound good. But I feel as though 31 years of fitting in working, with 11 years working two jobs, raising a family (even with the help of my village), furthering my education with three master's degrees, my duties at home and my duties at the church have consumed me and there was not much time for me. God will always be first, and I have more time to build a better relationship with God. I am also available for my church when a need arises. But I changed my mindset that "me" would be my priority after God. This became more urgent after the 2020 pandemic. But I will talk more about my ministry later in this book.

What do I want for "me"? What do I want to do and not do? How do I want my life to look, feel, and be like? While learning to live in retirement with my husband, who unexpectedly retired technically five months before me in February of the same year, 2015. Having an empty nest without the distractions of our jobs or children, enjoying our new life separately, and enjoying each other together. This, too, was an adjustment and a learning experience. We jokingly said what if we find out that we do not like each other, and our jobs and our children were a distraction all these years. The song by Bill Withers and Grover Washington Jr. comes to mind; "Just the two of us we can make it if we try…" After forty-two years of marriage and over seven years of retirement together, I guess that we are making it. Our children and grandchildren know that we are always available for them even though our Interstate 95 southbound drives to Virginia to see our daughter and North Carolina to see our son and his family are starting to become less frequent as we explore other parts of the United States.

What will I do as a retired person? What do I like? What do I not like?

What I do not like:

I am starting with what I do not like. I know that I do not like getting up early. Actually, I do not like having to get up early, even if I automatically wake up early. Waking up early does not mean getting up, and I give myself permission to do that. I found that I really do not like driving, now that I do not have to, especially after dealing with crossing the always congested George Washington Bridge, leaving New Jersey to go to New York, and then to the Major Deegan Highway going either south when I worked in the Village of Harlem or north when I worked in Westchester for 28 years. Now, I would rather walk than drive. When I told someone that I did not like driving anymore, she asked, "What is that all about?" thinking that it was a mental flaw. It is a conscious awareness and a decision I chose to make. I do not like being in traffic. I do not like paying for or wasting gas at any price. I do not like rushing. I do not like time restraints; I gave away my alarm clock and stopped wearing watches as soon as I retired. I started wearing a Fitbit, and then a Samsung fitness tracker watch to calculate my steps. I do not like arriving at places early because I do not like waiting. I prefer getting places on time with the expectation that I should not have to wait. The calculation of my estimated time of arrival often tends to make me rush, and I already said that I do not like rushing. I do not like getting to places late, and late people annoy me (not mentioning any names, but you know who you are). I am constantly reminding myself, and now, post-pandemic, it has helped me with many of my choices so that I do not have to do the things I do not want to do. I do not have to do things that I am not comfortable doing. I do not have to go places I do not want to. I can now say "no" and "I don't want to" and be okay with my decisions. After all, no is a complete sentence! I tend to overload my calendar and daily agenda, but I am working on doing better through therapy so that I will always feel content and embrace my decisions. I do not have to be a people pleaser; no thank you is okay. I stand on this new platform, and stress does not live here anymore.

What I like:

I like a clean and organized environment. My OCD and my anal retentiveness are still on heightened alert even in an orderly setting because I am still mentally checking and double-checking my surroundings. First, Marie Kondo helped me declutter every part of my house and life after retirement, and now Home Edit helps keep me organized. My therapist, Lorna, is trying to help me not obsess over this and not drive others around me crazy (she would not have used the word "crazy") with my obsessions.

Workouts: I now have time to work out! I always wanted to fit in more time to exercise. I joined a gym before retiring but was only able to take Saturday Zumba classes and then Saturday Aqua classes. Now, in retirement, I can increase my gym time. Being in classes as a senior and following directions helps with improving my seemingly deteriorating cognitive functions. I did Zumba religiously in two different 24-Hour Fitness Gyms in Paramus, Englewood Cliffs, and the Rodda Center until I repeatedly hurt my knees, ankle, and lower back. Even long before Zumba classes, I hurt my knees taking African dance classes barefoot. I love dancing. I am still doing the weight classes called Body Pump at 24-Hour Fitness Gym in Paramus twice weekly. I am also taking a Body Flow class comprising Thai Chi, Yoga, Pilates, and a cycling class. Before the pandemic, I also did Pilates once a week at the gym and Body Combat because I love kickboxing when my body feels healed.

I was finally eligible to join the senior center at the Teaneck Rodda Center after retirement. I also tried some of their exercise classes, but I stayed with yoga because it challenges my body more than any other classes offered. I understand the need and benefits of physical fitness on every part of your body, including my brain and heart. I am taking every opportunity to stay active.

Walking: I love walking. Walking is my favorite form of exercise, and now I have time to get out and walk. I can walk forever; I literally have to put a time limit on my walk using the timer on my phone. I set my phone to either 45 minutes or 1 hour and then come back so that I am walking 1½ to 2 hours per walk. I found that even though I have two beautiful parks near me in Teaneck, New Jersey (Votee Park and Overpeck Park) with one-mile tracks, I get bored easily, so I moved on from these parks, and now I walk the neighborhood; from Teaneck to Hackensack, or from Teaneck to Bergenfield to Dumont, or Bogota, or Lodi. This allows me to change my walking routes and scenery. I must confess my sense of direction is terrible, and I have gotten lost in many of my own neighborhoods. You will probably hear this again, but I thank God for GPS because I often have to use GPS to find my way back home. I walk whenever I can. I cannot say that I am a year-round walker. I do not like cold, but now, because of my sister Shelley's encouragement, I layer up and even walk in the winter in what I call my Shamanie ski pants (ski pants given to my sister Shelley and then passed on to me by my niece Shamanie). Again, I express my gratitude for directional devices that help my directional challenges because, even though I should, and my daughter and my husband constantly remind me, I am often unaware of my surroundings while walking, and I frequently get turned around. I got lost so many times when we were traveling that Willie now has a Life360: Find Family & Friends tracker on my phone. My son, his trainer, and my unofficial trainer (Tasha) think I might be walking too much. Of course, I had to look it up and ask my brother in the ministry, Ken. I found that too much walking might affect my muscle strength, especially since I am not taking in enough daily protein. So, now I have to reduce my cardio from 5 days per week to 3 days. I am also trying to increase my resistance/weight training from 2 days per week to 3 days per week. Finding a third day to do weight training is becoming difficult because I prefer classes over using the machines at the gym. My classes are on Tuesdays and Fridays now, and you are not supposed to do back-to-back weight training of the same areas of your body, which leaves me to commit and try to fit in weight training on Sundays, my day of sabbath rest. We will see how that works. I do have a weighted battle rope in the garage that I might have used twice. The only obstacle to this is that I do not like wasting clothes and would have to change from my Sunday best to workout clothes. I am a one-outfit per day and then lounge wear or pajamas type of girl in retirement. I admit that I am not feeling as strong as I used to, which is evident with my planks, push-ups, and my upward-facing dog, but I am determined to improve every part of my body and strive for optimal fitness.

Stretching: Stretching your body and mind is important, especially as you age. I was introduced to the thought of yoga when I heard on one of the morning television shows that if you do yoga, you probably will not need a hip replacement. My daughter Tileah (from another mother/Monica), Shené's best friend since middle school, and my sister Sharon have encouraged me to try yoga. Being in an environment now where everyone is talking about their body parts replacements or their need for a knee or hip replacement, I started taking yoga at the Rodda Center. My yoga teacher, Mr. Martin Bland, has taught and encouraged me to continue and to practice. Surprisingly, even though I have a way to go, it is paying off because even as a child, I was not flexible. I am now seeing and feeling gradual improvements. I also mentioned that I started taking a Body Flow class at 24-Hour Fitness Gym and a Pilates class that has not resumed since the pandemic. All these classes are challenging for my body, but I am seeing a steady improvement in flexibility, strength, and balance. I strongly recommend yoga to people of all ages and genders.

Bible Study: I wanted to increase my study of God, so I started attending Institute of New Dimensions (IND} classes. I consistently attended Bible as Literature classes, going through the Old Testament books as literature until the pandemic in 2020. I chose not to continue the class when they resumed virtually. I am now a faithful student of my former church, St. Mark Baptist Church, in NW Washington, D.C.'s Saturday morning Bible Study class, taught by a phenomenal instructor, Felicia Boggan. Her depth of knowledge, thorough research, and love of teaching mesmerized me. I started with her teaching of Revelation and continued as she went back to the Old Testament, starting with Genesis. Felicia's teaching reminds me of my first Sunday school teacher, Mrs. Gloria Strong, who was also Felicia's teacher and mentor. I also attend my own church's Wednesday Bible Study and Sunday morning Church School lessons. I have been a sponge for the Study and understanding of the Bible since I became a Baptist at age 22 in 1979, first at St. Mark's Baptist Church and then in 1990 at my current church, First Baptist Church of Teaneck. Two amazing Bible teachers taught Sunday School from the commencement of my discipleship at my two churches that are no longer with us. These two teachers fed my initial hunger for knowledge: Sister Gloria Strong (who I just mentioned) of St. Mark Baptist Church in NW Washington, D.C., and Brother Ernest Davis of First Baptist Church of Teaneck in Teaneck, New Jersey.

Art: Some type of art and creating things were always part of my retirement plan. I thought about designing blank greeting cards. I even visualized and sketched some of the figures that would be on all my designs in different poses. I thought about designing inspirational workout hand towels. I wanted to put my creativity to work and make some extra coins by turning it into a business. Quilting was never in the cards for me, but it is now my new vocation or my 2ndStitch.

A Second Language: I used to be fluent in Spanish. This is a perfect example of using it or losing it. I visited Spain and

Mexico with my Spanish classes in high school. I minored in Spanish while in college. I have also been back to Mexico as an adult several times, as well as to Puerto Rico, speaking and understanding the language. I think leaving the Bronx (where I grew up) and leaving East Harlem (where I worked for my last two years in Harlem) took my opportunities to use the language frequently. My pronunciation is so bad now that my son said he cannot believe I used to speak Spanish. I attended, for a short time, the Teaneck Rodda Centers' Senior Spanish classes. I realized that studying was needed, and that was on my 'what I do not want to do list.' I tell myself that I will eventually use an app like Duolingo or Babbel and continue to brush up on my Spanish. My upcoming trip to South America is to Brazil, where they speak Portuguese, which has a 90% lexical similarity to Spanish. I pray that when I do go, it will be like riding a bike, and my muscle memory will kick in. Jayla, my granddaughter, was surprised at how much French she remembered when we went to Canada this summer after one year of French class that she took two years ago.

Mindfulness: My therapist, whom I will talk about later, suggested that I take a mindfulness class at Ramapo College because of my inability to stay in the present. Unfortunately, because of the pandemic, this class has not resumed. However, Ramapo College offers Mindfulness Meditation, which I have been participating in once a week when it does not conflict with my yoga class. From these sessions, I realized my extreme difficulty in staying present, but because of this class, I now have an awareness of this, and I can bring my mind back more than before. I am currently completing a mindfulness course through the Krame Center to help me both focus and reduce stress. I can write a whole chapter on the importance of mindfulness, but since I am a novice, I advise you to investigate it on your own and try it.

"

I feel that it is time to retire when every day at your place of employment becomes a chore when there used to be excitement and joy about even the day-to-day challenges.

"

Sixteen

What is Sixteen? Although this book is based on my life after retirement, I had to include my last sixteen years of working, which made my retirement so necessary. I was always told, and I tell others, that retirement is an individual decision. It's not just when you reach a certain age or have that magic number of years. At least for me, it's when you know you cannot go on anymore. I know of people who are not ready to retire, and they are in their 70s, 80s, and even 90s, needing to do something to keep busy. I remember my neighbor and very close friend of the family, William Moon; even after retiring, he found things to keep him busy at age 90+, even if it was working on his immaculate manicured lawn or helping others like what he calls his old ladies, taking them or picking them up from work. I feel that it is time to retire when every day at your place of employment becomes a chore when there used to be excitement and joy about even the day-to-day challenges. So, I knew it was time at age 55, but I had to wait three more years.

I always said that I would write a book about my last School District because what was going on was such an unbelievable experience. But I guess that could be said of any workplace once you get a peek behind the curtains of their inner workings.

I was an educator for 31 years. I taught for fifteen years, and I was an administrator for sixteen years. My first seventeen years as an educator were in the Village of Harlem, what used

to be called District Five. Fifteen years at Public School 129 John H. Finley Elementary School as an elementary school teacher, and two years at Community School 30/31 Rafael Hernandez / Langston Hughes Elementary School as an assistant principal and then continued to be an administrator for fourteen years in both middle schools and elementary schools in New York's Southern Westchester County District schools.

I love teaching. I went to Howard University in Washington, D.C., to be an Elementary School teacher. Teaching is in my blood. I played being a teacher when I was growing up. In High School, at John F. Kennedy High School in The Bronx, New York, I was part of a Future Teachers program. I was assigned to a school in Washington Heights to work with children in small groups. My mother was a retired elementary school teacher, also in District Five in the Village of Harlem. I spent a lot of time in my mother's first-grade and second-grade classrooms while I was growing up; I graded spelling and math test papers a lot of weekends for my mother and helped with the design of her bulletin boards. When I started teaching, my classroom and bulletin boards often resembled my mother's classroom and bulletin boards. We did similar school plays and often went on the same trips to New York City's World Trade Center, The Circle Line around Manhattan, New York City's Central Park Zoo, or the Bronx Zoo, and would meet each other with our classes at Van Cortlandt Park in the Bronx for our annual end-of-the-year cookout which would always consist of Sabrett grilled hotdogs. Two of my sisters,

Sharon and Shelley, are also retired educators who also started in District Five. We were known in District Five as either the Burns Sisters or Loni Burns' daughters. When I was a classroom teacher, I sought leadership positions or was selected for positions such as third-grade leader. My Assistant Principal, Mrs. June Cardwell, encouraged me to supervise student teachers from City College so that I could get vouchers to take free leadership classes toward a second master's degree. Even though I told her, I love being in the classroom and having my own group of children. The experience of seeing these young minds developing, going from point A in September and the progress achieved by June, was such a rewarding experience that I could not imagine giving it up. Mrs. Cardwell insisted that with my talent and leadership abilities, I needed to be prepared when certain doors opened, even if it was not as an assistant principal or principal.

I had a master's degree in reading and wanted to be a reading teacher in my school. At that time, those positions were lifelong Title I-funded, and no one was retiring.

Doors began to open for me. Ms. Beverly Ford became the principal at P.S. 129. I did my supervisory classes under Ms. Ford's leadership as she began making some creative changes. I left the classroom because I was given the opportunity to facilitate a Science, Mathematics, and Technology mini-school within my same school building with some amazing, dedicated teachers. This was before charter schools in New York City and schools within a school. The mini-school became very successful as we partnered with City College. Companies began donating their old computers as they upgraded to newer ones. Our speech teacher and my Sistah-friend, Karen VanDerHorst, became our computer repair person during her lunch breaks and before and after school. Teachers became excited about being able to be more inventive in their teaching.

Teachers were able to extend their time for teaching various subjects, leading to more student-led lessons and more autonomy in their teaching and their student's learning. Students enjoyed the hands-on learning, the outings, and the comradery. Unfortunately, we were abruptly introduced to the politics of education as we closed the doors of the mini-school and were thrust back into the regular population. I can honestly say, and those colleagues around me can attest, that I lost my fervor in my last years as a teacher and my last years as an administrator. I was always told I only have two speeds; I am either all in or I am going through the motions. Something broke in me, and I could not bounce back after the mini-school shut down. I've never done well with disappointment and still do not (that's the spoiled brat in me). In New York City, I became what they call a Cluster Teacher, teaching 45 minutes of science using a SMART, Science, Mathematics, and Technology curriculum to several grades. The SMART curriculum was a great program for grades kindergarten to sixth grade, but it was an unrealistic feat trying to facilitate hands-on science once a week for less than 45 minutes to back-to-back different grades. Even with having my own science classroom, the setup and clean-up took at least 20 minutes, no matter how you prepared for the day. This time in my life was becoming taxing, and it seemed like I was disagreeing or complaining about something at work daily. When you know that something is working, especially for the students, it's hard to go back to mundane, overcrowded, textbook-driven, time-restraint curriculums.

God opened another door or an escape hatch for me in 1999. I was at my good friend Quentin's retirement party in Washington, D.C., when I got the news that I was being offered a new position. The Chancellor took over some of the failing New York City Schools, and I applied and became an Assistant

Principal. Being a school administrator was not my dream; it was more like an expectation. It was a challenge. It was my next step. I wanted to continue at P.S. 129, which became one of the Chancellor's District schools, as an administrator, but I was sent to another District Five school on the east side of the village of Harlem. Although I was disappointed that I could not stay in my familiar surroundings, I felt blessed because the school's new principal was a well-known, outstanding former assistant principal of another District Five school who became principal and happened to know my mother. Ironically, both of our birthdays are on January 16. It was a great fit, and I was learning so much from Mrs. Harriett Fortson as I did from my last principal, Ms. Beverly Ford, at P.S. 129. But again, the politics of education reared its ugly head, and Mrs. Fortson was removed from C.S. 30, just like Beverly Ford was removed when P.S. 129 became one of the Chancellor's schools.

I must stop and let you know that I do not do well with politics, not in my teaching career or even as a minister. The mini school at P.S. 129 was successful for the students, parents, and teachers who were a part of it but not for those who were not a part of it, so the state said it had to be dismantled because improving the rest of the school would take extra funding. Does that make sense to you? That is exactly why we have so many failing inner-city schools. I've taught talented and gifted classes for several years, and the disparities in funding and special attention were so evident. There have been so many controversial discussions about gifted programs in schools. My children and nieces attended a Talented and Gifted School in East Harlem. Intelligent and gifted students deserve the additional funding to help address their needs, as well as Title 1 students, lower functioning students, and special needs students. However, I notice that groups always seem to fall through the cracks in our educational system. Schools and school districts, especially in the inner cities, are disproportionately funded. Charter Schools seem to be the answer, but even with that, the funding, students, and involved parents are being taken away from the performance needed in the public schools. I cannot go down the rabbit hole with a discussion about the school system. I thank God for principals like Ms. Beverly Ford and Mrs. Harriet Fortson, whose priority was the education of their students and not playing the political games that would ultimately hinder their students. I thank God for placing role models like this in my path, but unfortunately, these leaders had to be removed. I later realized that this type of thinking is why, when the time came, I would not be successful as an interim principal in Southern Westchester. I was never able to play the political game. My first principal at P.S. 129, Mrs. Vera Smith, reminded me that I needed to be more diplomatic when meeting with parents. I was a stern teacher with high expectations. I had the same high standards for all of my students; I expected my students' parents to do their part. I was never able to stomach those who hindered young people's progress, be it a teacher, parent, staff, or administrator. My priority was always on the students and those who were truly committed to their education. God has blessed me with the gift of discernment to recognize those who are, I will not say, fake but insincere colleagues. Did I really want to be a part of this? I worked closely with the next principal at the East Harlem School, but she chose to leave and was replaced by another (3rd principal in two years) principal. The Chancellor's District Schools' curriculum was a SFA – Success For All program. SFA was a scriptive program. I had to strongly encourage creative teachers to become robots in their teaching. While at this school, one of the teachers introduced me to the book The Prayer of Jabez by Bruce Wilkerson. The book is based on 1 Chronicle 4:9-10 and enlarging your territory. This time, I knew that it was my time to exit. God enlarged my territory. The second principal left the Village of Harlem and took a Curriculum position in Southern Westchester. She urged my sister Sharon to leave her assistant principal position at P.S. 161 in the Village of Harlem and apply for a Principal Position in this Southern Westchester School District. After my sister got the principal position, they both encouraged me to apply for a position also, with the promise of greener pastures. My antennas should have gone up when I interviewed for an elementary school assistant principal position at an elementary school, was offered the position, and more behind-door politics prevailed, unbeknownst to me at the school board meeting, they decided to place me in a middle school, when all of my experience was elementary pre-k to 6th-grade, as a teacher and as an administrator.

Praying the Prayer of Jabez and asking God to enlarge my territory did make changes in my life. It was not only the beginning of a new position in Southern Westchester but also the beginning of my ministry. I did not understand then that you need to be careful what you pray for. I realized that I needed a change. I also recognized that a lot was going on around the same time. My son was leaving to start college in August 2001. I would start seminary at New Brunswick Theology in five months, at the beginning of the year in January 2002. I was also going to be licensed as a minister in January 2002. All of this could only be God's way of blessing me abundantly. I prayed for financial blessings to make these additional financial ends meet. This new position included a financial increase in salary; I began making more money in ten months in this Southern Westchester School District than I was making in twelve months in the New York City Chancellor's District school. I began working at a middle school as an Assistant Principal on Monday, September 10, 2001. We all know what happened to the world the very next day. On September 11, 2001, it became chaotic in the school. It seemed like every teacher was tuned into the current events, watching the airplanes hit the Twin Towers, and wanted to leave the school to get home, pick up their own children, or just try to make sense of what was happening in the world. Parents were picking up their children early. At the end of what seemed like a never-ending day, when we finally emptied the building, I was able to leave. I could not get in touch with my own family or get across the George Washington Bridge to leave New York and get into New Jersey because the bridge was completely shut down as a precaution for more terrorist attacks. I made it to my mother's house in the Bronx but could not stay. This was the first time I can remember that I had to choose between my mother and my husband and daughter (my son was away at college). With all the unknown outside of my mother's door, I still had to get home to my family to feel as though I was safe.

It had me asking God if this was a sign. If it was a sign, I did not adhere to His warning. I still resigned from my position in the Village of Harlem instead of taking the recommended leave of absence to test the new waters. For some strange, unknown reason, I knew in my spirit that God orchestrated this new move.

God's enlarging of my territory came when tuition payments were needed for my son, who started North Carolina Agriculture and Technology in August 2001. I was beginning New Brunswick Theological Seminary working toward my Master of Divinity Degree in January 2002, which was an additional and unplanned tuition.

I spent one year at that middle school, and as always, I befriended some amazing teachers, staff, and administrators. But it was the first time in my adult life I found out (this is hearsay) that I was referred to as "that Bitch" by my principal.

I can go on and on about my trials and tribulations in this district. It was obvious that I was not wanted. As I said before, I could write a book, but all I can say is that during my time there, I was constantly reminded that I was an outsider. I was told that I did not grow up in this town. I was reminded that I was not a product of this town's school system. I was even told that I did not pay property taxes in this town. People constantly pointed out that I lived 'all the way' in New Jersey. You would think that New Jersey was on another coast instead of the next state south of New York, approximately 17 miles, a 45-minute drive away in traffic, and less than 30 minutes away without traffic. I lived closer than many of the teachers and administrators who lived in upstate New York who commuted for over one hour daily.

In my 14 years in this Southern Westchester school district, I was in two middle schools, two elementary schools, and then back to my second middle school, which moved, and the name was changed twice. I had eight principals, one interim principal, and five superintendents. The mixing around of the leadership seemed to be the district culture when I was there. You do not have to take my word for it, but in 13 out of the 14 years as an administrator in this district, I was very good at my job. Ask any of my colleagues, dedicated teachers, parents, or students whose path I have crossed. My priority has always been the students first, and encouraging and assisting conscientious teachers and staff members second, as well as aiding and helping in the development of those marginal teachers and staff members who wanted to improve. I fought tirelessly with the teachers' unions and those individuals who were harmful to our students. As an assistant to nine principals in this district, I always aimed to carry out their vision for the school. One principal became like a brother to me at the time, especially since I had recently lost my only brother to a fatal car accident in 2000. Two of the principals were my mentors, and we are still good friends. With everyone I worked with, we as colleagues were all cordial and respectful of each other's roles, except for one which I already mentioned.

I seriously hurt my lower back twice breaking up fights in two of the schools I worked in; the first incident was between a female and a male student in the elementary school, and the second one was preventing a physical altercation with a female cafeteria worker and a male student in the middle school who allegedly repeatedly disrespected the cafeteria worker. As a result, my lower back is still a reoccurring issue that has caused other issues with other parts of my body.

Each of the four schools was a learning experience. I am not a fan of change, but I learned to embrace it as I waited for what God had for me.

I do not know if you caught it, but I said 13 out of the 14 years as an administrator, I was very good at my job. I said I was ready to retire at 55, three years before I retired. We were without a principal again. We also had a new superintendent again. Superintendent number 4 for me so far. She asked me to be the Interim Principal until they could find someone for the position. I accepted the challenge, and it was a challenge every day from August to June of the 2012 - 2013 school year. One of the most memorable encounters was on a Sunday. On Sunday, October 28, 2012, Super Storm Sandy hit; according to Wikipedia, "It was the deadliest, the most destructive, and the strongest hurricane of the 2012 Atlantic hurricane season," About three months into my Principalship, our school became a shelter on a Sunday while I was at Akil and Stephanie Davis's wedding. I got calls from the district administrators throughout the event about what was happening in "my" school. December was another memorable time for the whole country. On December 14, 2012, the Sandy Hook Elementary

School Shooting occurred in Connecticut while I was at a Westchester County Monthly Principals Meeting. Twenty-six people were killed, and twenty of the victims were children. Heightened safety protocols were put in place immediately. I was instructed that as the principal during lockdowns, because of an active shooter or other dangerous situations, I had to be on hand with our security officers to ensure the building was secure until the police took over. That did not sit well with my family or me. I felt responsible for everyone in the school building, but honestly, the captain going down with the ship was not anything I signed up for. My husband reminded me that I, too, have a family to come home to.

I thank God that I never had to make that decision. Violence in the schools and school shootings has continued, and I am grateful that I am no longer at the helm of a school.

As interim principal, working in the same building as an assistant principal for nine years, I began to see my relationship with the teachers and the staff change. I realized that it is true that it is lonely at the top. The buck stopped with me, and I did not have a principal to go to advocate on others' behalf. I missed the days when I was the intermediary or could pass on issues and concerns or collaborate with my principal. I also cannot forget the parents who loved me one day and then ran to the superintendent's office to complain about me when they could not get their way. I struggled daily with the decisions of consequences for behavioral issues: are the penalties too lenient or too severe? Dealing daily with some of the teachers who lack classroom management skills and, even worse, sometimes their lack of caring for some of their students became insurmountable. Almost daily, I felt as though I was the rope or the flag in the middle in a 'tug of war' with parents and/or the district on one end pulling and teachers, union, and/or staff on the other end pulling, with a large puddle of muddy deep water that I can fall into with either side having more strength on any given day. There was no victory for me in the middle.

I think the only thing that God was telling me during my one year as interim principal is that you will be retiring soon. The only positive takeaway that I took from this experience was a boost in salary, which resulted in a boost in my pension.

Surprisingly, a principal from another Westchester School District told me that I could not be successful because I cared too much. I did care too much, and that would never change. I cared about every child, every Black and Brown student in any school. I am (not was) concerned about every Black and Brown boy's past, present, and future as we prepare them to take their rightful place in a world that is trying to extinguish their very existence. I care about the success of every special-needs child and their teachers. I am pointing this population out because I first had to be a strong parent advocate for my own large-built, dark-skinned, very outspoken, extremely intelligent son since he was in pre-school. As an elementary school teacher, I had to ensure that all of my students were treated fairly and knew that they were supported. Also, when I started in the middle schools of this Southern Westchester district, the special needs classes were in the basement until two special education supervisors who were advocates in these two middle schools fought to give the students an equal place at the table of what we call equal education. These advocates and dedicated special education teachers and aids forced us administrators and general education teachers to see each student's potential. I cared about the personal lives of my teachers because they could not always leave it at the door and do business as usual. I cared about the sacrifices and struggles of the parents in this community. I cared more about the wholeness of everyone in the school than (God forbid that I am saying this aloud) the scores that were not the true reflection of the success of our students and teachers as well as believe it or not, our parents' efforts. I went through 31 years of the blame game. Teachers blamed the other teachers who had their students prior to the students coming to them. I do not have any high school experience, but I know that the middle school teachers blame the elementary schools for the student's lack of progress. The elementary school teachers blame the earlier grade teachers, and everyone blames the parents, society, poverty, inequality, lack of funding, lack of resources, and lack of support.

As a principal, I continued with innovative ideas and measures to improve teaching and learning, but I struggled and was bogged down daily with the daily, ongoing nonsense (lack of a better word) that did not benefit anyone's learning. Was I a good principal? Was I successful? All I can say is that God placed me in that position because, as an assistant to 9 principals in Southern Westchester, there were always areas that I felt that I could do better. I found out that it's hard to do better when your hands are tied one day, or you feel like you are drowning the next day. So, all I can say is that I made it through and that I gave it my all.

I suffered from stress-related illnesses and pains, which also resulted in having less hair on my head during my Principalship. With the Grace of God, again, I say I made it through one of the most difficult times of my life. I must say that in all my years in education, I have loved young people. The young people were never the problem, not even the most challenging students; it was the adults. I often wonder if I would have been better off staying in my first corner room 301 classroom at Public School 129, enjoying my students each year until it was time for me to retire. My daughter recently asked me what I would do if I had a career do-over. I told her that instead of being an administrator after teaching, I would prefer to go the counseling route. I enjoy spending time with young people, assisting and guiding them along their life and educational journey. My office was not only a place for discipline as an administrator but also a safe haven for the students. I was glad that I could set up small advisory groups in the middle school before I retired because all children need their voices heard, even in school. I have students from my teaching and administration days with whom we keep in touch. There is one student that I have known since she was in second grade, and I tutored her in an after-school program at Harlem Dowling Family and Children Services before she became my student in my third-grade class. She has gotten married and has children. She lives in Florida. She is now working on her doctorate. The two of us never lost touch with each other. Many years ago, she reminded me that it was because of me that she knew her multiplication tables. As a teacher, I was determined that you were not going to leave my third-grade class without knowing your times tables. I have other students and parents who have found me on social media, and we keep in touch with each other. Even though I have many fond memories and success stories of being in the educational field, I will say it again and again: I thank God for retirement. When I am asked if I miss it, my answer is always not at all. I love that I wake up with my own agenda and say, "Heaven must be like this." I know I am being repetitive again, but my last 18 years out of 31 years of working have been beyond stressful.

Until I got into the groove of retirement, I thought that this is how life is supposed to be. I thought that life was supposed to be stress-filled. Jeremiah 29:11 reminds us that God knows the plans he has for each one of us. Plans to prosper and not fail. I thank God for the teachers, principals, administrators, supervisors, staff (secretarial, custodial, paras, aide, cafeteria workers, counselors), students, parents, and superintendents that God placed in my life to guide, help, and even love me on this journey of 31 long years. I pray that you know who you are and the roles that you played in my life.

As I end this chapter, since my first paraprofessional when I began teaching third grade at the John H. Finley Elementary School Public School 129, Mrs. Delores McCain recently went home to be with the Lord. I must acknowledge publicly that she saved me during my first year of teaching a very challenging third-grade class, and she taught me how to be a teacher. I thank God for Mrs. Delores McCain not only for your acceptance, assistance, guidance, love, and friendship during the 15 years at P. S. 129 but also for remaining part of my life until death do we part. I dedicate this chapter to you. You were with me through the death of my father, brother, and mother, as well as in the raising of my own children, and I thank you for your unselfish, agape (unconditional) love!

"

We need to look at the foods and the food preparations of our family and begin making better choices and pass on healthier recipes.

"

5

Work It!

People think that I am more conscientious with food and workouts because I talk a good game about what I should be doing all the time, but I have my moments. I have to work on it constantly and intentionally! It is so easy for me to fall back into bad habits with both eating and working out. I have to work out regularly because I am a confessed bonified foodie. Food soothes my emotions. I will eat if I do not restrain myself, when I am bored, or when I am frustrated, (I was going to say some of the time) most of the time, I am a stress eater, or I eat just because. I am what they call a grazer and can eat all day long. My husband does not understand why I do not get full after a meal, I do not understand it either because with my size it cannot be because of a fast metabolism. Commercials will entice me to go out or order a particular type of fast food but then I am 99% disappointed because fast food does not do it for me most of the time.

Good health and fitness are another generational plan, in addition to wealth, that I want to pass on to the next generation. Passing on the importance of your own wealth, a healthy lifestyle, and exercising regularly will change the course of the next generation towards a better life. A health provider once informed me that you do not have to inherit the diseases of those before you, like high blood pressure, high cholesterol, diabetes, and gout. We think prescription medication is the answer to correcting these conditions instead of preventive measures like lifestyle changes such as a healthy diet and exercise. We need to look at the foods and the food preparations of our family and begin making better choices and pass on healthier recipes. I also want to pass on traveling and seeing the whole world to the next generation and you also have to be healthy to achieve that.

I might be repeating myself in this chapter but as I sit here today. I struggle with losing the last 10 pounds, AGAIN! Women do not tell their weight, but my plan is now to stay under 170 pounds. I feel as though I literally look at food and gain weight. My goal is 165 pounds because I need five pounds to play with. I question if the National BMI is for people of color. At 5'5", according to their standards, I should be less than 140 pounds, which was fine in my twenties before childbirth. On my good days even at my lowest, I am overweight according to the BMI calculations. I am constantly slipping back into the obese range of 30. Now I struggle to stay in the 28 range which is still considered overweight. According to their standards to be at a healthy weight I should be 23. They do not take into consideration being "big-boned" and the struggle of being naturally flabby and wanting to develop a more muscular frame. I may be considered overweight by BMI standards, but I am feeling and looking good by my standards and, just as importantly, by my doctors' approval.

I have what my mother's friend, Annette Lee, calls the 'Burns Butt.' Everyone in my family both females and males with strong Burns genes has this feature. My primary care doctor, Dr. Michael Denker, wanted me to weigh no more than 180 pounds. I've struggled and have gotten to 180 pounds many times. My cardiologist, Dr. Tariqshah Syed, informed me that because of my family history of heart disease, he wanted me to be down to 170 pounds. Both my mother and her father died of heart disease. 180 pounds was hard enough, so I thought 170 pounds was impossible for me. But I did it… Thank God!

One of the things that I could not wait to do because work got in the way was going to the gym regularly. When I was working, I used to get up before daybreak to do Tae Bo with Billy Blanks for many years. We kept a VCR player just so I could use my outdated Tae Bo VCR tape. I had two treadmills, one burned out and my husband thought that it was a good idea to buy me another one, which I eventually gave away. My neighbor when they moved gave us a sitting elliptical that my granddaughters used more than I did and they are only with me one month in the summer, but I figured that this machine would be perfect for my husband since you can sit and use this machine. Using these machines is boring to me and I cannot always self-motivate myself to exercise at home. I joined a gym while working but was only able to muster up enough energy on Saturdays to do a class. Saturday workouts at the gym, eating salmon and chopped salads for lunch, walking up and down four flights of steps all day at work, even though there was an elevator. I would encourage and sometimes force my colleagues to walk up and down the stairs with me. Some of them would run away when they saw me coming. I was also drinking tons of water, and all of this was not giving me the needed results. I later found out that this did not mix well with the stress of the job.

Retirement gave me an assortment of workout opportunities; I told you that I love walking, so I started walking in the parks and around the neighborhoods. I found a way to walk every place I went while traveling. I prefer working out in classes instead of doing it on my own because it forces me to challenge myself. I tried various classes at the gym, looking for my right fit: Aquacise, Zumba, Silver Sneakers,

Pilates, Yoga, Body Pump, Body Flow, Body Combat, and Spin Classes. Like everything else in my life, I overdid it at the gym. I often spent two to three hours at the gym, taking two or three classes. My mindset was that I was not going to drive to the gym for only 1 one-hour class, to me at the time felt like that was a waste of gas. At the beginning sometimes I would work out five to six days per week. The only day that is off-limits at the gym is Sunday. I hurt my knee, my ankle, my foot, and my lower back. I love my Zumba classes and my Zumba instructors, especially first Mark and then Lele and Kim. I was doing Zumba three to four days per week until I finally had to give it up because of my knee, then my ankle, and then my knee again, not to mention persistent reoccurring lower back pain. I befriended one of 24-Hour Fitness Gym's best instructors, Trey Jackson. Trey subbed one Saturday for an aqua class when I was still working, and she said that she normally taught the Friday morning aqua class. As soon as I retired, I joined her Friday aqua class. I also joined her Silver Sneakers class and occasionally her spin class. She was the one who showed me how to adjust the spin bike so that it would not be painful for certain parts of my body during and after the class. Trey would end every Friday's aqua class by saying, "Make healthy choices." Her words would ring in my ears all weekend, often stopping me from making unhealthy choices. Trey from 24-Hour Fitness Gym was the first person to change my eating mindset. Then my "coach," Tieandra in Florida, and my unofficial trainer, Tasha from T-2 Fitness in Virginia started holding me accountable for my workouts with workout challenges and suggestions on the foods I should eat and not eat. Trey also would give me tips on how to use the weight machines and which machines would be best for what I was trying to accomplish.

When I first joined the gym, it was with my husband. We joined Bally's in Englewood Cliffs before it became the 24-Hour Fitness Gym. I would take a Zumba class with Mark, which I loved. Mark's classes became so popular that I always had to get there early, and sometimes, numbers were given out so that the room would not fill over the required capacity. At Bally's, my husband and I would use the weight machines together as well as the pool. I cannot forget the first classes that I took at the Paramus 24-Hour Fitness Gym. I started with Aquacise. I started with Phil on Saturday mornings before retiring. After I retired, I could do weekday mornings with phenomenal instructors: Aqua with Ceribet on Wednesdays and Trey on Fridays. KaTonya, another extraordinary instructor, would sub for some aqua classes. I bonded with wonderful women and men in the pool, hot tub, and sauna as we strived to maintain better health. Eventually, I joined additional classes after the aquacise classes. I joined Laura's class after Ceribet's water aerobics on Wednesdays with Pilates. I joined Kim after Trey's water aerobics on Fridays with Zumba. I would do Danny with kickboxing, aka Body Combat on Thursdays, which changed my philosophy about only taking one class. Danny's classes are absolutely worth the gas. Danny's Body Combat was like more than one class. I even forced myself to do a night Zumba class because Travis, an outstanding instructor, was teaching the class. Travis is another instructor who is worth the sacrifice to attend his class. When I would leave Travis' night class, my body would not shut down so that I could fall asleep at a decent hour. I was also blessed to have three exceptional Body Pump 24-Hour Fitness instructors who deserve recognition: Maryanne at Englewood Cliffs, and Danny and Fanny in Paramus. I am still taking classes with Fanny. The three classes (Spin and two Body Pumps) I now take three days per week are with Fanny.

Gym

I saw my body slowly chiseling down, including my Burns Butt. I have learned through the constant ups and downs of my weight loss that slow, intentional weight loss is the most beneficial. In an article through Holy Name Hospital by Dr. David Shaker, I just read that "there is no one-size-fits-all approach to weight loss." I went through years of fad diets throughout my life. I remember running into a Senior Saint church member, Sister Rose Scott in Walgreens and she told me that the ups and downs of my weight are not good for my body. She is no longer with us, but her words have stuck with me, and I am trying to do better. Once again God has placed someone in my life to plant a seed. Traveling has been the only thing altering this new revelation. For some reason, I have not been able to eat as healthily as I want and need to while traveling. It seems impossible for me not to partake of breads and potatoes, not to mention irresistible desserts which are all my weight loss kryptonite while traveling.

After stopping with Aquacise, even though it is a great form of exercise, I stopped because they changed the equipment, and I found the new tubes difficult to work with. The instructor asked that they replace this new equipment with equipment similar to the old equipment but that still has not happened. But I needed to change my routine because my body became used to it, and I was not seeing too much of a change anymore. I was advised and I also came to realize that it is best to change up your exercise routine every once in a while, to continue to see weight-loss results.

The gym and my gym buddies, Tasha Turnbull, and her book The Last 10 Pounds, Rosemarie Dunham holding me accountable with Monday weigh-ins, as well as Tieandra Cole whom I call Coach, challenging me to walk 20,000 steps, checking in on me, and giving me some great suggestions, such as looking at a Keto food wheel of do's and don'ts, all helped with a healthier lifestyle and weight loss.

My workouts were consistent. My eating habits became more intentional until March 2020 when everything shut down because of the pandemic. Like many others, I became isolated and started eating my mixed emotions. I must confess that I am still eating my disappointments. I even started cooking (cooking is not my fortè). I cooked real meals for breakfast and dinner for my husband and I and learn and implemented new recipes.

As a minister, I was getting almost daily (no exaggeration) prayer requests and sadly reports of too many deaths because of this horrific disease called COVID-19.

In January 2021 Tasha in T2 Fitness started a 30-day workout challenge that included food preps and healthy food choices. I joined (I can be very competitive). I won the challenge, and the changes began… Tasha started virtual classes. Tasha gave me exactly what I needed, I was held accountable for my workouts, my cardio, my eating, and my daily choices of food and exercises. It was a small group effort and we encouraged each other virtually as we worked out and posted on Facebook our cardio workouts, our food preps, and our meals. I lost 30 pounds and went down 3 sizes. I must confess that maintaining weight loss might be more difficult than losing weight. I now struggle with balancing my last 10 and sometimes 15 pounds because of my traveling.

Usually, when I travel, I gain at least 5 pounds. I've learned to accept that as a fact. When I travel, I usually eat carbs and sweets (which I already mentioned are my kryptonite), especially breakfast foods. Breakfast foods are my favorite meal. I find it next to impossible to travel by car or airplane without eating fast food. When I am with my grands or my daughter, I usually have sweets too. After my Panama Canal Cruise in January 2022, I gained 12 pounds. It was after gaining weight after the Thanksgiving and Christmas holidays. After the cruise, I tried a 7-day detox for the first time because my sister Sharon is always talking about detoxing and cleansing. The cleanser was to prayerfully get rid of sludge, and water weight and to deter the cravings for carbs and sweets. During this cruise, I ate 3 meals per day. I had French toast, waffles with apples and almond toppings, potatoes, and an omelet. I would eat lunch, which consists of a hardy, healthy, dark green salad but a sandwich and cookies accompanied the salad. For dinner, I would have an appetizer, entree, and dessert often trying more than one of each. Even with doing 2 to 3 classes; sunrise stretch, abs or body workout, cycling, before breakfast on this cruise, and then walking around the deck several times after lunch. I drank at least 50 ounces of water daily too. I still gained 12 pounds.

When I went to Dr. Denker in February this was the first time that I felt as though he was disappointed in me. This is why I love him as my doctor, he keeps me accountable. He did not even do blood work because of what the results might show. I gained 14 pounds since my last doctor's visit 4 months ago. He stated that it was like I gained a pound a day on this 14-day cruise. I vowed to myself to not let that happen again.

Then in the summer of 2022, we went on a 17-day Canadian road trip in July and an August Alaskan cruise which caused an added weight gain before I was able to lose what I was trying to lose from November through January gains. The gains were not as bad with these next two trips, but I do know that I cannot keep doing these ups and downs to my body.

Once the Rodda Center opened back up after the pandemic, I returned to yoga. We started with spring and summer 2021 yoga classes outside in Votee Park. Then we continued in the fall, winter, spring, and winter again of 2021-2022 yoga classes indoors.

I cautiously returned to the gym in March 2022, facemask, and all, taking Spin classes on Monday mornings, then a Body Flow class, and then thirty minutes of weights using the machines. In April I returned to a Friday Body Pump class. My body yearned for the return of all these classes. Eventually, I added a Tuesday Body Pump class too, and stopped the weights on Mondays. I tried adding the pool on Fridays after the weight class, but I am not consistent with that because of the hassle of changing clothes. I want to go to the pool with my husband but he goes in the evenings but my body has already shut down for the day.

When I get up each morning and say my prayers, while I am down on my knees I usually do push-ups, as well as leg and back stretches and a plank (I need to do better with my morning planks). I continue to maintain my weight by walking every chance I get. I was walking for two hours while listening to audible books or music. Drinking 50 to 100 ounces of water per day. I should be drinking 100 ounces or at least half my body weight each day but I must be strategic with balancing bathroom opportunities. I was drinking 100 ounces to a gallon of water each day while doing T2 Fitness and my doctor stopped me because he said that I was flushing out needed nutrients. This was another way that I was overdoing it and hurting my body.

I am now working out at the gym in classes three days per week and at the Rodda Center one day per week. I always choose walking over driving whenever I can. I am intermittent fasting, eating my first meal after noon. I am starting to be more intentional with eating more protein for muscle strength. With intermittent fasting, I try to eat my dinner around 6 p.m. My choice of beverage is always water because anything else is wasted calories.

Even with eating salmon, which I love, I had to limit my intake to three times per week because of possible mercury. I also had to stop the smoothies because my glucose levels elevated. I am sure that my travel diet contributed to both the elevation of my glucose and the elevation of my cholesterol. I can now only eat one fruit a day, and although I did not want to give up my morning blueberries, my one daily fruit is an orange. Oranges are supposed to help lower your cholesterol. I am very conscientious about knowing my numbers and keeping my numbers in the normal range. I take supplements to help maintain both my blood pressure and cholesterol as well as being mindful of the foods that I eat. I love avocados but it is on the eat-in-moderation list for my cholesterol. I love, love, love fruits but that too I had to limit. The first time that I cut out fruits from my diet I lost 10 pounds. Bananas are filling but I had to stop with them because they are too high in sugar for me. I also try to eat steel-cut oatmeal because Michelle at Dr. Denker's office advised me to start eating oatmeal to lower my cholesterol. Once I get my numbers in an acceptable range and maintain the numbers I need to find wild blueberries because I just found out that wild blueberries help prevent Epstein Barr flare-ups. I need to do better with my eating on weekends. I usually eat what my husband eats on Sundays; the only day we eat breakfast together (grits, red salmon, and sausages), and also dinner together. We also often order out for food on some Fridays but most Saturdays. But no matter what I must report my weight losses or gains to my BFF Rosemarie on Monday mornings. Now my sisters Sharon and Shelley and I are also reporting our weight on Mondays to each other. You need to have at least one accountability partner.

Intermittent fasting, water, and little to no carbs are all working for me in addition to workouts. The fact that weight loss is 80% food intake and 20% exercise keeps me intentional most of the time about what I eat. Carbs will put 5 pounds on me in one day, as well as foods high in sodium. I do not cook with sodium, but I have to be mindful of reading labels for their sodium content. Including spices, sauces, and dressings. Also, any dining out or ordering out you do will contain high amounts of sodium, which can be a problem for me on weekends. I was raised without salt as a seasoning because of my father's high blood pressure, and I raised my children with a saltless diet (which they might not have continued the practice). They now refer to my food as bland. My husband will grab the saltshaker without tasting his food when I cook. With all the health-conscious eating that I do, 'all bets are off' when 1) I travel 2) I am with my daughter or grands 3) If I go to a dinner or an event. I seem to not even try to restrain myself. I can say that I am good at my eating at home alone (with Willie), most of the time but Willie can be a bad influence at times (if I let him) with his food suggestions. I must confess that I do not always have the willpower and am not always strong enough to resist!

Age and weight are two things that women seem to not want to talk about, but I told you my age already. As for weight, I was at my heaviest in seminary, at 5'5" I was 216 pounds busting out of a size 16. My lowest in the last thirty or so years was 163 pounds working out with Tasha and T2 Fitness. I wear a size 10/Medium and I am happy with this size as long as it does not become tight-fitting. Most of my dresses are a size 12. Now, I struggle during my travels to stay below 175 pounds. I think I already mentioned my goal weight, but that changes with my mood…, it's those last 10 pounds that I wrestle with.

Tasha helped me through the COVID-19 times both physically and mentally, but they say all good things must come to an end. I will never believe that. I believe that you make your own good. I have always been a half-empty type of person, while Willie has always been a half-full person, but now I try to always focus on the positive and possibilities in more and more cases. I try to think and speak positively. Tasha "broke up" (my words) with me at the end of September 2021 after 10 months and 30 pounds. Did I say that I can be selfish? I kept convincing myself that I understood that Tasha needed to stop with the virtual classes and get back to her in-person studio and clients in Virginia Beach now that the world was getting back to its new normal since the pandemic. My daughter had to convince me that I should not look at it as a negative and look at how I benefited from being with Tasha. I got so used to that daily accountability and commitment with both workouts and healthy foods. I guess eventually the training wheels had to come off and with the tools she imparted to me, I can now ride on my own. Thank you, Tasha! Also thank you for always being here for me. I always have questions and you are still taking the time to answer them. I now know that God sent me another Angel. You are truly a blessing, and you helped change my life, especially when this world seemed upside down!

My Monday morning Body Flow class recently switched to evenings. My evening class days are over even though I know I needed this extra stretching of all parts of my body. I used to feel, before my many injuries, as though it was a waste of gas to drive almost 5 miles on Route 4 to the gym for one class (I know that you are saying that it is less than 15 minutes but I do not like to drive at all), as well as how I used to feel the need to be at the gym five days per week and walk two hours daily. Now, as of the end of October 2022, at age 65, my workouts are four days a week even though I have to explain to the gym regulars why I am not at the gym every day.

Monday mornings are my Spin class. I take this class to rectify my weekend mishaps. This is truly a strenuous one-hour cardio workout. Because I want and need to tone my body, especially after my weight loss, I attend a one-hour Body Pump class at 24-Hour Fitness Gym in Paramus, New Jersey, on Tuesdays and Fridays. The use of free weights and the bar in this class addresses my arms, shoulders, back, legs, and abs. Thursday afternoons are my yoga class at the Rodda Center (Senior Center) in Teaneck, New Jersey. Yoga is so significant for my well-being because it slows down my inner and outer being and mindset. Mr. Martin always gives us seniors tips on improving various parts of our body concerns. He shows us neck, shoulders, lower back, and hip stretches that will help improve our mobility. I try to stretch my lower back and hip daily since I have issues with both reoccurring pains in my lower back and stiffness in my right hip. Sitting crisscrossed was impossible for me when I began yoga. I am now able to sit in a crisscross position, I am working on improving this position so that it will be a comfortable sitting position. I was told to use a block, and that has helped, but now I can sit crisscrossed most of the time without the block. This needs to be a daily practice if I want it to be a natural sitting position.

Balance is also something that is constantly being encouraged by Mr. Martin. My improvements in balance are more than remarkable. Since I am being brutally honest in this book; I know that in yoga sun salutation is so necessary because it addresses every part of your body, but I dread doing it even though Mr. Martin encourages us to do it daily. I feel as though I can do downward-facing-dog all day long but I struggle with staying in an upward-facing-dog position for too long. It uses the same muscle strength as the planks that I struggle with. While doing yoga, I realize that I am not as strong as I think I am, especially in my upper body. This is the reason why I need to do them daily… someday, I promise! I will also stretch daily my back and hips by doing stretches like; Child's Pose, Cat and Cow Stretch, Spine Twists, Knee-to-Chess Stretch, Happy Baby Stretch, The Pelvic Tilt, Bridge Pose, Frog Stretch, and (I did not know the name of this, so I had to look it up, it is great) Supine Figure 4 Stretch, plus various leg stretches laying down and in a seated position. I must tell the truth and shame the devil, it is rare that I do these exercises outside of my classes, but now that I am confessing this, I will try to do better with these and my physical therapy hip exercises, I promise this too!

I am being more intentional about giving my body a break; therefore, Wednesdays are my break days because of the noon prayer, but sometimes, I will walk after the prayer line. It is the same thing on Saturdays; I have 10 am Bible Study, and sometimes I will walk afterward. Even in retirement, I find myself doing housework and laundry on Saturdays, even though I can do it any other day of the week except Sundays. On Sundays, I walk home from church, which is only a 15-minute walk. Right now, my walks are on Tuesdays and Thursdays to and from Physical Therapy, which is fifty minutes each way, but my physical therapy will eventually end. I am walking less and beginning to bulk up because of less cardio. I am continuing with weight classes and a spin class. Now, I am trying to figure out what works for me and my weight-loss journey. I need to be under 170 pounds. How many of you know that you have to change up your exercise routines and even your foods in order to continue to see weight loss results or to even maintain your weight? Or is it just me?

Note:Because our body and our body needs are always changing, since I finished this chapter I am now on a meal plan developed by my church daughter Andrea Ceasar. With this meal plan, I eat 5 small meals per day, with plenty of protein that includes some carbs and healthy fats. I eat ¼ cup of almonds, a half a cup of blackberries or raspberries per day, and I drink a gallon of water a day. I use the app My Fitness Pal to make sure that I eat my recommended 1200 calories per day. I have also made some changes to my workout regimen and I now weigh under 160 pounds.

Hobbies such as jigsaw
puzzles, knitting, crocheting,
quilting, or assembling model
forms of transportation
can help with your mental
health and the mental acuity,
hand-eye coordination, and
sharpness of people of
all ages.

6

Putting The Pieces Together

Putting The Pieces Together is a short chapter that I feel is important to remind us that we all need an outlet, a hobby. My hobby is putting The Pieces Together. It is a hobby and sometimes an obsession. Yes, I love the challenges that come from assembling numerous odd shapes and various colors of pieces that go from a bunch of nothing to becoming eventually something recognizable. If you have not guessed yet, my hobby is assembling jigsaw puzzles, which I call puzzling. You might still ask why we have a chapter about puzzles. Hobbies such as jigsaw puzzles, knitting, crocheting, quilting, or assembling model forms of transportation can help with your mental health and the mental acuity, hand-eye coordination, and sharpness of people of all ages. Before my 14-year-old granddaughter became enamored with puzzles, I would have addressed this chapter to my fellow seniors. Right now, as I am going to bed past my bedtime because I was puzzling (probably not a word yet), Jayla is still up doing the puzzle that we are supposed to be working on together. I like her tenacity, but I wanted to do most of the puzzle myself (if this was a text, I would put the thinking or the rolling my eyes emoji right here).

1000-piece jigsaw puzzles have become my sanctuary. I needed puzzles to help me de-stress from self-imposed stress. Puzzles help me focus and concentrate on one thing (which is usually difficult for me), as well as enhance my problem-solving strategies. But on the other hand, it also feeds into my anal retentiveness and obsessive personality. I become obsessed whenever I start a puzzle. When I am puzzling, I am mesmerized by each piece of the puzzle to the point that everything around me vanishes from both my hearing and sight. I must refrain from my OCD tendencies of not having completion and staying up all night completing the borders of the puzzle or completing a particular section of colors. Puzzles will relax me when I let them; it gives me a breather. It calms my ADHD.

My love for puzzles is so well known that for Christmas, my grandchildren and even my Pastor, Reverend Dr. Marilyn Monroe Harris, gifted me with puzzles. My granddaughters know that when they come to visit for the summer, we are going to start a puzzle. I am a real #puzzlehead, and now my granddaughter Jayla has drunk the Kool-Aid, and also stays up late, is mesmerized by the pieces of the puzzles, and has the same determination towards the completion of certain parts. I feel that she is lackadaisical about everything in her life, but when it comes time for puzzling, she is all in. She has even put her iPhone down to do jigsaw puzzles.

This puzzle hobby keeps my mind occupied. I have to vary my puzzle time because even in retirement, my husband and I have dissimilar schedules. I squeeze in puzzling in between activities during the day or night and try, but not always successfully, not to be so consumed with my puzzle that I do not acknowledge my husband's presence. My puzzles serve multiple purposes that also serve to improve my mental health. But I space out doing my puzzles by months because of the intensity and my self-imposed commitment that comes with this hobby for me, while others can leisurely work on one puzzle for a long period of time, but for me, it becomes another obsession towards completion.

My grandchildren gifted me with a 2000-piece puzzle of World Landmarks 360 (a 360-degree puzzle) last Christmas when I usually do 1000-piece puzzles. I started the puzzle after Willie came home from neck surgery, thinking that it would keep my mind occupied while Willie recovered. I also thought that my son and daughter would want to help me with this 2000-piece puzzle while they were home assisting in the care-giving of their father. The puzzle is so large that I had to purchase a 40x60 board from Blick Art Materials and cut it down for this 38.5 x 26.5 puzzle. I first started separating the pieces by color using thirteen box tops to hold the sorted pieces; then, I assembled the frame/sides before putting the rest of the puzzle together. Unlike my granddaughters, my children did not want any parts of this puzzle. But I, as usual, became fixated, spending almost every waking hour either putting pieces together or thinking about the pieces. I would stay up past midnight some nights puzzling when normally I am sleep at 9pm. It took around three weeks to finish the puzzle; I was like a hermit, only coming out when it was absolutely necessary, even when company came over to see my husband during his recuperation at home. But being a #puzzlehead, I enjoyed every minute of this intense task. I will glue and mount it to the board, but what happens after that? I have no idea. When a puzzle is completed, I glue the front of the puzzle, and then after the front dries, I glue the back of the puzzle to a board. I have had many unsuccessful mountings, but I think I finally found the right type of board from Blick Art Materials in Paramus, New Jersey, on Route 4 West. The glue has varied from puzzle glues to Mod Podge. I do not understand how people can dismantle their puzzles after all the work it takes to assemble them and then put them back in the box until the next time. But "to each his own". My mother always reminded me that "God did not make us all alike."

Route 66 Puzzle

I do not know what to do with all my assembled puzzles. I have puzzles stacked upright in my basement. I am open to suggestions on what I should do with all these completed puzzles. However, even though I stopped hanging things on the walls in my house, I have framed some inspirational Completion puzzles and have them hanging in my room which has become my everything room. Since my children no longer live with us, Willie and I each have an extra room. I framed and hung up the puzzles that inspired my travel: a puzzle of the world, a puzzle of the United States, and a puzzle of the western United States titled Sunset. I also have a completed unframed Route 66 puzzle with the world's smallest 1000-piece puzzle in my room.

My two granddaughters and I did a Coca-Cola puzzle for Willie because that is his drink of choice that is on display in our hallway until we can find a place for it. The last puzzle that I put together and gave to Willie after his back surgery was destroyed in his room because I used the wrong type of board and the wrong type of glue to attach to the board, 'live and learn.' I also have a 14"x 39" long Grand Canyon puzzle on my table/desk in the basement. I completed puzzles during my visits to North Carolina and left them for my grands after we completed them and mounted them. I have given completed puzzles to others, too. My latest puzzle purchase was a Canada puzzle which I purchased while I was in Toronto this summer; now I am debating if I should do the puzzle by myself or wait to do the puzzle with my puzzle partners when they come to stay with us next summer since they were part of the Canada puzzle adventure.

I think that everyone should have some type of calming force that will occupy their minds and distract them from the rigor or even the routine of their everyday life, puzzles do that for me.

7

Golden Plus Years

How many of you have watched and enjoyed the television show *The Golden Girls*? That was my mother's show, and her granddaughters also followed in these viewing footsteps. The show reminded me of the joy of our golden years. There are so many perks to becoming an official bonafide senior, and the Teaneck Township's Richard Rodda Community Center's Senior Center is one of those perks. The Senior Center is such an intricate part of my life that it had to be part of this book. My business #Her2ndStitch was birthed because of the Senior Center. I attribute improvements to my mind and body to the Senior Center. The township of Teaneck supports its senior community. The well-being of this community of people is enhanced through the Center. It unveils the talents of individuals through the various classes offered. It also improves health through the multi-level exercise classes. Nurse Kathy Powers and Social Worker Alex Cerbone are on staff in the Township of Teaneck.

We put our children in various programs while they were growing up that the Township of Teaneck in New Jersey offered for children prior to the Rodda Center opening in 1998. Both of my children did Biddy Basketball, my son played football and baseball, and my daughter started dance classes through the town at age three and later did cheerleading, art, and ran track. They both attended Sports and Arts summer camp. My husband coached both the Teaneck township's Jr Highwaymen football teams for my son and basketball for both our son's basketball teams as well as our daughter's basketball teams. Later, he also coached a friend's son's basketball team. He brags that both my son and daughter won championships when he was their coach. He still has good relationships with the young men that he coached in basketball and football over thirty years ago.

My son got his first job in the town; he "manned" the sprinklers at Teaneck's Marie Andreas Memorial Park. But we teased him that he mostly played in the water because Andreas Memorial Park was unpopular except for parents with small children.

I now remember taking several African Dance classes through the town's programs and a couple of African-American Studies classes at night at Teaneck High School with the late Coach Curtis March. I remember going to a Black educators' conference in Atlanta, Georgia, with a group of Teaneck Black educators through that connection. My mother joined us for the conference. It was my first time in Atlanta, and I got a chance to explore the historic city. Visiting the Rev. Dr. Martin Luther King's Ebenezer Baptist Church and other civil rights historical sites. Of course, my mother and I had to shop at Atlanta's underground mall.

Now, I take advantage of the free senior classes offered at the Rodda Center's Senior Center for Teaneck residents under the director, Mary Beth Hubbard, for seniors 55 and over and two outstanding office assistants, Elaine Polakoff and Mary Beth Flynn, before she retired. Since I do not have children at home anymore, and through the encouragement of Marlene Davis, Carrie Johnson, and Rosalind Chambers from church, I felt compelled to take advantage of what the town has to offer, especially since we are paying such high Bergen County taxes.

After retiring, I took several classes at the Senior Center, starting with cardio and Zumba with Patty Swartz and quilting with Dee, aka Delores Butler. I even tried Spanish classes with Kathy Glowski. I was too advanced for the beginners' class and did not want to put in the brain power effort to continue in the intermediate class. I also tried the Strength and Toning with KaTonya Rochester, but the time of day that it was offered did not work with my schedule. I wanted to take the class with KaTonya because I knew her from the Paramus 24-Hour Fitness Gym. Several people like Naomi Blumenfeld and Wilhelmina Jackson are regular Pilates students, and they both love it, so I tried one Pilates class with Judy Sbrocco, especially since my gym has not offered Pilates since they reopened from the COVID-19 shutdown. Because of COVID-19 precautions, the Rodda Center's Pilates class was only doing standing Pilates and was not using mats. Even though the exercises we did address our core, I needed the core strengthening that the floor exercises provided, so I did not continue after that class.

In the quilting class, Dee and my fellow quilters have helped me with various sewing and quilting techniques and ideas that are now assisting me with my business #Her2ndStitch. Every time I am pinning and/or ironing pieces for my string-quilted pillows, I can still mentally hear Leslie reminding me that I need to use pins and iron each piece, which causes me to slow down and not cut corners.

The Rodda Center offers Introduction, Beginner, and Intermediate Yoga classes. Surprisingly, they are all classified as level 1 classes. For me, the Yoga class, even the Beginner class, is more challenging than the level 3 Zumba class because cardio comes easier for me. I am taking the Intermediate Yoga class with Yogi Martin Bland. I started with the Beginner's class and was truly a yoga novice when I began. Yoga challenges both my body and my state of mind. Yoga is so needed for strengthening, flexibility, balance, breathing, and mindfulness. It is so difficult for me to stay present, to keep my mind from wandering, and my yoga instructor, Martin Bland, constantly reminds us that our focus should be on our bodies and mats. It also forces me to slow down my movements. I mentioned before that if doing yoga stretches can keep me from replacing body parts later in life. I will continue to challenge my body through yoga. I also need yoga to slow the pace of both my mind and body. I am always in a rush, both mentally and physically, not to mention spiritually, too. Yoga is helping with my ADHD and focus.

I have never been flexible, but my flexibility has improved so much. I have a very stiff right hip, and my doctor, Dr. Denker, said that continuing with yoga will help to loosen my hip, it has gradually improved, but of course, I am so impatient and want faster results. I recently discovered through my orthopedic that this stiff right hip is bursitis, so I am now doing physical therapy, yoga, and Voltaren rub to improve the mobility in this hip.

I appreciate the fact that I have continued a sewing friendship bond with those whom I met in the Rodda Center quilting class, as well as yoga class friendships. I also love the noticeable improvements in my body through yoga classes. I pray that I can continue to get into this popular yoga class each session, and I pray that God will continue to bless Mr. Martin Bland to be able to continue to teach the classes.

8

#Her2ndStitch

I had a Pre-Launch Party for my new business venture, #Her2nd-Stitch on Sunday, September 29th, 2019. #Her2ndStitch officially launched on Tuesday, October 1st, 2019, when my handcrafted string quilted pillows with my signature back pockets were placed on display for sale at African Heritage Fashions in Teaneck, New Jersey.

#Her2ndStitch

Several years before retiring, I thought about creative small business outlets that I would pursue when I retire. I did not want to work as many retirees do, but I wanted to find a way to use my creative juices with my assumed free time. I was an art major in high school at John F. Kennedy High School in the Bronx, New York. I expressed an interest in being an artist as a career, but my father quickly shut that down and told me that I was not going to be a starving artist. As an elementary school teacher, I was able to express my artistic abilities throughout my classroom, hallway bulletin boards, school performances, and students' projects in all subject areas. When I became an administrator, all of that was put on hold except for advising or making suggestions to teachers on how to enhance the visual appeals in their classrooms. Elementary school teachers know the importance of a colorful, vibrant, stimulating classroom, but not many secondary school teachers or their administrators that I encountered, when I was in the schools, thought it is necessary to enhance learning through visual stimulation.

I started thinking about designing blank greeting cards. Once upon a time, I pictured my small greeting card store with my logo-styled cards, stationaries, and motivational signs. This dream was before electronic greeting cards. I still love browsing unique, eclectic card stores, but I am not interested in sitting in a store waiting and praying for customers. Maybe someday I might decide to dabble in online cards.

When I retired and began working out in gyms, I thought about my logo-styled drawings again and began drawing markups. With the help of my son, we started researching the possibility of creating my logo-styled inspirational hand towels. For some reason, we could not figure out a cost-effective way to get the logo and wording on the towels. I even reached out to my Howard University first-year roommate at Howard University Truth Hall, Sarita Watson (now Sarita Brewer), who has an embroidery business, as well as Naomi Blumenfeld from my quilting class, who also does embroidery. For some reason, this project would not fall into place. But as I am writing this, my mind is thinking of the possibilities of revisiting this venture as well as greeting and occasion cards.

I spoke recently at the 2022 United Missionary Baptist Convention of New Jersey Women's Conference about my start of #Her2ndStitch. The theme of the conference was 'Hanging Up Your Hang-Ups.' I testified publicly that I realized that I was getting in my own way with God's plans for me. I was resistant, but God was placing people, places, and opportunities in my path to start #Her2ndstitch.

#Her2ndStitch began with my mother's Delta Sigma Theta, Inc. t-shirts. In 2017, my mother was getting older and was not well at age 89. We were packing up her things because it was decided that it was time to sell her house, and she was moving in with my sister Shelley and my sister-in-law Soqui. We packed up all of her Delta t-shirts that she had accumulated throughout the years from conventions and regional meetings from vendors. When we gave the Delta t-shirts and Delta paraphernalia to my daughter Shené, who is also a Delta, she asked me to make her a quilt with the t-shirts. I knew how precious these shirts were to my daughter, but in my mind, I was "hung up" on the fact that I do not sew. My father was a tailor, and my sister Sharon and I took sewing classes at the Harlem YWCA on 125th Street in the Village of Harlem when we were children. We were good at it, too. We made clothes. We stopped sewing because someone asked Sharon if she had made the outfit that she had on, and she decided to stop sewing. As her little sister, I stopped sewing too. Now that I think about it, I also stopped sucking my two fingers too when she decided to stop sucking her two (different) fingers. Now that I am writing this, I realize that my sister Sharon had a bigger influence on me than I thought when we were younger. I remember her using our dog Dinogetta and me to see her boyfriend on Undercliff Avenue in the evenings under the pretense that we were walking the dog and she was not allowed to go by herself once it was getting dark outside. But becoming a teacher is something that I decided on long before she did. We were in classes for our master's degrees in reading and administration, but I think I also took the lead on that.

I think that I might have been 10, and she was 13 when we stopped sewing, and I have not done any real sewing since. No, I did do a little sewing (more observing than sewing) after spending so much time in the middle school Home and Careers classroom. The Home and Careers teacher became my friend, confidant, and now my travel agent. I am transgressing again, but she also taught me some cooking techniques and the usage of various cooking tools. Before her, I did not know the difference between measuring cups for liquid and smaller cups for dry measuring. I only owned the large liquid measuring cups before her teachings. When I took Home Economics in Junior High School at John Peter Tetard JHS 143 in the Bronx, New York, I only remember learning how to make hot chocolate and cinnamon toast. When my son took cooking in High School, he learned how to cook as a prospective chef. My son taught me about the various knives and their usage. I think before him, I basically used steak knives and butter knives for all my cutting needs. I guess you now know that I am not a master in the kitchen, but my son, as a side gig, owns a catering business with his wife. My son is a chef. He did not get his cooking talents from his mother, or maybe he did because of my lack of cooking (another thinking and smiling heart emojis).

But back to #Her2ndStitch. My daughter asked me to make her a quilt, so I started inquiring about quilting classes. My BFF Rosemary Dunham informed me that the Rodda Center had quilting classes for seniors. When I spoke to people in my yoga class, and I also spoke with Elaine Polakoff, who works in the Senior Center's office, about the quilting class, they told me that the ladies in the class are very friendly and helpful, which ended up being so true. I registered for the class. When I started the class, I told them I had my mother's T-shirts, and my daughter wanted me to make a quilt. They asked me if I had ever made a quilt before, and I said no. They asked if I sew, and I answered that I had not since childhood. They informed me that I had to start with the basics before I could make a quilt. Did I mention before that I am so impatient?

I started with the basics, and I made a Nine-Patch square with the fabric that the center provided first, then I made a

Friendship Star. The third project was a Dresden Flower with my fabrics, which allowed me to graduate from the beginner's seat to the next step. Because of my impatience, I also enrolled in one of JoAnn's Fabrics quilting classes, hoping to start the t-shirt quilt there. But again, I had to start as a beginner, and I realized that I am truly a beginner, being around other experienced quilters. I made a nine-patch square in a nine-patch class at JoAnn's. I turned two of my patches into pillows.

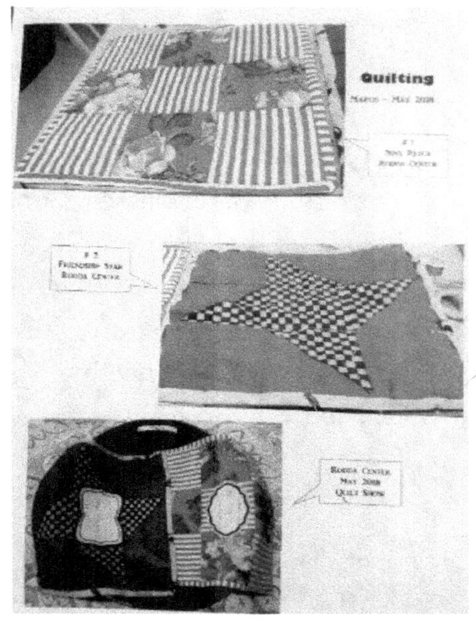

Beginning Quilting

I displayed my beginning works, my patchwork, and two pillows at the May 2018 Rodda Center Showcase. Roz Chambers from the church, who also worked at the Rodda Center, asked for one of the pillows and I still have one.

The comradery, helpfulness, and encouragement in both classes were so motivating that I spent many late nights sewing. Yes, my OCD kicked in for completion.

Some of my fellow quilters and I have formed a text chain group during COVID-19 that we have continued (Amala, Janelle, Janet, Leslie, and Judy). Janelle and Leslie have relocated, and Judy and Janet now facilitate the quilt classes.

The quilting classes at JoAnn Fabrics & Crafts started in June 2018 in Paramus with Margaret Piccolo. Margaret is the one who made the recommendation for my first sewing machine. I purchased a Singer's Patchwork sewing machine from JoAnn Fabrics & Crafts. I started with basic block quilting in a class called Block Along, and then I attended a couple of Quilting Social classes. I already stated that the quilting community was very friendly, encouraging, and helpful.

While taking classes at both the Rodda Center and JoAnn's, I was told that t-shirt quilts are a more advanced quilting technique because of the stretchiness of the fabric, so I decided to start with regular cotton fabric quilts for my granddaughters. I purchased a Connecting Threads – Square Deal pattern and learned how to quilt using a pattern. I made a pink quilt for Darby and then a purple quilt for Jayla using the same pattern.

Looking back at the numerous emails to Margaret (I must have been an insistent, annoying, determined, and ambitious student). I began at JoAnn's in June 2018. The next month, I was enrolled in a July 27, 2018, class to start on the memorial t-shirt quilt, creating my own 18x18 block pattern for a queen-sized bed. I Googled different ideas for my pattern design versus following a pattern like I did with Darby's and Jayla's quilts. I bought red and white and black and white triangle fabrics from JoAnn for the trims/sashes and borders (there are probably technical terms, and I apologize to real quilters). Creating this Delta Sigma Theta, Inc. memorial t-shirt quilt became very emotional for me because my mother passed away in March 2018. I felt her spirit as I

Delta Quilt

put together her t-shirts, bag, and line sisters' group picture to make a quilt and two pillows for my daughter. One pillow had my mother's Delta line on it, and the other had my daughter's Delta Line on it. I gifted this quilt to my daughter for Thanksgiving in 2018, eight months after her grandmother's passing.

In 2019, at the Rodda Center quilting class, I was told many times by classmates about a store in Rahway that sold African print fabrics. On the Cultured Expression website, I discovered that the owner, Lisa Shepherd, also offered classes. I enrolled in a string quilting class that was held on June 14, 2019. I started one string quilted block in the class and finished it as soon as I got home, then decided to do three more string quilted blocks to make a pillow with the scraps of leftover material that Gina Asante from African Heritage Fashions gave me for my son J's African Print quilt. I decided that I would make an African print string quilted pillow to gift to Gina. I could not go to bed until I finished the four blocks for the front of the pillow. I asked Gina for a recommendation for a Mudcloth, aka Bogolan fabric, for the back of a pillow. She did not know that the pillow was for her.

Gina displayed the pillow in her store. The pillow created interest, and customers asked about buying Gina's pillow. Gina was the second person to suggest that I sell pillows. Janelle of quiltsandmoreby-janelle was the first one to suggest that I sell pillows. I said "no way" when she made that suggestion. Janelle invited me

Gina's Pillow

to see her quilting workshop, where she made quilts and pillows and bags. I did not want to venture into anything that might look like work. Now, I, too, have converted part of my basement into my own sewing space. These are some more examples of God placing people in my life.

With me passing on sewing to another generation, my granddaughter, at age 11, took a 3-day kids-summer-camp sewing class with Lisa of Cultured Expressions in July 2019 in Rahway, New Jersey, where she learned basic sewing machine operation, safety tips, fabric cutting, seams, pressing, and more. She continued doing some sewing in an after-school program when she got back to North Carolina. Jayla and I sew together when I am in North Carolina because Jayla now has a sewing machine. Darby, my youngest grand, has also made a pillow for herself and now wants a sewing machine. Lisa from Cultured Expressions sent Jayla an Ankara Charm Shoulder Bag kit, and Jayla made an African patchwork shoulder bag when I went down to North Carolina for Christmas in 2021. Now that Jayla is starting high school, she is considering starting her own business, making and selling accessories to her classmates. There might be another entrepreneur in the family.

Lisa Shepherd of Cultured Expression in Rahway, New Jersey, and #Her2ndStitch have continued their relationship by providing consultations and advice to enhance my business. I also benefited from being one of the recipients of the Cultural Expression Business Grant in 2021.

The majority of #Her2ndStitch fabrics are either from Gina at African Heritage Fashions in Teaneck, New Jersey, or Lisa at Cultured Expressions in Rahway. New Jersey Gina's fabrics are exported from her native land, Ghana. I also get my African print fabrics, fat quarters, and other Afrocentric items, mostly by shopping virtually, from Lisa at Cultured Expressions in Rahway, which are exported from various parts of Africa, including Ghana and Mali.

Making quilts is time-consuming and expensive. I found an incredible quilter through the ladies at the quilting class at the Rodda Center, in Union New Jersey, to finish up my quilts through top quilting and binding. Because of the time and expense, I had to tell several people no, when they asked me to make a quilt for them; including my sister Shelley (whom I never say no to), who wanted a baby quilt for her youngest grandson Legend, who was born in 2021. I also had to say no to Gwen, my former apartment-mate and friend since my first year at Howard University; she also wanted a baby quilt for her first granddaughter. I reluctantly also had to turn down Essence Cohen-Fields, whom I have known since she was a child. She wanted a t-shirt quilt from her collection of memorable T-shirts from throughout her life.

I made a total of nine quilts, most of them with matching pillows: from two baby quilts to a throw, four twins, a queen, and a king. Prayerfully, I will make a quilt for myself eventually. There is one person who would not take no for an answer about me making a quilt for them, and that is Sister Edith P. Green. As long as I have known her, probably since 1990 at First Baptist Church of Teaneck, she has supported my husband, my children, and me in every possible way, so it was my pleasure to do something for her in return by making her a throw quilt. I call Edith my right and left hand. My prayer is that it will bless her and her home as she has blessed me and mine.

My quilt quilting days are probably officially over because my top quilter and binder person, Janice, whom I trust with my precious works, unfortunately, has not been taking in work since the pandemic. I pray that she is well!

My nine quilts were made in the following order:

Darby (pink), Jayla (Lavender), Shené (Delta t-shirts), Szymon (blue/green bow tie dinosaur), Dasaiah (red/black/white shadowbox), J (African Prints), Edith (city lights rust), Shannon (baby quilt gift), and Tileah (baby quilt gift). I pray over everything that I sew, be it a quilt, pillow, or even a face-mask. My prayer is that God will bless the receiver and its surroundings.

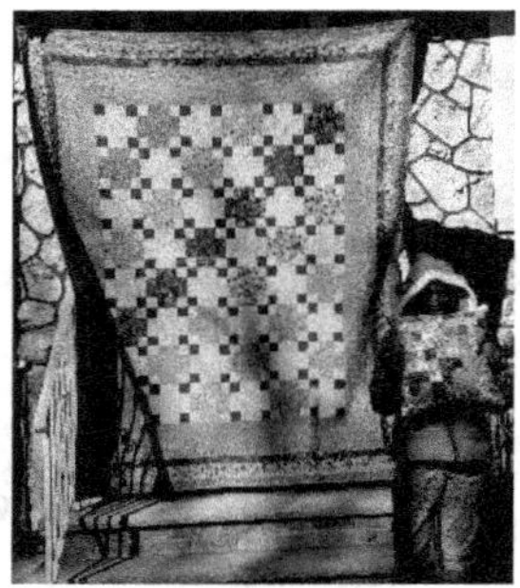

Rodda Center's Showcase. Displayed the Delta T-shirts Quilt that I made for Shené out of my mother's t-shirts

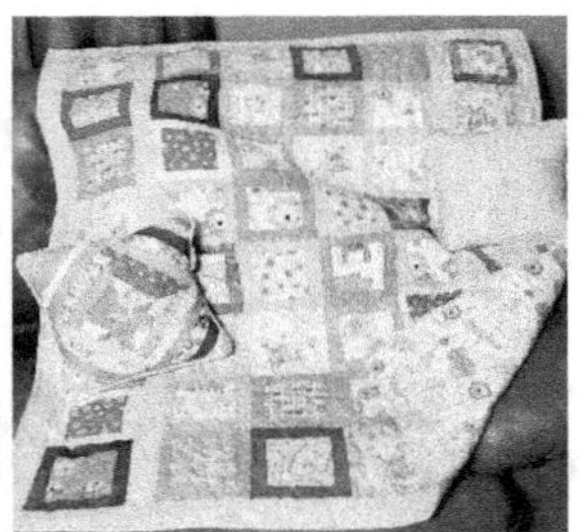

The business end of this industry is not my forte. I have often heard that you must spend money to make money. In starting the business, I purchased a lot of supplies in bulk. I also purchased a large variety of fabrics so that customers would have plenty of designs, African prints, and theme fabrics to choose from. I did not know that having such a large inventory at the end of each year would keep #Her2ndStitch at a loss, no matter how many pillows are sold.

#Her2ndStitch handcrafted string quilted pillows with back pockets have been sold in African Heritage Fashions in Teaneck, New Jersey, since its inception on October 1, 2019. I thank my friend Gina Asante for this. #Her2ndStitch is also on Facebook, Instagram, and Twitter. But #Her2ndStitch needed a wider audience, which meant spending money. Now, #Her2ndStitch is also on Google, Etsy, Shopify, and Pinterest. I am also doing email marketing through Constant Contact, sending emails to those on my #Her2ndStitch email list. I am not as aggressive with my selling as I should be, and my accountant, Lonnie, advised me that 2022 is my last year of not making a profit. While I have less than zero patience and cannot imagine just sitting, I am considering maybe opening up a pop-up shop and inviting other artists to join me or participate in pop-up shops. Participating in vending opportunities for additional sales and exposure is also something that I need to consider. In addition, I am looking into the possibility of placing my pillows in stores on consignment, which Lisa advised of Cultured Expressions in Rahway during our consultation session.

#Her2ndStitch pillows are handcrafted string quilted pillows made from various fabrics with back pockets to hold your favorite books, magazines, or television remotes. Ready-made or custom-made pillows are available. I started #Her2nd-Stitch because of the artistic beauty that goes into making each pillow. Crafting these pillows allows me to express my artistry and is also therapeutic because it causes me to focus and relax. The pillows may seem expensive for some, but it is because of the intricacy that goes into the craft-woman-ship of each pillow. My pillows would enhance any décor, be it in a home, an office, a hotel or a building lobby and it also makes a perfect unique gift. I pray over each pillow that I create. I pray that each pillow will bless the receiver and their environment. #Her2ndStitch was birthed as an artistic outlet, and I pray for its success.

9

We Honor Our...

We honor our... The Bible states as a commandment to "honor thy father and mother, that your days may be long in the land the Lord your God is giving you." (Exodus 20:12). I added this chapter on Monday, May 9, 2022, the day after Mother's Day in 2022. I feel honored because my daughter Shené decided that we should start a new Mother's Day tradition where we meet up and spend Mother's Day or, because of her unpredictable college work schedule, at least around Mother's Day together. Since this is the first year, we decided on a place within a short driving distance of each other. I was leaving from New Jersey, and Shené was leaving from Virginia.

Our Mother's Day has always centered around my mother, the matriarch of the family. When Willie's mother was living, he would go home to Washington, D.C., to be with his mother for Mother's Day. My children and I, along with my two sisters and their children, would attend a 7 a.m. worship service with my mother at her church in the Village of Harlem. I always searched for an orchid corsage to pin on my mother in church on Mother's Day. The Mother's Day corsage tradition began to fade away more each year, and it became harder to find corsages. I remember when mothers would either have on a white or red carnation corsage on Mother's Day. The colors represented whether your mother was living or not. I graduated from carnation corsages to orchid corsages for two reasons: orchids are beautiful, delicate flowers deserving of my queen mother. Secondly, I could not wrap my head around wearing a badge of your mother's life or death status.

After church, we would go to the diner and meet up with the rest of the family for a big breakfast. My nephew Joshua would always have flowers for all the mothers. After breakfast, our farewells were long as we stood in the parking lot, taking pictures, talking, and hugging each other goodbye.

On our first mother/daughter Mother's Day weekend, Shené and I spent an extended weekend, Saturday through Tuesday, in Bethany Beach, Delaware at the Bethany Beach Hotel, directly on the beach. The hotel was perfect, it had a beautiful view of the amazing beach but unfortunately, it was so unexpectedly cold, in the 50s, rainy, and unbelievably strong winds coming off the water.

We had to go to the outlet stores to get Shené a jacket because it was so cold in Delaware. It was around 75-80 degrees in her home in Hampton, Virginia. Shené packed for Virginia weather and not 50 degrees on the water unforeseen Delaware weather. She now admits that she was not prepared for the trip because mentally she was still at work and school. Shené wanted the weekend to work for us despite her busy schedule. That is another reason I love her. I am so honored, and I am so proud of her. Shené has always tried to make time to provide happiness for others her priority as she juggles her overwhelming calendar. Shené literally walked off stage at work from the Inaugural Black Alumni Weekend at William and Mary in Williamsburg, Virginia. She was the moderator for a panel discussion on Being Black at a PWI (Predominately White Institution) Past and Present. Ironically, her dissertation is on The Relationships Among Race, Sense of Belonging, and The Experiences of Selected Black Students at a Predominantly White Institution.

My Mother's Day gift (besides spending time with my daughter) from my husband, son, and daughter was three spa treatments at the Spa at the Bellmoor in Rehoboth Beach, Delaware. Shené could not get an appointment for herself, so as I was luxuriating in my pampering, she was working. I had a De-Stress massage by a young Black cute guy. He was so gorgeous that I had to ask God for forgiveness because I felt like I was cheating on my husband being completely naked under a sheet with this man giving me a massage. The second treatment was a Vanilla Latte Scrub; I felt like I was at Starbucks. It smelled and felt so invigorating. The third treatment was a first for me, and I had my first facial. Shené knew that I always wanted to try a facial. With facials costing the same as a full massage, I always opted out and got a massage instead. I had a Signature Facial. My family always finds it difficult to gift me with something that I truly like but they definitely found the right gift for me this time.

Just an FYI, I am happy with less expensive gifts such as an essential oil candle, a nice journal, or even a 1000-piece puzzle.

All of the weekend time spent on schoolwork paid off because Shené said it was the highest grade she got in that class, and she passed it. I did not mind Shené during her schoolwork. Not only was it too cold to do much of anything else, but I was also working on my manuscript. Even though it was a little disappointing because of the weather, it was a great weekend, and we know that God was in control!

Even though food is a huge part of the essence of our mother-daughter relationship, there was no place that we ate at that we can say was memorable, not even the lobster rolls at a chain establishment or at the seafood restaurant with the great view. As much as I love walking, we had to drive to places that were right down the street because it was so cold being directly on the water. Shené planned to have a soft ice cream cone while in this beach town, but it was just too cold to even think about eating ice cream. We took deliberate trips to Wawa for hot tea with lemon and honey to warm our insides.

Before we left to go to our separate homes, we had to walk out to the beach to take pictures together, bundled up from the harsh May cold and winds.

Mother and Daughter/Delaware

I recommend treating yourself by pampering yourself with de-stressors like spa days, massages, facials, reflexology, hot tubs, saunas, steam rooms, or even a bubble bath with candles of essential oil scents. If you are not impatient like me, even having a mani-pedi or going to a hair salon or barbershop to be pampered. Treat yourself often because you deserve it. What you may think is nothing, a simple walk or sitting in the park or beach can be a de-stressor. Always remember that you earned some me-time!

Since COVID-19 in 2020, I have not seen J and Shené as much as I used to. Now, knowing that we have set a month that we will spend time together makes me overjoyed. Of course, I have notes in my phone of all the places I want Shené and me to go together for future Mother's Days.

I want us to visit our roots in South Carolina. Our roots are in John's Island, South Carolina, so of course, we will visit John's Island, my mother's land, and the big oak tree that she fell out of when she was a child in front of where her house used to be. We will also go down the road to my grandparents house on River Road, where my father grew up. We will honor and follow in my childhood footsteps (even though all the roads are now paved) and go where my Uncle Joe and Aunt Emily lived and had their store that sold 'Hot Soul Sausages'. I was recently reminded that the sausages were not cooked, they came right out of a jar of vinegar. We will also go down that same road where my Uncle Walter and Aunt Janie used to live. A visit to the family's cemetery at Saint Stephens AME Church on Maybank Highway is a must. Memories of walking down River Road with my siblings still bring joy to my heart.

Growing up, my father would always take the last two weeks off in August from "The Shop," aka Reliable Cleaners on 141 Street and Lenox Avenue. My parents, Sharon, Julius, Shelley, and I would load up in his Lincoln Continental. Cars were huge then because it was the six of us traveling from New York to South Carolina, and somewhere along the way, we would pull out a thin mattress like what you see in pull-out couches, and the three oldest would sleep on that mattress in the back seat. Shelley, the youngest, would sleep in the front with our parents with her head on my mother's lap. I am still trying to figure out how the luggage for two weeks for six people, a large cooler (because we always brought back crabs and shrimps as well as fresh okra and pecans from our cousin Roosevelt's pecan tree), and that mattress all fit in the trunk of the car. Also, I cannot figure out how the whole mattress fitting worked in the back seat.

Often, my parents' cousin Leslie, who lived in Queens, New York, and his family would drive down to South Carolina with us. We departed from either our apartment in the Village of Harlem or later from our house in the Bronx. Leslie was both my father's and mother's cousin. He introduced my father to my mother when he and my father were in the army together. Imagine this: I want to introduce my cousin to my other cousin, and they eventually marry. Leslie and his family, wife Lynn, son Leslie Jr. aka Junebug, and daughter Lynnette, would coordinate with my parents on the ride down south in his Cadillac. My Uncle Ernest, Aunt Arlene, their son Alvin, aka Junie, and three daughters Joann, Karen, and Delores, aka DeeDee, would also drive down from McKeesport, Pennsylvania, in their Buick around the same time. It was always one big family gathering on John's Island in August. I had to mention the cars because these three men loved their brand of cars. The cars were either brand new, or they always looked new because of the attention, care, and love that they had for their automobiles.

I remember being in the outhouse and being frightened because of the possibility of being met by a snake. I also remember the slop bucket, aka pee-pot, under the bed, and it seemed like we always had to go to the bathroom when it got dark, and by morning, the bedroom where our parents slept reeked of urine. I remember the big washtub and washboard that was used for washing laundry on the back porch or the tub being our bathtub in the kitchen near the stove. I remember the outdoor water pump we used to fill the wash basins. I remember going grocery shopping at Piggly Wiggly. I remember the summer that my grandparents got their own indoor plumbing. We watched the digging and installations.

The water pump looked something like this [Wikipedia]

Water Pump

My father loved these visits with his parents, siblings, family, and friends. When it was time to go back home, we were sure that we saw a tear coming down my father's face. We instinctively felt our father's pain, and the car was so quiet. It would be hours before anyone spoke a word. No one spoke until my father broke the veil of silence. While vacationing on Johns Island in South Carolina, we, as children, had so much fun with our cousins. But now, as I am writing this, I do not think that this was as much of a vacation for my mother, even though she, too, got to visit her family, especially at Saint Stephens AME Church. It had to be a lot of work for her: taking care of the four of her rambunctious children, washing our clothes by hand, and ironing (there were no permanent-press fabrics back then) our clothes, in addition to hauling and heating water for our baths. She also had to cook or help with the cooking and clean-up. She did not drive then, but she had to be driven to the grocery stores by my father to go grocery shopping, too. The grocery stores were not close to my grandparents' house. As men, it seems as though my grandfather and my father did absolutely nothing as the women worked and served them. The only work that I remember us children doing was closing up and putting away the roll-away beds that we slept in. We played from sun-up to sun-down. Running in and out of the house. Running up and down the road to our cousins' houses. We enjoyed our rocking chair races with our grandparents' two rocking chairs facing each other. Being reminded constantly not to bang the rocking chairs against the wall. We would play with stray dogs, which was a no-no in the South. We wanted to bring the dogs into our grandparents', uncles', and aunts' homes. My grandmother always called them mangy dogs. We would go crabbing and shrimping and we also caught mussels in the river behind my mother's cousins' house. Now that I am a grandparent in an empty house where my grandchildren come for a month every summer, I now get a glimpse of how my grandparents' lives must have changed every last two weeks of August. God bless their souls.

We had so many cousins to play with. Some of Uncle Walter's and Aunt Janie's children were older, Lee, Robert, and Annabel, but Evonne and Chris were about my siblings' ages. Uncle Joe's and Aunt Emily's children, Wanda (recently found out her government name), aka Vonnie, Joe Jr., aka Junie, and Concetta, aka Connie, were also around our ages, and we all had fun together along with our cousins from Queens and Pennsylvania.

I added these memories to this chapter, as well as the honor that should be given to the family because family and family history have been and should always be important in our lives. Our grandparents and parents always shared their stories, but this oral tradition seems to be getting lost in my generation and the next generation. As well as passing on our southern cuisine recipes that we should cherish, we should use, teach, and pass on to the next generation. The only recipes that I can think of that have been passed on from our grandparents' generation to my parents' generation, to our generation, and our children's generation are the Soul food meals that we fix at Thanksgiving. The collard greens, turnips, okra, yams, and macaroni and cheese. Of course, in addition, as Geechees, the white rice (which I personally do not try to make). We have also passed on my Aunt Marie's biscuit recipe that she passed on to my Aunt Janie and she passed on the recipe to my mother. My mother has passed on the recipe to her children and grandchildren. We each make a version of the recipe, adding or subtracting the amount of sugar and cream cheese, as well as interchanging whole milk, buttermilk, and even almond milk. Even though we still occasionally fry fish like our grandmother Sissie and our mother did on Fridays, I do not think any of us perfected their red rice or shrimp with brown gravy. It makes me hungry just thinking about it. Let us pass on our history. Let us tell their stories. Let's make our own stories. Let's tell our stories...

Family Picture South Carolina

In October 2011, my mother sponsored a family trip to South Carolina. Twenty-nine of us came together from New York, New Jersey, Connecticut, North Carolina, Virginia, and Georgia. We took a family picture in front of the Angel Oak Tree with my mother and the three generations that were made possible because of her.

On one of our future mother-daughter Mother's Day trips, I want to stay in the heart of Charleston, on Market Street or Meeting Street. Even though my daughter was with us for the South Carolina trip ten years ago, she did not get there in time for Charleston's Gullah tour. I do want her to have that experience because this tour is part of her heritage.

I would also want to figure out how I can also stay in the Clevedale Historic Inn and Gardens in Spartanburg, South Carolina because that is one of the 10 Domestic Black-Owned Hotels and Resorts found on Ebony.com. Oak Bluffs Inn, on Martha's Vineyard in Massachusetts, is another one of the ten hotels and resorts that I want to visit with my daughter.

In addition, I want to visit Savannah, Georgia, Chicago, Illinois, Detroit, Michigan, Houston, Texas, and the mountains of Colorado and Utah, which are all on my list of places for Shené and me to go together. I guess I should check to see what is on Shené's list too, but I am the mother being honored.

10

Go...

While on a Holland American Panama Canal Cruise in January 2022, I changed the title of this chapter from 'Travel' to 'Go...' with elites because that is what I am doing and will be doing. Go and see different places, Go and meet people, Go and experience other cultures, Go and make new memories, Go and create new stories.

One of the things that I said I would do when I retire is travel. I always had the desire to travel. In my last two years of high school, I mentioned that I had the opportunity to travel to Spain and Mexico. I am now encouraging my granddaughter to travel with her school. Her first trip with her school in eighth grade was to Rome in 2022. Prayerfully, she will continue to travel throughout high school, starting with Greece in the fall of 2023. My youngest granddaughter will also have the opportunity to travel with her school in three years in sixth grade.

St. Thomas 1990 - After my father passed away in March 1990 at age 59, that November 1990, my mother, my two children, and I went to St. Thomas for Thanksgiving. My father had just started traveling. My father and mother traveled to Saint Martin twice before his death using their friend Florence Coleman's timeshare. My father was returning from his first cruise when he got sick with a headache that turned out to be a brain aneurysm. His plan was to travel more. They actually put a large nonrefundable deposit on an RV / recreational vehicle because we were supposed to go on a family camping trip the next month in August. We had been family camping using tents almost every summer since my brother Julius and sister-in-law Stacey introduced us to camp life through their wedding in 1982, but that year (1989), we finally decided to RV it instead. I feel like I am fulfilling my father's travel plans.

St. Thomas PJs

In St. Thomas, as always, my children enjoyed swimming. My mother and daughter wore similar nightgowns and called each other roommates because we had two connecting rooms and they roomed together. (They were usually roommates at Shawnee in the Poconos too). St. Thomas was our first Caribbean excursion. My son's three memories of this trip at age 7 are that his 4-year-old sister jumped in the pool not knowing how to swim, and he jumped in and almost drowned to keep her head above water. He remembers eating clam chowder for the first time. I do not remember this, but he said he remembers getting stuck in the hotel's elevator. Do not judge me and my parenting skills, this was the early 90s and we felt comfortable allowing our children to explore on their own.

We ate a Caribbean Thanksgiving dinner in St. Thomas while Willie was home. Willie attended the Teaneck High School vs Hackensack High School annual rival football game in New Jersey with his brother London. To this day, he talks about the Thanksgiving when he ate Big Bites (large hotdogs) from 7-Eleven for his Thanksgiving dinner.

Caribbean - After the St Thomas taste of the Caribbean, we began going on group Caribbean cruises during either our

February winter school breaks or our spring school breaks, visiting various Caribbean islands. These cruises were organized by Liza, my co-worker at P.S. 129, and her friend Latifa. We cruised on the Carnival Cruise Line. I mentioned before that my children would save up change in a jar throughout the year to have their own spending money for their trips. They would cash in the coins and decide how much they could spend each day based on the number of days for the trip. Shené's memory of these cruises was dressing up for dinner, especially the Captain's Ball. (She always loved dressing up, even as a young child. My chic daughter wore Harvé Bernard pantsuits in fourth grade). My own memory was having to go to Payless to find white patent leather shoes for the winter break cruises for Shené because I could not find them anywhere else. With her growing feet, I could not buy the white shoes months in advance. I also remember four people in a stateroom, and J and Shené slept in pulldown bump beds that they loved. We stopped taking them on cruises with us because the staterooms became too cramped as my children grew. Several of these Caribbean cruises departed from Puerto Rico. We enjoyed touring Old San Juan. Our Caribbean cruises have taken us to various Caribbean islands. The most memorable islands are St. Thomas, St. Maarten, and Barbados, and we cannot forget Aruba because of its beauty and its winds. My family decided that we would all wear red and white as we explored the island of Aruba.

Jamaica 1992 - I also took advantage of an educational trip to Jamaica and even Cuba in 1992. My sister's co-worker Teresa of P.S. 36 organized this trip. I went with my sister Sharon and her principal and coworkers. We visited schools in both Jamaica and Cuba. I love Reggae music and Caribbean food, so I did a lot of dancing and eating, in addition to enjoying the beach and the hotel pool.

Jamaica 1993 - The island of Jamaica deserved a second trip, so my sister Sharon and I went back during our February 1993 winter break with our families. We stayed in Montego Bay again, but we visited Negril and Kingston. In Negril, my son, at age ten, jumped off the cliff at Rick's Café. In Kingston, we visited the Marcus Garvey Museum. After the museum visit, my son wrote a report on Marcus Garvey for school. J also brought back artifacts to show his class. I believe that traveling is the most memorable education. My son will always know the contributions of Marcus Mosiah Garvey to our Black History. He will also always be a fan (like me) of Bob Marley's music. Both vacations in Jamaica were beyond amazing. Everyone spent a lot of time in the sun and had fun. You would think that I would have learned after the first visit to Jamaica that even as black as I am, my skin could still get burned. Sunburns are uncomfortable, and I was peeling for weeks when I returned home both times.

Mexico 1993 - We went on a family trip to Mexico that same year as our second trip to Jamaica, in August 1993. My mother arranged a two-week trip in August through her time-share exchange to Puerto Vallarta, Mexico. My mother, sisters Sharon and Shelley, and our children Shamanie, J, Shené, and Shequé were able to stay for two weeks. My husband Willie, my sister-in-law-to-be Soqui, and niece Tammy joined us the second week. We stayed in two different villas these two weeks. The first villa was a beautiful hotel-type villa with a beautiful large pool that we all enjoyed. The second villa was a one-story hut-type villa down the street from the Corona factory. I am not a beer drinker (I only drank beer as a child when my grandmother, Sissie, gave me a taste), but others enjoyed the brew. I remember doing a lot of swimming in the first villa and the children doing arts and crafts in the second villa, which we still have somewhere in the attic. Let me correct that; their beautiful works of art are lovingly packed away upstairs.

Puerta Vallarta

Hawaii - I have been to Hawaii twice. The first time was one year after Willie and I got married in 1981; we went with our church at the time, St. Mark Baptist Church in Washington, D.C. We were 24 years old, not only scraping to live but also scraping to go on this trip that we did not have sense enough to know that we could not afford. Truth be told, like most of our trips, there was no extra travel budget. My priorities had always been screwed up. My mother-in-law probably gave us a helping hand with paying for this trip. It was a seven-day trip with a stop in Los Angeles before getting to Hawaii. My college apartment-mate, Ronda Robinson (now Ronda Robinson-Kirk), lived in Los Angeles then and took my husband and me on a grand tour of L.A.

In Hawaii, we enjoyed the beach and feasted on fresh fruits, especially pineapples. We attended a Luau. We even went to a Japanese restaurant for our first anniversary, and at that time, we could sit on the floor and get up on our own. If the trip was seven days, I think that we probably ran out of money after day four. We had no concept of money, especially on an expensive island like Hawaii.

Our second trip to Hawaii was a cruise. We were invited by my mother's friend Christine Hughes, whom she met in the hospital when my mother was giving birth to me. My mother, another one of her lifelong friends' Annette Lee, my husband, and I went cruising in Hawaii. All I can say is that it was an interesting experience, realizing that both my mother and Mrs. Lee were aging and needed more attention than we expected. It was a beautiful trip. This was our first cruise with a stateroom with a balcony. We could sit out on our stateroom balcony and soak up the beauty. The ship was gorgeous and full of entertainment and, of course, food and fun.

We had to reschedule our third trip to Hawaii. We planned to take two cruises for our 65th birthday as we did for our 60th Birthday but after a 14-day Panama Canal cruise in January for my birthday and also plans for May, we decided that an April cruise would not be feasible. My mother always said, "Listen to your body". At 65, our bodies were saying to pace ourselves as well as our wallets. Traveling can be exhausting, especially with time zone changes. After 14 days on a ship plus two days before embarking in Fort Lauderdale and two days after debarking in Santa Monica, we knew another cruise in four months would be taxing, especially when we both had travel plans for May too. Willie was going to Selma, North Carolina, for his family reunion in May. I was meeting Shené in Bethany Beach, Delaware, in May for our Mother/ Daughter Mother's Day meet-up. Hawaii was supposed to be state number 49 in our 2019-2022 50 states plan. We still count Hawaii in our 50 states visit because we have been there two times. When I reschedule the Hawaiian cruise, I want to go on the cruise that I saw that includes Bora Bora or Tahiti.

The **Bahamas 2008** - For my mother's 80th birthday, we gifted her with a family cruise to the Bahamas. Shelley, Soqui, Shavon, Jabari, Shamanie, J, Denetra, Dasaiah, Willie, and I. Jayla wants me to include her because she was also there in utero. Shené reminded me that she was not there because it was her senior year in college, and she had classes that she could not miss. The Bahamas cruise was a great trip. We visited the beautiful Atlantis Bahamas Resort. I remember us trying to all agree on excursions as well as haggling with drivers for the best rate. We will not let Shamanie forget crashing into a bush with her rented scooter. Shavon remembers that there was a lot of food. Shelley and Dee remember Dee being pregnant, sitting in the beach water, and getting stuck. Dee could not get up on her own. Dee also remembers that they stopped at a restaurant for their island cuisine and had to discard it because you could not bring outside food onto the ship. There were such great memories of this trip for everyone except Dasaiah because he was only six years old and remembers very little about the trip, but he recently told me that he remembered that there was a pirate ship that he could play on.

Turks and Caicos 2012 - When my daughter received her master's degree in counseling in December 2011 and walked in May 2012, we decided that we would go on a mother-daughter celebratory trip. My daughter and I cruised to Turks and Caicos with Carnival Cruise Line. We danced to Caribbean Reggae and Calypso music every chance we got on the ship, even in the dining room with the Waite staff. We went horseback riding which was a beautiful but scary and rocky experience. We rode on the beaches and mountains on the edge of cliffs. We both had massages (usually my must-do when I go away). I think it was our first hot stone massages. As foodies, we tried every exotic item on the daily dinner menus. We cruised with the Carnival Cruise Line, and our stateroom had a balcony,

Turks and Caicos

but it was on the side of our room, so we were not able to enjoy the roominess feel of a balcony room. Live and learn.

St. Thomas 2012 - Since St. Thomas was the first island that my son visited as a child, he decided to have a destination wedding in St. Thomas also in November, around Thanksgiving again. We had a wonderful Thanksgiving weekend with family and friends with a lot of dancing, swimming, all-inclusive drinking, celebrating, and of course, eating delicious Caribbean buffet cuisine, as J and Dee said, "I Do". I thank and appreciate those family members and friends who joined us for my son's nuptials weekend and who continue to be part of his village as long as you have known him.

In January 2017, for my 60th birthday. We spent a few days enjoying ourselves in one of my favorite places, New Orleans, Louisiana. In New Orleans, I am in awe of the feeling of freedom and entertainment throughout the streets, which is so interesting because I tend to be so strait-laced. I spent my time walking all over the streets of New Orleans, especially near the water. I walked through the street in rhythm, drinking some huge oversized frozen blue drink. Soaking up the entertainment spilling from buildings. As well as, of course, eating the scrumptious New Orleans cuisine. From New Orleans, we cruised from the port on the Norwegian Cruise Line's

Norwegian Dawn to Cozumel, Mexico, Honduras, Costa Rica, a private Cruise line-owned island of Belize, and Costa Maya, Mexico. Not going to the city of Belize was disappointing, but it was a great cruise. We spent a lot of time enjoying the islands' beaches. I was even able to zipline in both Costa Rica and Honduras. This was my second opportunity to zipline. My first zipline experience was in the Poconos for an all-girls weekend celebration for my sister-in-law Soqui's fiftieth birthday. This time I did the Superman zipline, laid out with my arms extended like Superman flying across the beach waters and sand. My husband was so busy talking to some people that he met on the beach that he missed seeing me fly by, and I wanted him to take a picture (frown emoji).

In April 2017, we cruised for the first time out of New Jersey for a Bermuda cruise through the Royal Caribbean Anthem of the Seas for Willie's 60th birthday, not knowing that Bermuda's weather is similar to North Carolina's weather, and it was unseasonably cold. Unseasonably cold seems to be our MO, aka modus operandi. It was too windy on the deck for me to do many outdoor activities, but I did join some line dancing. To sit out on our stateroom balcony, you had to layer up but since we did not expect cool weather we mostly packed for warm weather. To top it off, the last shore stop was (of all places after being cold) we stopped in Boston, Massachusetts, and went on a tour.

I remember two previous trips with unseasonably cold weather. When we visited Cancun, Mexico, and Orlando, Florida. For both trips, like this cruise, we packed for hot weather. With the Florida trip, we even rented our first convertible and froze.

The Royal Caribbean cruise ship had a variety of fun activities to choose from, including go-carts, surfing, and I-Fly. I did I-Fly! Skydiving is on my to-do list. It was colder on this cruise than it was years later when we went on an Alaskan cruise.

I-Fly 60th Birthday Cruise

Florida - We have been to various parts of Florida numerous times, especially when my son lived in Florida for a few years. We spent plenty of time in Fort Lauderdale, Miami, and Hollywood, Florida, when my son and his family lived in Hollywood, Florida. I went to Tallahassee, Florida, when I was in college. We went to Orlando three times; once with just our children, a second time we arranged a trip with the church youth group and parents, and a third time for a family trip for Thanksgiving. We were in Key West during a horrific storm. Also, we enjoyed Miami when we went on the Bahamas cruise and the Turks and Caicos cruise. We rented a house in Hollywood, Florida, for Jayla's ninth birthday because she said she wanted to visit the place where she was born. Jayla was four months old when she and her parents moved from Florida to North Carolina, but Jayla makes sure that she lets every-one know that she was born in Florida. It is like my son being from Maryland because he was born there, and we moved to the Bronx, New York when he was a little over one year old; my daughter was born in the Bronx, and then we moved to Teaneck, New Jersey when my son was four years old, and my daughter was eleven months old. I digress, but are you from the place where you were born or from the place where you grew up? I spent my first nine years living in the Village of Harlem and the next nine years living in the Bronx. So, where am I from?

We drove to Miami from Hollywood because I remember suggesting a visit to Miami's famous South Beach, not know-ing that it was not appropriate for children. All I can say is that the elaborate, sometimes 'R' rated scenery was a sight for sore eyes.

"

I was not sure if it was doable,
but my belief in speaking
things into existence sparked
determination.

"

11

All 50 States

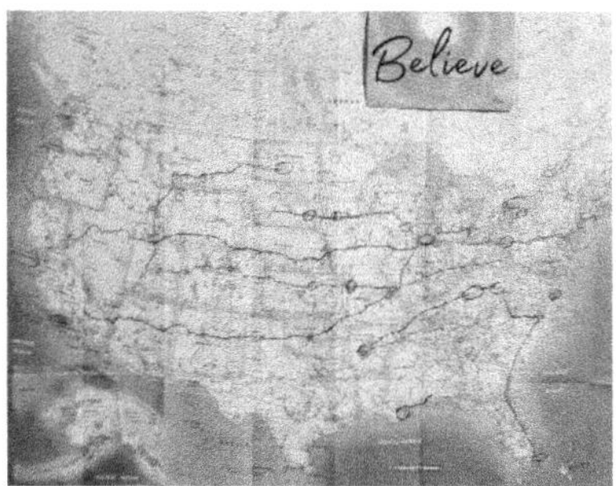

Map USA

I remember when we were traveling to various Caribbean countries, someone asked me, "Have you seen all of the United States yet?" It's like living in New York and New Jersey most of your life and never visiting places like Times Square, The Statue of Liberty, or the Empire State Building. I did not think anything of it until many years later when I was having a conversation with my friend Karen Lewis's mother, Marion Elizabeth Watson, in August 2017 at a pool party celebrating Quentin Gore's birthday. She told me through her travels for work, she has been to 48 states in the United States. That is when I had my aha moment and decided that was what I would do. I was not sure if it was doable, but my belief in speaking things into existence sparked determination. My mind went into planning mode. I started the conversation with Willie, my husband, about the States. He informed me which states he would not be going with me, but I knew that I had my sister Shelley and my daughter Shené as travel partners. I started planning and strategizing. Shené had conferences in other states and said I could join her. I met her in Arizona twice before, in June 2013 and October 2014, when she had to go to Arizona for school. Because of Shené's conference, I was also able to go to Indianapolis, Indiana, in March 2019, which was the start of my 50 states.

My strategy was to visit states in clusters and take advantage of whatever opportunities came my way. I created a vision wall in my room with the United States map and post-its with listings of clusters of states. I also indicated projected seasons for some of my explorations. My original timeline was visiting 50 states by age 70. I was 60 when I had the conversation with Mrs. Watson and 62 when I visited my first state. My carefully planned initial calculations had me finishing in 2027.

Through my travels being a native New Yorker and living in New Jersey for the last thirty-five years, I knew the general mentality and cultures of this multifaceted Middle Atlantic area. I was also familiar with the southern ways of those from Maryland to South Carolina and maybe even further to Florida. But venturing out northeast to New England, south to the Gulf Coast, to the West Coast, west through middle America, and across the northern United States, I did not expect to immerse myself in some of their proclivities as though I was a sociologist or an archeologist as I traveled through many of the states. My eyes were opened, as well as my thinking in many ways. Not only did I witness the many changes in landscapes and cultures. I also traveled during COVID-19 restrictions, controversies, and political presidential upheaval. I stepped on lands of middle America not only observing but also feeling their strong partisanism views of a party that was basically against everything that I strongly believed in. I listened to and witnessed the praise for their leader, who, to me, was determined to ruin our democracy. I have spent a lot of time in southern states that adorned the confederate flag and cringed, but it seemed as though middle America breathed its own self-righteous image of their red, white, and blue patriotism.

2019

Indiana

Tennessee

Connecticut – Rhode Island

Massachusetts

Vermont – New Hampshire – Maine

8 States

#1 Indiana - God kept placing opportunities in my path in 2019. The first was my March 2019 trip to Indianapolis Indiana because Shené was attending the American Association of Blacks in Higher Education (AABHE) conference.

My focus in life, especially when traveling, is to try new things, so I tried floatation therapy at 'A Place to Float' at 425 West South Street in Indianapolis, Indiana. I am including this because I suggest that you try it. Try it if you are trusting with floating on your back and not claustrophobic. According to the brochure, "Float therapy is the practice of lying in saltwater solution in a tank devoid of external stimulation. This method yields multiple benefits like stress reduction, enhanced creativity, help with sleeping, treatment of chronic pain, and

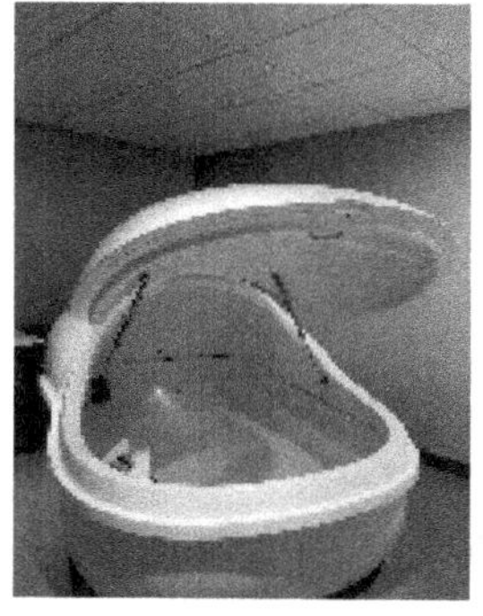

Float Therapy

muscle soreness. The saltwater solution is made from Epsom salts which are rich in magnesium, a mineral in which most people find themselves deficient. Some believe that floating gives them the quiet and space they need to soften their minds and easily find answers to problems that have been causing them stress." I encourage you to undertake this endeavor. Unfortunately for me, I have 3 major issues; #1 I have real issues with relaxation, and this was in 2019 before I had a therapist to help me with this issue. #2 I have a real fear of floating on my back, even though the water is not deep. It's that trust issue, which brings us to #3 I am extremely claustrophobic. I had to keep the pod door open, with it closed I felt like I was in a casket. This floatation treatment could have been a relaxing experience if I had let it.

The foodie in me, of course, had some delicious food in Indianapolis. I decided that another one of my many quests was to compare chicken and waffle entrees. I wish I had taken notes during that time of the restaurants I visited or had taken more pictures as I walked all over downtown Indianapolis. Still, I can say that Maxine's Chicken and Waffles at 132 North East Street was scrumptious. The chicken and waffles at the hotel were good, too. I am not a coffee drinker, but I had the best coffee in this coffee shop known for its coffee. I risked my life going back a second time just to get more coffee. You might ask how I risk my life. My family will get angry with me again, as I tell you. Shené and I attempted to have breakfast at a highly-rated coffee shop (I wish I knew the name). I am extremely allergic to strawberries, airborne allergic allergies, EpiPen, and emergency room allergic allergies, , = airborne allergic – emergency room allergic just being near them. I have two trips to the emergency room to attest to my sensitivity to this beautiful, red, small, delicious fruit. I cannot leave home without an EpiPen. At this restaurant, we noticed that it seemed like every breakfast item was garnished with strawberries. I had to leave the restaurant and we took our order to go. The food was delightful, but the coffee was definitely the best coffee that I ever tasted. During my walk the next day, I took my life into my hands and went in and got a second cup of coffee to go and also risked the wrath of Shené Vivetta Owens, who sometimes forgets that I am the mother. My mother always said, "Once a man (a woman in my case), twice a child."

I explored the city of Indianapolis while Shené attended conference meetings. She said I only joined her in Indianapolis to get a magnet to start my 50-state magnet collection. But we all know it was so I could spend time with my only birth daughter.

We were going to go to the restaurant Dicks Last Resort where they are rude to you on purpose. Shené went to their chain in Baltimore, so I insisted that I wanted to give it a try. Shené said her line sisters took her there without telling her the premises of the restaurant. But I decided that I could not intentionally accept rudeness, so we left and went to a steakhouse instead. [3/23-27/2019] #1state

#2 Tennessee - In April 2019, because we usually go to North Carolina for my son Willie J and daughter-in-law Denetra's annual pre-Easter cook-out and then spend time with the grandchildren during their spring break, we decided to take a road trip to Tennessee. Willie, Dasaiah, Jayla, Darby, and I took a road trip from Raleigh, North Carolina, to Knoxville, Tennessee. We drove through the mountains of North Carolina to get to Tennessee. We stopped at the Welcome Center in Tennessee before going to our hotel. We stayed at the Hampton Inn & Suites in downtown Knoxville, Tennessee. We saw the huge golden globe while entering Knoxville. We visited Knoxville College. Willie attended Knoxville College in 1975 before transferring to Bowie State University in Bowie, Maryland.

Tennessee Golden Globe

Knoxville College

This was his first time returning to Knoxville since 1976, 43 years ago. Even though the college has closed its doors, Willie was able to show us what used to be a beautiful campus. He pointed out his former dorm, the library, the cafeteria, and the Towers, which were the upper-class co-ed dormitory. We saw the remnants from the various fraternities and sororities plots and, of course, the gymnasium and football field. Willie played football for both Knoxville College and Bowie State University, as well as football and basketball at Coolidge High School in NW Washington, D.C. It was heartbreaking to see this Historical Black College University with a rich history, which was founded in 1875 by the United Presbyterian Church of North America in this condition. There are plans to rebuild and reopen the campus. I recently read that Knoxville College is partnering with The University of Tennessee to help speed up the re-accreditation process. My husband mentioned that one thing has not changed about Knoxville College, and that is the neighborhood. The neighborhood is still surrounded by what seems to be low-income Caucasians sitting in front of their small homes on their porches, but we were greeted by a Black woman who lived across the street from the college entrance gate. [4/18-19/2019] #2states

#3 Connecticut - I surprised my husband with a trip to Connecticut and Rhode Island for his birthday, which checked off two more states at the end of April 2019. We stayed at the Foxwoods Resort and Casino in Connecticut using a Groupon discount for a night. I am not a Groupon spokesperson like Tiffany Haddish, but I do endorse using Groupon's discounts. The resort is beautiful. Even though we did not gamble, we enjoyed Junior's famous cheesecake and burgers. Here I go, talking about food again. We also walked through their shopping outlets, mostly window shopping. Willie said that we went dancing for a little while, but I do not remember. [4/29/2019]

Juniors Connecticut

#4 Rhode Island - We stayed a night in Newport, Rhode Island, at the Wyndham Newport Hotel the next day, but unfortunately (which is the story of our lives), the weather was unseasonably, unexpectedly cold, and rainy. We also rode around looking for a Rhode Island magnet.

It was a good, quick getaway. We have been to Connecticut many times before but even though we do not gamble, it was good to spend time at this casino that we have heard so much about. I was disappointed that the weather in Rhode Island was not good, especially since this was our first stay in Rhode Island. [4/30/2019] #4 states

Newport Rhode Island

#5 Massachusetts - I said I would take advantage of every opportunity. Reverend Edna Dismus organized an AARP 5-day, 4-night bus trip to Cape Cod, Martha's Vineyard, and Providence Town in May 2019. Willie does not do bus rides, but he agreed to accompany me on this trip. This trip not only checked off the state of Massachusetts but also allowed me

AARP Trip

to visit three places that I always wanted to visit: Cape Cod, Martha's Vineyard, and Provincetown. Our first stop was in Connecticut, the Foxwoods Resort and Casino, allowing the two busloads to hit the slots and shop at the Tanger Outlets. Since Willie and I were just there last month, Willie and I basically walked around (I walked, and he sat), and of course, I ate. Surprisingly, we had scrumptious lobster rolls from Subway Sandwich Shop, which is another one of my must-try comparison meals.

After Foxwoods, we went and spent the night in Cape Cod.

We had a delicious lobster dinner. I think that is the first time I had a whole lobster on my plate instead of just the lobster tail. I am glad they cracked and shelled it for me because

I would not have known where to begin. But like the tail, no matter how big it is on the outside, there is no equivalent amount of meat inside. But it was delectable.

During our 5-day stay, we toured the towns of Hyannis and Sandwich. We visited the John F. Kennedy Museum and its exhibits to learn more about the Kennedy family's history. We also saw the historic scandalous Chappaquiddick. We had a fascinating visit to the Zion Union Heritage Museum, which celebrates the history of African Americans and other people of color on Cape Cod. I really enjoyed this history lesson. We took the ferry to Martha's Vineyard, a place

Cape Cod Lobster

Lighthouse

I always wanted to visit and will return to soon. I spent so many years hearing people of color rave about their annual summer visits to Martha's Vineyard because they either own a home there or they had a friend who did. I am still waiting for an invitation if you are reading this (hint, hint). I finally saw the iconic, colorful gingerbread cottages of Oak Bluff. We took pictures around the Gay Head Lighthouse in Aquinnah as part of our Massachusetts tour.

My sister Shelley and her wife Soqui always talk about their frequent, used-to-be almost yearly, trips to Provincetown, and now I know why. P-Town was magnificent with its unique culture, eclectic artists' homes, beautiful galleries, stores, and boutiques, not to mention its delightful restaurants. We had delicious seafood for lunch, and we went to a bakery I would return to if I could find it again. [7/15-19/2019] #5states

I want my three grandchildren, Dasaiah, Jayla, and Darby, to experience the wonders of traveling, and they usually spend part of their summers in New Jersey. We decided to travel by car to a timeshare in

Vermont

Vermont, then leave for a day and go through New Hampshire to spend a night in Maine at the end of July into August 2019. That checked off three more states.

#6 Vermont - We stayed at Smugglers' Notch Vermont America's Family Resort. It was a ski resort. Dasaiah said it felt like we were in the clouds as we passed through the huge mountains. The grandchildren enjoyed Fun Zone, the Vermont swimming pools, and miniature golf. We learned Ben and Jerry's Ice Cream was created in Vermont, and we definitely enjoyed it at the resort. I discovered that I love Ben and Jerry's Cherry Garcia ice cream

Smugglers

as much as I love my favorite Haagen-Dazs Vanilla Swiss Almond ice cream. The resort had plenty for the children to do. As well as many hills for me to walk up and down for my daily walk. The grands went on their own nature walk. The resort was having a festival with country music, dance, and food. [7/29 -8/3/2019] #6state

#7 New Hampshire – Basically, we drove through New Hampshire. We did stop to pick up a magnet because I am collecting refrigerator magnets from each state. Now that I am finishing up states, I realized that New Hampshire (and Iowa) are the only states that I visited but did not spend the night in. Which means that I have to go back to spend at least one night in these two states. On our drive through New Hampshire, we passed

New Hampshire

through quaint towns with shops that we were able to explore as we hunted for a refrigerator magnet of the state. Jayla actually remembered the New Hampshire motto on their welcome sign because she said that it scared her "Live Free or Die". [7/31-8/1/2019] #7state

#8 Maine - We stayed at Beach Cove Waterfront Inn in Boothbay Harbor, Maine. It is a beautiful, charming Inn in Maine with both a pool and a lake with rowboats and canoes. We stayed on the top floor with a large balcony that overlooked the back of the property. We went row boating in the lake. The grands went canoeing by themselves

Maine

to the other side of the lake. The grands also went swimming in both the pool and the lake. They would jump off the pier into the lake. Because of my cautious nature, I had to hold my breath and pray as they enjoyed their daring stunts in the waters around them. It seemed like they were trying to outdo one another. Of course, we found a seafood open-air shack-type place for dinner, the Boothbay Lobster Wharf, where we sat at picnic tables to eat our jumbo-size shrimp and fries. Except for Dasaiah who does not eat one of my favorite foods; shrimp. My grandson remembered that all along the roads there were advertisements that marijuana was legal.

Jayla claimed that she was traumatized in Maine. I probably should not add this part, but my granddaughters made a song about Willie, aka Big Daddy, in Maine. After taking their showers, as always, they wet-up the bathroom floor. When Willie was leaving the bathroom after his shower he slipped and fell. The girls started singing "I won't go to Maine anymore-more-more because Big Daddy fell on the floor-floor-floor." [7/31-8/1/2019] #8state

After our enjoyable Maine visit, we went back to Smugglers' Notch to finish out the week with more fun and games. We all had the best time ever in both Vermont and Maine. It was a great retreat exploring the coast of New England.

Since I started collecting refrigerator magnets along the way, this became an additional adventure for my granddaughters and then for Willie and me. Luvs and Travel Lodge became our friends as well as charming little shops and sometimes Walmart, collecting state refrigerator magnets.

#9 Ohio - Because my mother passed away in March 2018, she graduated from Central State University in Xenia, Ohio, now Wilberforce, Ohio. She wanted at least one of her children to follow in her footsteps but that did not happen. She supported her alma mater both financially and by attending homecomings with former classmates over the years. In honor of her, Tanyunekia Mitchell, a church friend of mine, my mother's Delta Sigma Theta, Inc. Soror, and fellow Central State University Centralian alumni helped me plan an October 2019 Homecoming trip with my daughter

Shené, and my grandson Dasaiah, who was a high school junior. I wanted to expose Dasaiah to as many college campuses as I could, as well as be able to show Dasaiah and us his great-grandmother's alma mater. We had the opportunity to not only visit my mother's college for their Homecoming. We also drove to HBCU's Wilberforce University and walked around the campus of Ohio State University. Ohio State University is massive, especially compared to the two HBCUs - Historical Black Colleges and Universities. We sat in the bleachers of Ohio State University's huge football stadium. We did the Homecoming experience at Central State University; we were sideline spectators cheering as the marching band marched down the streets to the football field. We ate food from food trucks, shopped at the University bookstore for memorabilia, and at vendors' stands (Shené purchased a chunky elephant necklace that she wore later in November as she accepted her Greek of the Year 2019 Award in honor of her grandmother. The Delta Sigma Theta, Inc. Sorority collects elephants, and my mother and daughter are part of the Greek sorority, Delta Sigma Theta, Inc. Sorority). We hooped and hollered for the maroon and gold Marauders throughout the game but unfortunately, Central State lost their homecoming game. This might have been my first HBCU homecoming since I graduated from Howard University in Washington, D.C. in 1979. I am so glad that I got to share this experience with both my daughter (who has attended many Hampton University in Hampton Virginia homecomings even after graduating), but especially the

Ohio

memories that will always have of this new experience with my grandson.

Ohio State University

I must also point out, even though you probably already know, that there is a huge disparity between both HBCU - Historical Black Colleges and Universities campuses that we visited, and the predominately White Ohio State University. Let us continue to support the United Negro College Fund and our Historical Black Colleges and Universities. [10/11-13/2019] #9state

#10 Florida - That same November, my son rented an Airbnb in Florida for Thanksgiving, so we took a road trip. My husband and I flew to North Carolina on November 22, 2019, on JetBlue (our favorite airline), and we drove many long hours as a family to Florida: J, Denetra, Jayla, Darby, Willie, and I. Our first stop was South of the Border, looking for a South Carolina refrigerator magnet. Our second stop was Savannah, Georgia, to have breakfast at the waffle house before searching

Disney Florida

for a Georgia refrigerator magnet. Shelley, Soqui, Szymon, Shavon, and Shamanie met us at the house in Florida. J and Denetra and their children, Shavon and Shamanie, and Willie and I stayed at the house, while Shelley, Soqui, and Szymon stayed at their Orlando timeshare. The house was beautiful in Kissimmee, Florida. The house was spacious, with a pool, a pool table, and a popcorn popper machine. My son ended up putting both a pool table and popcorn popper machine in the loft of his own house after seeing them in this house. We all had Thanksgiving dinner together. Friends and family came by; Jhovany and his family; Shavon and Shamanie's Aunt Heather and her husband Norman, who live in Florida, came by to spend time with us. Some of us went to Universal Studios and met up with J's co-worker Dorothy and her son Shawn. Everyone had fun but me, and I came back home. In addition to Universal Studios, with Harry Potter's Diagon Ally, my son got three wands, and his children thought one would be for them, but it was not. They gave out free butter beer at the Ally. They (not me) went to Disney World. Another thing about me that some might think is strange is that I do not like amusement parks or rides. I never did! Even though I went on many rides as a child. I do not know if it was peer/ sibling pressure or an expectation that I am supposed to enjoy the ups and downs and spinning around of rides. We had a great time in Florida. As always, the drive down was full of excitement. I think the two Willies did most of the driving, I know that I did not drive, but I am not sure if Denetra drove. I do not think that these non-stop drivers appreciate having to stop in each state so that I could get a magnet. The drive home was long and exhausting for everyone especially the drivers because there was a lot of traffic. On our way to Florida, we checked off the states of #11, North Carolina, #12, South Carolina, and #13 Georgia. Even though we did not spend a night in South Carolina and Georgia, we stopped in both places, and I have stayed in both states before. Entering South Carolina and stopping at the South of the Border brought back memories of my family's summer drive to South Carolina. My family always either stopped or acknowledged that we were at the South of the Border when I was growing up.

Jayla reminded me that when we stopped at the Waffle House in Georgia, it had a lake behind it that had a warning sign about alligators. Willie and I flew back home from North Carolina on December 3, 2019. Thank God that we did not have to drive home! [11/26 – 12/1/2019] #10/11/12/13states

I did not realize that we traveled so much in 2019 until I started writing this chapter. I went on 7 trips, stayed in 9 states, and saw 13 states in 9 months. I went to Indiana in March with Shené. Willie and I took the grands to Tennessee in April.

Georgia Alligator Warning

Willie and I went to Connecticut and Rhode Island in April and then Massachusetts in May. We took our grands to Vermont, through New Hampshire, and Maine in July/August. (I have to go back to New Hampshire). Shené, Dasaiah, and I went to Ohio in October. Then, in November was the Florida family road trip, and we left from North Carolina, including South Carolina and Georgia.

Before I go on, some states are a given because we are constantly going to as well as through them, especially since we spend so much time on Route 95 and Route 80. These states are #14 New Jersey (live), #15 New York (family/work/dentist), #16 Pennsylvania (Poconos Timeshare/ Outlet shopping/ Returned 2021), #17 Delaware (pass through but stayed May 2022/ chapter 9), #18 Maryland (family/always visiting), and North Carolina (already checked off/ Son lives/always visiting), and #19 Virginia (Daughter lives/always visiting). Now we can check off 6 more states. #19 states #19down31togo.

19 States in one year is a lot, but 31 more states are a large number. That was 2019, and we all know what happened in 2020. I could not believe that we checked off 19 states in one year. I figured it would take years to do 31 more states. My plan-setting mindset set my 50 states travel planning for 8 years. I planned to finish the States by age 70. I even said that for my 70th birthday, I would get a tattoo on my wrist saying something like 50@70.

2020

Louisiana – Alabama – Mississippi

Illinois – Oklahoma – Texas - New Mexico – Arizona

– California

Nevada – Utah – Wyoming – Nebraska – Indiana

14 States

New Orleans, Louisiana, is one of my favorite places to visit. I spent three January birthdays in New Orleans. My first birthday visit was a surprise from my husband. Husband, when you read this, please know that I like this type of surprise (wink kiss emoji). Unfortunately, my husband was sick with some type of stomach virus from when he got off the plane until it was time to return home. On our last evening in New Orleans, he mustered up enough energy to go out to dinner. We dined at one of the many places I explored earlier on my own. I even went to a gospel brunch by myself. While we were at dinner, our rental car was towed away because I unintentionally, in my excitement, parked in a no-parking area in which I saw other cars parked in this location earlier that day, and we spent the evening getting our rental car out of an expensive tow yard. My husband and New Orleans did not seem to get along. Our second visit to New Orleans was prior to his back surgery, and he was in so much pain. I did a lot of exploring on foot again in New Orleans French Quarter and walked along riverbanks on my own, but we did go on a tour together that included seeing the New Orleans' cemetery and eating beignets. We also hopped on the bus and road from one end of town to the other end. This visit was prior to getting on a cruise ship. I decided that I wanted to go to New Orleans again for my 63rd birthday in January 2020. I invited my son, Willie, and my daughter-in-law, Denetra, to join us for his birthday, which is 3 days after my birthday. Of course, to add to the states, Willie and I flew into Louis Armstrong New Orleans Airport, we rented a car in New Orleans, and drove to Mobile, Alabama.

#20 Alabama – We began our Gulf Coast adventure in Mobile, Alabama, for a one-night stay with a birthday spa massage and dinner. We visited the Mobile Mardi Gras Museum. We found out that Mardi Gras began in Mobile, not in New Orleans. Willie enjoyed talking to whomever he ran into about sports in Alabama because he said that Alabama is a college football region. He said that it is bigger than the NFL and NBA. Bear Bryant, the former coach of the University of Alabama, is just as popular now as he was in the 50s and 60s, according to Willie's Sports Fun Facts. [1/16-17/2020] #20state

Alabama

#21 Mississippi - From Mobile, Alabama, we also spent a night in Biloxi, Mississippi. I always enjoy the food in Louisiana, but the seafood in Alabama and Mississippi was beyond delicious. The drive down the coast was a spectacular scenic beauty. [1/17-18/2020] #21state

Mississippi

#22 Louisiana – Although this was my third time in Louisiana for my birthday, this was beyond special because I was spending time in one of my favorite places (New Orleans and Sedona were my favorites at the time) celebrating my birthday with my firstborn for his birthday. There were so many places and foods that I wanted J and Dee to try and experience. My son does not like sightseeing, but he was ready to try the New Orleans cookeries, their Po-boy, Beignets, Cajun, and Creole cuisine. Willie and I have gone to recommended restaurants in New Orleans, usually by hotel staff. My son wanted to eat where the native eats, so we ended up getting takeout orders from a popular spot with a long

Louisiana

line in the back of a gas station. Yes, me, Sheila René eating and enjoying gas station food. It was plentiful and delicious. J and Dee explored and enjoyed New Orleans' nightlife. We also found a K & G Fashion Superstore in New Orleans. K & G is both Willies'- my husband's and my son's store for shoes and clothes. [1/18-22/2020

#22states

Because COVID-19 hit us in 2020 when it was time for my two granddaughters, Jayla and Darby, to go back to school in the fall, they had to continue with remote learning, and their parents had to go back to work. My husband and I went to North Carolina and brought them back to New Jersey to continue their virtual learning. We set up our living room and dining room for a first grade and seventh-grade classrooms. All of you parents and educators out there know that virtual school in the fall of 2020 was not a small feat. I applaud all of you for your dedication, sacrifice, efforts, and determination to allow learning to continue for children.

Once again, I had a bright idea that stemmed from when my sister Shelley retired, and the two of us went on a AAA

Grand Canyon retirement sister's trip in October 2018. When we were in Arizona, we saw signs for Route 66. We nonchalantly said that we should take a Route 66 cross-country trip. My plan when I graduated college in 1979 was to drive cross-country to California, but love and life changed that plan. . . I am digressing again. So, of course, my bright idea was to do it now because we would all go stir-crazy if we had stayed couped up until who-knows-when isolation, remote learning, and this pandemic would end.

I mentioned it to my sister, Shelley, who is always ready for an adventure, and of course, she was ready because she, too, was doing remote learning with her second-grader grandson, Szymon. What surprised me was that when I mentioned it to my husband, Willie, he said yes. So, in September 2020, with no preplanning, we rented a large RV - a recreational vehicle, from Cruise America in Cliffwood, New Jersey. Three adults, Willie, Shelley, and I, took our grands Jayla, Darby, and Szymon on 15 days of adventures from September 23rd to October 7th.

We did our test driving when we picked up the RV at Overpeck Park parking lot in Leonia, New Jersey. It took us about four hours to pack up the RV and we still had to move things around several times throughout the initial trip. As always, we overpacked with the what-ifs. Because it was during the pandemic there were a lot of what-ifs.

We drove up Route 80 incredibly early in the morning, so early that Shelley and Szymon slept in the RV overnight in front of my house. Checking off my second trip to Ohio and Indiana, on our way to Chicago, Illinois. We did not realize how long Pennsylvania and Indiana were. Indiana was miles and miles of cornfields.

Route 66 Postcard

Chicago is the start of Route 66. According to Wikipedia – "U.S. Route 66 or U.S. Highway 66 (US 66 or Route 66), also known as the Will Rogers Highway, the Main Street of

Historic Route 66 Sign

America or the Mother Road, was one of the original highways in the U.S. Highway System. US 66 was established on November 11, 1926, with road signs erected the following year. The highway, which became one of the most famous roads in the United States, originally ran from Chicago, Illinois, through Missouri, Kansas, Oklahoma, Texas, New Mexico, and Arizona before terminating in Santa Monica in Los Angeles County California, covering a total of 2,448 miles. It was recognized in popular culture by both the 1946 hit song "(Get Your Kicks on) Route 66" and the Route 66 television series, which aired on CBS from 1960 to 1964. In John

Steinbeck's novel, The Grapes of Wrath (1939), the road «Highway 66» symbolizes escape and loss."

Checking off Illinois, Missouri (we missed Kansas because route 66 ran through the tip of Kansas, and we were back and forth on the main road because not all of Route 66 is drivable anymore), Oklahoma, Texas, New Mexico, Arizona, and California, we ended our Route 66 trip in Santa Monica, California. Our return trip consists of Nevada, Utah, Wyoming, and Nebraska. We spent one night in each state except for Chicago, Illinois, and Los Angeles, California, where we spent two nights. We stayed on campsites, mostly KOA - Kampgrounds of America sites, sleeping in the RV most of the time, but we also stayed in cabins some nights. We stayed in a hotel in Chicago, an Airbnb in both Mexico and Los Angeles, a motel in New Mexico, and a Teepee in Arizona.

We stopped at many of the Route 66 sites to take pictures and collect memorabilia from those places that were open. Even though schooling remotely in an RV presented some challenges, especially with time changes. In California, the children had to start school at 5 am for 8 am classes. They also had music and art classes that they had to participate in a small space. Their gym classes were usually done during a stop. Darby and Szymon basically had classes at the dining room table facing each other with their tablets and their headphones on.

Route 66 Passport

Shelley and sometimes I sitting with them. Jayla did her classes on the side couch with her headphones on and her tablet in her lap. It took us a while to get the hang of staying connected to the internet, but we made it through, and it was an unbelievable, spectacular, once-in-a-lifetime, experience for all. No classroom would have given our grands the educational experience that this trip provided. The Grand Canyon alone with its topography; flatlands, mountains, oceans, rivers, sunrises, sunsets, and all types of animals, birds, and insects were an education in itself. #34states #16togo

Route 66 RV

Headphones

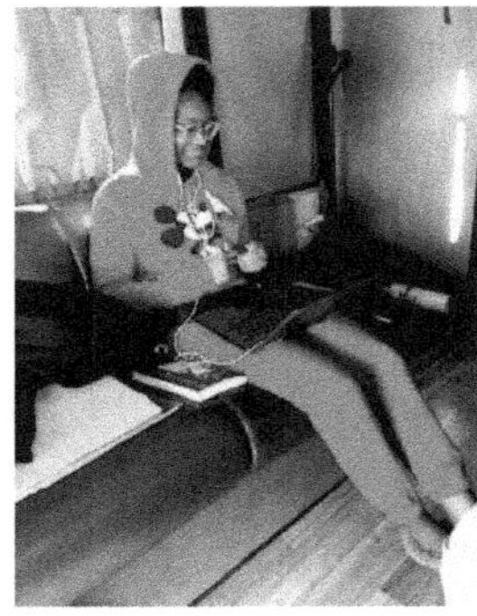

Route 66 RV

Jayla in Red

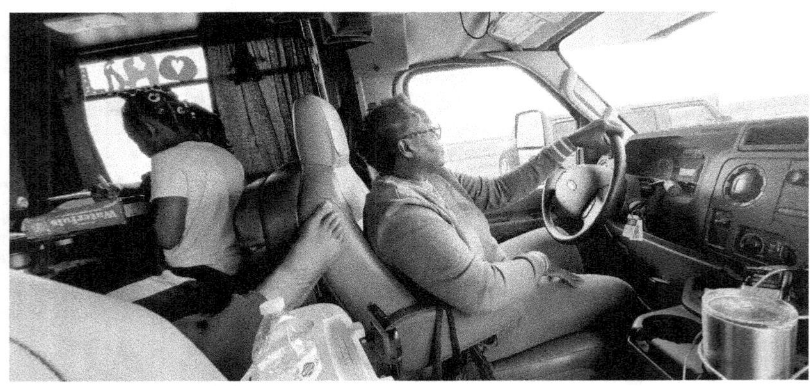

Route 66 RV Willie's foot

Willie did most of the driving, but Shelley gave Willie breaks and also drove. The one time that I drove to give Willie a break I could not stay awake. This was too big a vehicle to not be fully conscious and coherent. He did relax some. Do you see his right foot as he sits on Jayla's bench side seat supposedly relaxing, but I am sure that he is still overseeing?

#23 Illinois - In Chicago Illinois, we were able to park the RV in McCormick Place Parking Lot B and stayed at Home 2 Suites by Hilton Chicago McCormick Place for two days. There was a Starbucks next to the hotel and Jayla did what was probably her first big girl errand and picked up my favorite fall drink pumpkin spice, orange juice, and muffins while as always Big Daddy supervised from a distance.

We took pictures at the Chicago Route 66 landmark, designating the start of Route 66. Of course, we had to try the Chicago-style pizza from Giordano's and hotdogs with pickles from Portillo's. We saw the Chicago Bulls and Chicago Blackhawks' United Center, the largest arena in the United States, the Bean, and huge sculptures in the park. We also went to Harpo's (Oprah's) studio. We did a whole lot of walking in Chicago, exploring the city on foot. There was a sign in this Chicago hotel about no firearms, which reminded us that we were in a different part of

Route 66 Chicago

the country. We are used to acknowledging the different mindsets throughout our lifetime when traveling from the north of New York and Washington, D.C., to the south to South Carolina for Shelley and me and North Carolina for Willie, and now we are preparing to experience the Midwest mentality. Because of one of our southern family summer vacation drives, probably in the 1960s, we were not able to eat or stay in a Howard Johnson establishment, which was a nationwide roadside restaurant and hotel with a signature orange roof. My sister Sharon was young and needed to use the bathroom, and she was not allowed to use the bathroom because she is colored; since that experience, no more Howard Johnson for any of us. However, I just saw that Howard Johnson is connected to Wyndham, as well as many other hotels. Now, back to Chicago: A lot of the stores were boarded up because of the aftermath of George Floyd's murder on May 25, 2020. I loved our time in Chicago, and I definitely want to go back and spend more time there. [9/23-25/2020] #23state

On our way from Illinois to Missouri on Route 66, we saw a mural town in Pontiac, Illinois, by the artist Robert Waldmire. "Robert Waldmire was an American artist and cartographer who is well known for his artwork of United States Route 66, including whimsical maps of the Mother Road and its human and natural ecology," according to Wikipedia. We saw the World's Largest Rocking Chair, the Route 66 Red Rocker rocking chair, outside of Cuba in Fanning, Missouri. They also had a wide selection of bottled sodas such as Shirley Temple, Celery, Red Hot, Cinnamon, Maple Syrup, Red and Black Licorice Soda Pop as well as well-known lime, black cherry, ginger ale, cream, root beer, orange, grape soda pop. Of course, we had to try a variety of their flavored sodas.

Route 66 Sodas/Chair

#24 Missouri - St. Louis West / Historic Route 66 KOA in Eureka, Missouri was our first campground site. We slept in the RV. Shelley and Szymon on the overhead front of the RV fold-out mattress bed, Jayla and Darby on the dining room table-turned bed in the middle of the RV, and Willie and I in the back of the RV. The RV was surprisingly comfortable. [9/25-26/2020] #24state

Route 66 RV Bedtime

#25 Oklahoma - From Missouri to Twin Fountains RV Park in Oklahoma City Oklahoma is a beautiful family-owned campground. They had beautiful water fountains in the middle of their lake in which Willie enjoyed the serenity of it as he sat on the bench facing the fountain... On our way to Oklahoma Shelley did an art project with the grands cutting out construction paper letters O-K-L-A-H-O-M-A and hanging them up on the side window of the RV. We sang the song Oklahoma as we

Route 66 RV Oklahoma

drove down Route 66 and Route I-40 to Oklahoma. "Oklahoma, where the wind comes sweepin' down the plain. And the wavin' wheat can sure smell sweet. When the wind comes right behind the rain..." [9/26-27/2020] #25state

Route 66

We stopped at the National Route 66 Museum in Elk City with antique cars, barns, old-fashioned gas pumps, barn, and old-fashioned tractors and farm tools.

#26 Texas - Our next site was an Airbnb in Canyon Texas. The house had a beautiful landscape and statues. Even though we were being extremely cautious about going to restaurants because of COVID-19, we could not be in Texas without going to a Texan Steakhouse. We ate at the Big Texan Steak Ranch. The steakhouse gave the grands cowboy hats with their meals. We also purchased cowboy boots at Cavender's Boot City. Real cowboy boots are expensive. We went to the Cadillac Ranch, and we sprayed paint on Cadillac cars that were stuck in the ground. This was a great and fun experience because Shelley and I as well as Jayla, Darby, and Szymon consider ourselves artists. [9/27-28/2020] #26state

Route 66 Texas

Route 66 Texas Cadillac Ranch

#27 New Mexico - From Texas to New Mexico, we stayed at the Roadrunner Lodge in Tucumcari, New Mexico. They had complimentary moon pies in our rooms. We basically cooked most of our meals outside, mainly on my old electric skillet when we stayed at campsites but since we were staying in a motor lodge, and we are in New Mexico we had to have Mexican food. We ate Mexican food at an authentic Mexican restaurant. The lodge and the

Route 66 Tucumcari New Mexico

town of Tucumcari had a vintage appeal including vintage cars and a Texaco Gas Station. We purchased some authentic native jewelry as we explored the area. [9/28-29/2020] #27state

#28 Arizona – I already mentioned that I love Arizona, especially Sedona, as well as New Orleans. I have been to Arizona four times and now I am working on expanding my horizons by exploring other states too. Holbrook, Arizona was another wonderful experience with its unique artifact shops. We spent the night in Wigwams at the Wigwam Motel in Holbrook, Arizona, which had two beds and full bathrooms. Jayla remembered that the Wigwam also had a television because the 2020

Route 66 Arizonia Wigwam

Debates were on, and my 12-year-old granddaughter could not believe the arguing, rudeness, and disrespect of the two adult men. The Wigwam Motel grounds had vintage cars in front of their wigwams. We saw plenty of huge, petrified wood on the grounds. We found out that the difference between a wigwam and a teepee is a wigwam is made of mud and sticks and a teepee is made of animal fur or leather. I pray that we all learn something new each day of our new adventure. #28state

We could not be in Arizona without stopping at the Grand Canyon. This was Shelley and my second time visiting the Grand Canyon. We went together when she retired. But being at the Grand Canyon with our grandchildren was more than a blessing. They were overly excited and amazed at such a spectacular, humongous sight that touches four states. Being an eyewitness to these millions of years of the geological natural formation of layered rocks cannot compare to what can be seen in any book or slide. I am showing my age because I am sure that no classroom has slides anymore. When I retired, my school district was installing smartboards in every classroom. [9/29-30/2020] #28states

We stopped at a KOA campground in Arizona to dump and were given some RV maintenance instructions, including how to use the stove and a better understanding of our propane levels. Shelley, Jayla, Darby, and Szymon did gold mining while they waited. Shelley made every day and every aspect of the trip a memorable learning experience with teachable moments for not just the grands but the adults, too. We are sisters and both retired educators, but she is the one with patience, she is a free-spirit and a lover and appreciation of every aspect of her life and its surroundings. Again, I reiterate that people at campgrounds (owners, workers, and fellow campers) are so friendly and so helpful.

Route 66 Mining

#29 California - From Arizona to Encino, California for two days in sunny California. We rented another cute Airbnb. It had a rock garden-type pool. Even though you do not see people walking the streets in the suburbs of L.A., we walked around Encino Commons. We walked to the Enterprise Rent-A-Car and rented a car. We went sightseeing in Los Angeles and to the Santa Monica Pier's landmark, which is the end of Route 66. We went to the Staple Center, which was closed because of COVID-19. We went to the Hollywood Walk of Fame to see the Stars on Hollywood Boulevard, and we were surprised that the area that looked so elegant on television was not elegant at all. There were a lot of homeless people sleeping in front of buildings, including in front of the Jimmy Kimmel Show building. Jayla was upset with me because she wanted to get out of the car, which we did, and we ran into two sports stores to price Kobi jerseys (I was not paying

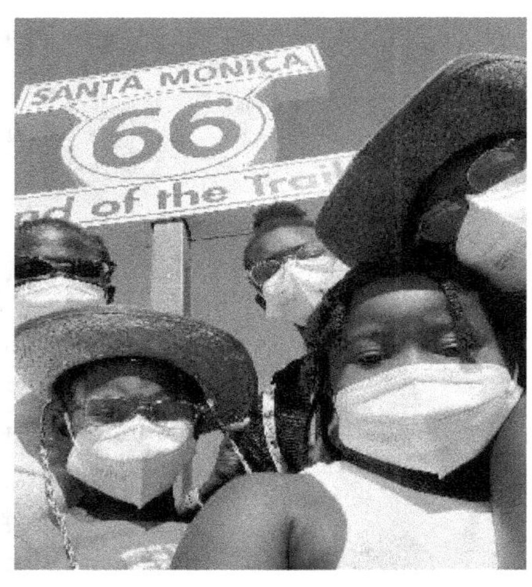

Route 66 Santa Monica California

$400 for a jersey, not even for my favorite birth daughter), then we got back in the car. I later found out that this moody Gemini preteen had an attitude because she wanted to see Michael Jackson's star, but she did not verbalize this request. I think that I made up for it when I went back to L.A. with her brother in May of 2021; we found the star, took pictures around the star, and sent them to her. If this did not earn me forgiveness, I took her to see MJ The Musical on Broadway in July 2022, so we should now be all good.

We were in California during the wildfires, and the sky was gray, we pray for all who have been affected by the fires and thank God that the fires did not alter our plans. We were advised to wear our N95 masks while outside in Los Angeles. It was really hot in New Mexico, Arizona, and California. Darby forgot and left her tablet in the rented car overnight in California and it fried the device. [9/30-10/2/2020] #29state

Now, it was time for our return trip back home. Route 66 was indescribably a wonderful adventure. Traveling during the pandemic had its advantages and disadvantages. The first plus is being able to take our grands on this trip and still have them in school virtually. Even though we noticed that at the time, six months after the inception of the pandemic, middle America was not taking COVID-19 protocols as seriously with mask mandates and social distances as we are in New Jersey and New York. We took advantage of the sparsity of tourists in most of the places that we visited for its historical sites, shopping, and also places for dining.

#30 Nevada - On our way back east, our first stop was the Reno KOA at Boomtown in Verdi, Nevada. It was a real Western experience and a spectacular view. The landscape with its mountains was beautiful. The campground is adjacent to a casino and hotel that we had access to but did not take advantage of the amenities because of COVID-19. We roasted marshmallows, and I made spaghetti

Campground Nevada

for dinner. Shelley, being a vegetarian, I fixed her TVP, aka Textured Vegetable Protein, while the rest of us ate ground turkey with our spaghetti and sauce. The campground had a gas grill and a fire pit. Jayla, Darby, and Szymon entertained us with a show using their flashlights. The next morning, we had grits and sausage for breakfast. [10/2-3/2020] #30state

#31 Utah - From Nevada to the Salt Lake City KOA Holiday in Salt Lake City, Utah. This was the only stop that disappointed us. The area of Utah where we stayed was an obscure area, not like any

Campgrounds Utah #1

Campgrounds of Utah #2

campground that we have become accustomed to. This campground was more like a trailer park than a campground, but there were still beautiful mountainous views. We passed a lot of homeless people while driving through Utah. I remember getting annoyed with my laid back sister in the morning because Willie and I were so ready to go, and Shelley wanted to explore the horizons. I am sure that Salt Lake City has other attractive aspects because the Utah Jazz Basketball team is located here, and Willie's Godson Christopher lives and works in Utah. [10/3-4/2020] #31state

#32 Wyoming - With my mapping out the trip using the KOA map, I thought that our next stop would have been Colorado, but we found ourselves in Wyoming (I have gotten a little better in my roadmap route mappings by the next

Campgrounds of Wyoming Cabin #1

Campgrounds of Wyoming Cabin #2

cross-country trip, but I still made mistakes with my mapping the second time around, too). Thank God Campgrounds of America provided us with a United States KOA book, so it was easy to find another KOA site. My sister and I were excited about staying in Colorado, but it would be easier to take a trip to Colorado than to figure out a visit to Wyoming. We stayed in a cabin at Cheyenne KOA, Cheyenne, Wyoming. The cabin stay was a change of pace and another adventure. We got to Wyoming late and ate hotdogs. Even though everyone was exhausted, we also celebrated Szymon's 7th birthday with cupcakes. [10/4-5/2020] #32state

#33 Nebraska - The next stop is Nebraska West Omaha/ NE Lincoln KOA in Gretna, Nebraska. The excitement must be wearing off because all anyone remembers about this campground is that we sat around a campfire, and of course we could not forget that it was a smores night (chocolate and melted marshmallows on graham crackers). We also all (except Willie) tried to get this beautiful bird in the cage to talk to us. [10/5-6/2020] #33state

As you can see schoolwork never stopped.

Nebraska Sign #1

Nebraska Campfire #2

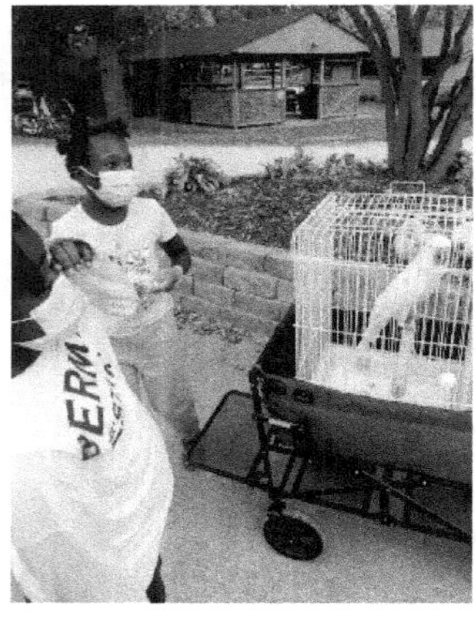

Nebraska Bird #3

Nebraska Campsite & Schoolwork #4

#34 Iowa – As I am writing this chapter I realize that we went through Iowa, but we did not spend the night in Iowa. That makes two states that I have been to, but that I did not spend the night. I will have to go back to both New Hampshire and Iowa to spend a night. New Hampshire is easy because it is a four-hour drive, but Iowa is a little more complicated, but of course, I will make it happen. #34state

Iowa &

Indiana, here we come, again, but this time we stayed at the South Bend/ Elkhart North KOA in Granger, Indiana. We saw miles and miles of cornfields. We sang The Jackson Five's song "We're Going Back To Indiana" as we traveled to and from Indiana. Jayla, Darby, and Szymon made glow-in-the-dark circles to put around their necks and wrists. They also put together wooden birdhouses and painted them with their Aunt Shelley. Once a teacher - always a teacher. Shelley was the one coming up with the entertainment throughout the trip, singing songs, and doing arts and crafts, as well as the nature observations, various activities, and nature walks. [10/6-7/2020]

Even our rest stops were an adventure.

Indiana Campground Nightlife

From Indiana back home. Our last stop was supposed to be at Mercer / Grove City KOA to stay in a deluxe cabin in Mercer, Pennsylvania but we canceled because everyone was ready to get back home to their own beds. Ironically, it became Willie and my first stop in September 2021 when we took our second cross-country RV trip but this time across the northern United States. This extra day also gave us more time to rest and clean out the RV before returning it.

Reststop

New York Highway Sign

Homebound here we come!

This adventure was our first RV trip. If we had to do it over, it would have been a longer trip with more stops so that there would have been shorter driving distances. I would plan more 2-day stays. Even though RV rentals are expensive, the cost is based on the number of days and the mileage, not to mention variant gas prices, especially in California. I definitely should have worked on enjoying the adventure more and not focusing on my OCD timeline. Also, I should have been in grandma mode instead of educator mode and focused more on enjoying the experience with my family instead of being so rigid with school schedules and completing virtual school assignments.

We made it through 2020. It was not easy, but we made it through because of God's Grace and Mercy upon each of us individually, and collectively. I pray for the families who lost loved ones. I pray for those who are suffering from long-COVID-19, and for those who struggled with school, work; especially small businesses, and/or finances because of this pandemic. The complete impact that this pandemic and disease has caused to each person, and each family, as well as the babies and children, physically and mentally has not been fully realized yet, but that too, is in my prayers. I thank God for all who are alive to tell their 2020 story.

Someone asked me, if I am so concerned about places reopening and people not wearing masks, how can I do all of this traveling? I am a germaphobe and was a germaphobe before this pandemic, and I am extremely cautious and try not to be too paranoid. I will still be wearing a mask in October 2022, and I decide what places I will go in, and my proximity to people, except for on an airplane, where I have little control of my space. I did find out that the aisle seat is probably the most exposed seat in an airplane. When we traveled with our grands, they wore masks every time they left the RV. They used hand sanitizer or washed their hands with soap and water (I prefer soap and water) when they came back to the RV. If a place was too crowded, we did not go in. But I already said that the advantage of traveling during this time was that there were very few people traveling.

2021
Washington - Oregon – California
West Virginia – Kentucky – Arkansas – Tennessee -
Pennsylvania – Michigan – Wisconsin – Minnesota –
South Dakota – North Dakota – Montana Idaho - Utah – Colorado – Kansas – Missouri – Illinois – Ohio
21 States

Now, in 2021, my grandson, Dasaiah, graduated from Wake Young Men's Leadership Academy High School in Raleigh, North Carolina. His dream was to see Los Angeles. So, I had him and his aunt Shené meet Willie and I in Los Angeles. His sister Jayla teases him, as siblings do because she was able to go to Los Angeles before he did.

Dasaiah left from North Carolina, and my daughter Shené left from Virginia. Unfortunately, I missed his High School graduation because the school schedule was changed, and the date for his graduation was pushed back. Also, limited graduation tickets were distributed because of the pandemic. My grandson had to change his flight date by a day because of the changes.

Another one of my brilliant ideas was to drive down the west coast. I always wanted to see Seattle and San Francisco.

#35 Washington - Willie and I flew to Seattle, Washington in May 2021. We stayed at the Residence Inn by Marriott Seattle Downtown Lake Union. The seafood at the restaurants

Seattle Washington

was indescribably delicious. We ate at the same restaurant twice because the food was so good. I had to try salmon in Seattle, but the first night, I saw halibut on the menu, and I had to try it first. You cannot be in Seattle without having their fresh seafood. Then the next night when we went back to the restaurant, and I tried Seattle's salmon. I also had to do a repeat of the restaurant's amazing seafood soup. Willie, who is a creature of habit had stuffed shrimps both days. The location was perfect, the restaurant was within walking distance from the hotel, and it was also on the water. I love being on the water whenever I can because water is so serene and relaxing for me.

Seattle sightseeing was great, and seeing various tech companies was amazing. We were told that Seattle is a place for young techies. We learned that the majority of the residents are under forty. We also found out that there are more dogs than children in Seattle. The tour guide explained that these young people's work hours prevent them from trying to raise a family. He told us how to recognize a self-driving car. We noticed the lack of churches and gas stations; we asked the tour guide and he confirmed that it is rare to see either one. The tour guide also let us know that Seattle has an underground city. I have to go back so that I can go on an Underground City Tour.

Seattle is the home of ten Fortune 500 companies: Amazon, Starbucks, Microsoft, Costco, Nordstrom, U-Haul, and Alaskan Airlines, to name a few. The wealth disparities are evident, with a large homeless population with tents lining the streets. The aging population can be found in the Asian area, where there is a Chinatown. We also saw boats and yachts at the marina and boathouses and rowing teams at practice. In riding around we saw Google, the first Starbucks, and Amazon stores everywhere. Most of the companies were closed and the employers and employees were working from home. We saw a beautiful colorful empty Google building. We were able to shop to Trader Joe's for road snacks. The Needle was also closed. Because of COVID-19 at the Wharf they were not doing the tossing of the fish. We definitely have to do a repeat of Seattle.

I am not a sports person, even though I went to football games in high school and college, I would even watch games with my father growing up, and Willie when we first got married. My husband is a diehard Washington fan; the now Commanders that was the Redskins. I decided it was time for me to have a team, mainly for team day/jersey day at the church, so I chose the Seattle Seahawks as my team because of the uniforms, and a Black quarterback, who is a community activist along with his wife Ciara Ciara. (Now Russell Wilson is playing for the Denver Broncos). I purchased my first jersey, a number 12 lime green jersey with a royal blue Fan on the back of the jersey because Willie explained to me that there are 11 players on the field and the fan is the 12th player. I am glad that I did not buy a Russell Wilson Seattle Seahawks jersey. We also saw Seattle's stadium, Lumen Field.

Did I mention that I love walking and exploring new places, but that I often get lost while walking? I got so lost in Seattle. Willie had to come to pick me up (this was before he had a tracker on my phone). I could not backtrack because I inadvertently walked through a homeless camp, and I did not want to walk through the camp again. There were a lot of homeless people in Seattle, there were a lot of homeless people on the West Coast. Thank God for GPS on my cellphone

Portland

because I was able to find a populated corner for Willie to pick me up. [5/16-18/2021] #35state

#36 Oregon - From Seattle, we drove down to Portland, Oregon, and stayed at the Portland Marriott Downtown Waterfront Hotel. Portland was in shutdown mode so we could not go on a tour. We rode around and I walked around but stayed close to the hotel. Again, there was a lot of homelessness, and the area was somewhat deserted because of closed restaurants. We thought of looking for Nike's home base but changed our minds. [5/18-20/2021] #36state

I keep mentioning the homelessness on the West Coast, and I want to stop and ask you to pray with me for all those who are without a home, shelter, food, and/or employment. As well as those who are not living in decent housing, who cannot afford nutritious food, and/or are underemployed. In Jesus' Name, I Pray!

We broke up the drive from Portland to San Francisco by stopping and staying overnight at the halfway point in Yreka, (not Eureka), California. We stayed at the Holiday Inn Express Yreka-Shasta Area, which was in the middle of nowhere. We went to an Italian restaurant for dinner that was nothing to brag about, as a lover of Italian food. Because of COVID-19 restrictions, for breakfast, the hotel gave out bagged continental breakfast.

I always wanted to visit San Francisco and it happened. We stayed at the Zelos Hotel in downtown San Francisco. Sightseeing in San Francisco was also spectacular. San Francisco was everything that I imagined it to be. The colorful architecture was very appealing to me. The steep hills were intimidating in a good way. I did not walk up or down the hills. The tour guide took us down a crooked steep hill on Lombard Street, which is known as the most crooked street in the world. We went across the Golden Gate Bridge.

We also saw redwood trees in the middle of the city. Like Seattle, San Francisco is a young people's town with both funk and jazz music communities. It has an Asian community, a lack of gas stations and churches, and it also has self-driving cars. We saw where the Black Panthers' headquarters was located in Oakland.

San Fransico California

We were staying in downtown San Francisco, and I did a lot of walking, but refrained from going into stores to buy, even though there were retail stores like Macy's right around the corner from the hotel. The Van Gough exhibit was also near the hotel, but I was not ready to be so close to people even with a mask and socially distancing. I am so ready to explore San Francisco, California again. I would go to the west coast again. The West Coast drive, I am starting to sound repetitive, but it was breathtaking.

Los Angeles, here we come! We were ready to meet up with Shené and Dasaiah. We rented a huge North Hollywood Airbnb. From the outside, you would never know that there was a gem inside. This is probably my favorite Airbnb to date. We were greeted with a huge welcome basket with so many items (mostly from Trader Joe's) that the four of us could not finish everything. Four bedrooms, a warm saltwater pool, and a hot tub. The décor and attention to detail were noticeable. Everything that you would possibly want was provided, including yoga mats. I was able to work out virtually to T-2 Fitness Facebook workout on the beautiful stone veranda, which my daughter posted on social media, which made Tasha happy that I was working out during my vacation. There were three washing machines and three dryers. I know I am using the word beautiful a lot to describe parts of the house, but the house is described in its Airbnb post as the Sanctuary Oasis Saltwater Pool and Spa, and it lived up to its title.

There was a rooster somewhere nearby in the neighborhood that Shené said woke her up every morning. We went on a tour that met at the Hollywood Walk of Fame. The tour took us all around Los Angeles. We went all the way up to the Hollywood sign. We went to movie stars' homes like Michael Jackson, Ditty, Kylie Jenner, and Justin Timberlake. The rumors about Los Angeles' traffic are probably an understatement. Now it's time for the foodie in me. The well-known In and Out Burger fast-food restaurant, known for its burgers and fries, did not live up to its reputation. Roscoe's Chicken and Waffles was beyond delicious.

Los Angeles #1

Dasaiah had two requests: he wanted to eat at Dave's Hot Chicken and go to La Ropa in L.A. Dave's Hot Chicken was so good that Dasaiah had more food delivered when everyone else went to bed. We saw a Shakey's, and we had to go there to eat and tell Shené and Dasaiah about our NIH (National Institute of Health)

Los Angeles #2

days where Willie and I met and worked while in college and would go eat and have pizza and chicken wings and that's exactly what we ordered. Unfortunately, it did not live up to our memories, but we probably would have still enjoyed it if we were in our 20s and it was 1977.

Dasaiah did purchase an expensive hat from La Ropa, and I shopped at Urban Outfitters. We went to Santa Monica Pier and also San Diego. Even though Venus Beach was on my must-sees, especially since I have not been there since Ronda took us in 1981, we were told that it is not safe now.

I left the west coast with #36states.

#37 West Virginia - We drove down to North Carolina in June 2021 and picked up Jayla and Darby during their summer break. We drove to West Virginia. We stayed at the Country Inn & Suites by Radisson, in Charleston, West Virginia. West Virginia was another state that I was not in a rush to see, but the mountainous landscapes were stunningly beautiful (I am

West Virginia

running out of adjectives – thinking emoji). When I asked Willie and the girls what they remembered about West Virginia, they said that we saw a lot of white people. In many of the places that we traveled to; we sought out people who looked like us. We saw a lot of hills and mountains. We also learned the West Virginia song and sang it over and over while we traveled through the state of West Virginia "Country Road, take me home to a place I belong West Virginia Mountain Mama take me home, country road." [6/23/2021] #37state

#38 Kentucky - I can lump in Kentucky as another one of my questionable states. I could not think of a reason to go to Kentucky, but I was pleasantly surprised. We visited the Muhammad Ali Center and Louisville Slugger Museum & Factory in Kentucky. We enjoyed both museums immensely. Both museums, especially the Muhammed Ali Museum, were very educational. We had to bring a souvenir back for Dea-

Kentucky

con Leary Puryear because, as a former boxer, he is a huge Ali fan. We stayed at the Best Western Central City outside of Louisville, Kentucky. We did not go to KFC - Kentucky Fried Chicken, probably because I did not think about it at the time, but my granddaughters said that they did... We saw a lot of distilleries. We also walked the grounds and steps of their Capitol building. [6/24/2021] #38state

#39 Arkansas - I could not imagine why I would want to go to Arkansas, and it turned out to be one of our best places. We exchanged our Poconos timeshare for a week in Hot Springs, Arkansas. In Arkansas, we stayed at the South Shore Lake Resort in Hot Springs, Arkansas. It was a very nice villa with an upstairs and downstairs living area. We let the girls convince us to let them

Arkansas

stay downstairs by themselves. They had a large bedroom with a walk-in closet and bathroom, a huge living room with a sliding door to a patio that extended to their bedroom, and a wet bar-type kitchenette. All I can say about our decision was that the 13-year-old and the 7-year-old were not ready. I will leave it at that.

I went to Quapaw Baths; one of the Hot Springs bathhouses and had a spa treatment and also soaked in three different temperature hot springs pools. This was such a relaxing experience. I am always rushing to get to my next, but this is one time I should have taken my time to luxuriate in these pools after my massage.

I explored the bath houses histories also while sightseeing in downtown Hot Springs.

Willie, the girls, and I went up the Hot Springs Mountain Towers that overlooked the city of Hot Springs and stopped on the road to drink the water flowing from a hot spring.

Hot Springs Arkansas

Little Rock Arkansas

Alligator Farm in Arkansas

We walked all over downtown Hot Springs. Jayla, Darby, and I also walked the grounds and steps of the capitol building. Visiting Capitols in states is starting to become our thing. We visited the statues of the Little Rock Nine. We also visited the Little Rock Central High School National Historic Site Visitor Center. We took the girls to the Arkansas Alligator Farm and Petting Zoo where they held baby alligators and some farm animals. [6/25-7/1/2021] #39state

On the way back to take the girls back home to North Carolina we went back to Tennessee, first to Nashville. Tennessee. Nashville was great. We stayed at the Graduate Nashville Hotel which was right down the street from Vanderbilt University. The girls loved the hotel with its playful luxe hotel room and lobby. The hotel advertises "surrounding yourself in history and legend at our funky, floral jewel box." The hotel had a vintage pop-up exhibit with vendors selling vintage clothing and jewelry the morning that we left. Jayla is into vintage and Big Daddy aka her grandfather let her pick out an outfit. She got vintage white cotton button-down romper shorts. Jayla and I walked around the area the evening that we arrived in Nashville. The next day we all rode through Vanderbilts' huge campus.

Nashville Tennessee

We drove by Meharry University and walked around Fisk University. We saw the statue of W. E. B. Dubois on the Fisk University campus.

We stopped and ate at the most amazing barbecue chicken place, Hattie's B's. Just thinking about their chicken makes my mouth water again.

We stopped in Memphis since Willie is a Federal Express retiree, and we drove to the FedEx Headquarters in Memphis. Willie was at the headquarters many years ago for a training, but because of strict security, he could not get past the gate this time without a current FedEx identification card.

The next day we drove to Knoxville Tennessee and visited Knoxville College again. We also

Knoxville College Tennessee

saw the University of Tennessee. We stayed at Home 2 Suites by Hilton in Knoxville. [7/1-3/2021]

Let's Do It Again!
Pennsylvania - Michigan – Indiana

The fall is a great time to do RV traveling, Willie and I decided that we wanted to do it again. So, we booked another RV in October 2020 for this 2021 trip. We rented a standard-size 25ft RV from Cruise America in Cliffwood, New Jersey to travel to the Northern United States. Our first RV was a large size 30ft.

There was a very friendly and knowledgeable young lady named Chrystal who assisted us both times and I want to give her a shout-out for putting us newcomers at ease with being able to not only drive these recreational vehicles but being able to maintain them. She gave us a quick tutorial both times on the black and gray hoses, how to dump waste correctly, how to refill the water tank, how to check propane levels and a reminder about the importance of turning off the generator at gas stations (that was Jayla's job on the first trip now I have to remember to turn it off before Willie pumped gas on this do over trip).

I must include that this RV thing is not all fun and games; we keep forgetting first, that it is a long drive from Teaneck to Cliffwood to pick up the RV and then return it. Also, it is exhausting packing and unpacking the RV, especially since you are paying by the day, and you usually pick up the day before your trip and return the RV the day after your trip. Plus, setting up and breaking down before and leaving each campsite is work; refilling the water and dumping waste is a job in itself. I would still do it again and again because the adventure outweighs all this. Willie and I, mostly Willie was concerned about being cooped up together for such a long time—just the two of us, together for 17 days in an RV. We did not know who was going to be the first one to throw the other out of this recreational vehicle in the middle of nowhere when we got tired of the other one.

We took a 17-day Northern United States road trip adventure, just the two of us, from September 14th to the 30th of September in the fall of 2021. We drove up Route 80 again to our first stop in Mercer, Pennsylvania's Grove City KOA. We have been to the Poconos many times. We also have been to McKeesport Pennsylvania to visit my family, which is in the same direction as Mercer, Pennsylvania. But for some reason, this scenic drive to Pennsylvania was more beautiful, peaceful, and surprisingly relaxing than ever before. My car rides are usually "Are we there yet?" but this five-and-a-half-hour drive was different.

The whole Northern United States travel was spectacular; the scenery of greenery, the changing colors of the clear sky, and witnessing up close the sunrises, sunsets, and the moon each day and night. Watching the variant mountain ranges, and the various lakes were all breathtaking. Even though we have been camping many times, staying at campsites, and sleeping in tents, these two cross-country trips were incredible. Waking up in the great outdoors, cooking and eating your meals outdoors, and breathing fresh tree surrounding air each day, were all so unnaturally natural.

On this trip every campsite was beautiful. We found with both RV trips that our fellow campers were very friendly and extremely helpful in every place we stayed. The owners of the KOA campsites that we stayed at were also extremely accommodating.

Mercer/Grove City KOA Holiday campground site is a beautiful campsite with a patio, a grill firepit, a table, and a

Mercer Campground

swing. I realized the bed of the standard-size RV is smaller than I thought compared to large-size RV. I was pinned to the wall this first night. Because Willie did all the driving and probably will be doing most of the driving, I decided to endure the discomfort and snoring from being over tired for this first stop. The next night I checked out the overhead bed so that we both could have a comfortable night's sleep.

#40 Michigan - From Mercer, Pennsylvania we drove through Ohio. We ran into a little bit of rain, but it was a beautiful day. Detroit, Michigan was another one of my many must-sees. We took a detour to Detroit, to try their so-called famous Detroit Style Pizza that we recently started hearing advertised at home and also to visit the Motown Museum. Because of COVID-19 changes, the Motown Museum hours changed, and it was closed on Wednesdays. Of course, I took pictures of this vividly bright blue building on Barry Gordy Jr. Blvd., adorned with the sign Hitsville U.S.A.

Motown Detroit

The building had a marquee with images of Marvin Gaye. I guess you probably already know that I do want to go back to Detroit to the museum. Just being on the grounds of Motown brought back memories of singing and dancing to the Motown music of the Supremes, the Temptations, Stevie Wonder, and the Jackson Five. Even though we found delicious pizza, it was not "Detroit-style pizza. We ate our Detroit meal at 1000 Degrees Pizza – Salad – Wings, across from Wayne State University. I am considering doing a Chicago / Detroit trip in the near future. I have not decided if it will be a road trip.

We stayed at Covert/South Haven KOA Holiday in Covert, Michigan. It was a beautiful campsite with a lake and a huge chair. I was able to walk the grounds and enjoy the beauty of nature. The campgrounds overlooked the orchards and vineyards of what is called the Napa Valley of the Midwest. We lit a campfire when it got dark and enjoyed the quiet. It got cool that night, but it warmed up in the morning. Even though camping and driving in the fall are great you have to be prepared for all temperatures of weather, which for me means overpacking with the "what ifs". I need to learn how to be a better packer for all types of trips. [9/15-16/2021] #40states

Michigan Campground

#41 Wisconsin – Wow! 40 down 10 to go… Hurray! From Michigan to Wisconsin. We stayed in Milton, Wisconsin.

This was my second visit to Wisconsin. My first visit was a conference in Green Lake, Wisconsin, for a conference through American Baptist USA Churches, while I was still in seminary.

Wisconsin Campground

I thought that both the Michigan campsite and the Wisconsin campsite would be closer to Lake Michigan based on my mapping markers, even though they were not Lakeview, they were beautiful. We stayed at another beautiful campsite, the Milton KOA Holiday in Milton, Wisconsin. The time changed before we got to Wisconsin. It changed as we drove through Indiana and Illinois. The site had a nice office with a store with cook food and snacks that they offered delivery to your campsite. The campgrounds and atmosphere were beautiful, but the sites were close together. We got to the campground early so we were able to relax. One of the mistakes that we made with the Route 66 trip was not getting to the sites early enough to relax.

I remember that here they were ready for Halloween with the huge, inflated decorations in front of their large clubhouse, another huge chair, and a big Laser Tag sign. We did not play Laser Tag or buy cheese even though there were signs everywhere about Wisconsin Cheese. We had our go-to outdoor cooking dinner of hamburgers, hotdog and I also had grilled broccoli. [9/16-17/2021] #41state

#42 Minnesota - Jackson, Minnesota was our next stop. Waze directions were our lifesaver, but I put in the wrong address for Minnesota in Waze. When we thought that we had less than two hours left to our destination, we actually had more than three hours. But of course, Willie was fine with the mistake, because that is his personality. But I on the other hand was kicking myself for making a mistake because that is my personality. I do not know why I cannot accept the fact that even with my detail-oriented brain I too can make mistakes. Another item on my list for my therapist.

Minnesota is another one of those states that I never phantom that I would visit. I did not know what to expect. We stayed at Jackson KOA Journey. The owners of this campsite, like most of the campgrounds, were so friendly and helpful. They purchased the campground in August 2020, and they showed me the renovations

Minnesota Campground

that they made to upgrade the place. I remember them because their site was near ours. Our site was next to their pavilion, and I was able to relax, do my morning stretching and a Tasha T-2 workout, and take a non-RV shower. I love outdoor yoga.

I also had enough time and was able to fix bacon, sausages, scrambled eggs, and in toaster waffles for breakfast. [9/17-18/2021] #42state

#43 South Dakota – I felt some type of way just entering South Dakota. The feeling was similar to the feeling when I was on the Central State University campus in Xenia, Ohio because both connected me to my mother and her past.

South Dakota

We stayed at Belvidere East KOA Journey in Midland, South Dakota. We grilled steaks and had a salad for dinner. I prefer outdoor cooking, even at home. We went to both Mount Rushmore National Memorial and to the Crazy Monuments Horse Memorial. I do not know how to describe the breathtaking specimens that we witness and the skills necessary to produce these humongous, majestic beauties. I did not know about the Crazy Horse Memorial prior to visiting the memorial but Willie and I was blessed to witness both monuments.

I was overly excited about finally going to South Dakota. I have been talking to my sisters for years about us going to South Dakota because after graduating college at Central State University in Xenia, Ohio, my mother went to Pine Ridge, South Dakota to teach on the Reservation. My sisters and I talked about visiting Pine Ridge even before my mother's passing. We wanted to take my mother back to Pine Ridge but as my mother became frail, we knew that it would be too exhausting a trip for her to endure. To get to Pine Ridge at the time it was an approximately seven-plus hours flight to Nebraska and then about a three-hour drive to Pine Ridge.

We stayed at the Prairie Wind Casino & Hotel in Oglala, South Dakota, right outside of Pine Ridge. I tried for months to book this reservation because it was the only hotel/motel listed as being in Pine Ridge, South Dakota.

This particular hotel was closed for a long time because of COVID-19. The Hotel, which was a motel looked like it should be in "Little House

South Dakota Pine Ridge

on the Prairie" both outside and inside. There was a notice about rattlesnakes. One of the locals said that if you leave them alone, they will leave you alone. The statement said, "WARNING Rattlesnakes – Rattlesnakes may be found in this area". I try to walk around everywhere that I go, but here I only walked from the hotel to the RV and back; quickly and cautiously looking all around for serpents. I definitely was not taking any chances with snakes. Our dinner was equal to our rooms and the hotel even though it was good to sleep in a real bed and to take a non-RV shower. There were times that I would refuse to stay in a place like this but this is my season of being adventurous. The dinner choices were limited (this was still COVID-19 time), I had a hamburger, and Willie had over-fried chicken wings. Just imagine this is the place that I waited months for in Pine Ridge to open back up so that I could book our reservations. But as underwhelming as it was, I have no regrets.

Too close for comfort but we were met by a huge hairy brown buffalo while driving down the highway. I am not sure if buffaloes are known for attacking cars but this one seemed preoccupied and we were glad.

In South Dakota, I felt my mother's spirit. I cannot explain my inner feelings, but it was like I was walking in her footsteps. Because of COVID-19, the Native American Reservation of the Sioux Tribe was closed to outsiders. We tried driving the RV to the Reservation to see

South Dakota Buffalo

the Reservation, but it was impossible to navigate the narrow, rocky dirt roads in an RV. We had to turn around on these dirt roads surrounded by what looked like a junkyard. It was a little disappointing, but the overall spiritual connection that I had with my mother in the Pine Ridge area made everything just fine, and for me, that is saying a lot. Maybe my sisters, I, and maybe our children will make the trip together by airplane, not a road trip (I can see everyone, except Shelley, shaking their heads no for a road trip). [9/19-20/2021] #43state

#44 North Dakota – We stayed at the Bismarck KOA Journey in Bismarck, North Dakota. It was a long drive, but we had a very restful night's sleep. That is one thing about sleeping outdoors: you can sleep well. The campground was serene and private. Willie and I ate our gourmet Parks Beef Hot Sausages on Martin's Potato Rolls with French's Spicy Mustard and Heinz Sweet Relish for dinner again. That was our fastest go-to flavorful meal. As much as I love trying new foods and restaurants, I can always eat hotdogs, hamburgers, french fries, and good pizza. [9/20-21/2021] #44state

North Dakota Campground

#45 Montana – We stayed at Billings KOA Holiday in Billings, Montana. This campground and our campsite were beautiful. It was advertised as being the first KOA. I expected an old campsite that probably needed upgrades but it was just the opposite with its overside

Montana Campground #1

patio with a swing for two, a bright yellow metal picnic table, and benches. We took advantage of a fire ring and made a fire. This was definitely one of my favorite campsites. I would definitely stay here longer.

Montana Campground #2

We also drove to Yellowstone National Park on our way to Idaho. I found out that there are campsites in the park. If I come this way again, I will look into staying in the Yellowstone National Park. [9/21-22/2021] #45state

#46 Idaho - We stayed at Pocatello KOA Journey in Pocatello, Idaho. It was our last stop westbound. Jayla was hoping that we would be going to Idaho on our Route 66 trip so that she could see the giant potato. We did not see a giant potato, but we did go to the grocery store to buy Idaho potatoes. We were informed that the best Idaho potatoes are exported to other places. Potato-potáto, we got our Idaho potatoes. The campsite was better than I expected. We were given a grill pit to fix our Idaho potatoes and barbecue chicken. A young lady, who I considered brave, was camping alone, across from us, in a car with a small, what I would call a pup-tent. The neighbors on the other side of us were extremely friendly; the husband was an inspector of campgrounds, and he told us that his son was a Pastor in

Idaho Potatoes

Stroudsburg, Pennsylvania. They had a huge bus-length long camper that had a king-sized bed. All I can imagine is how much it cost them to fill up that enormous thing on wheels. But I guess since it was part of his job he probably had a corporate gas card. [9/22-23/2021] #46 states

Utah

We stayed at Fillmore KOA Journey in Fillmore, Utah, on the way back east. It was a better experience than the last Utah visit, but again, Utah's campgrounds are my only complaint. Although the Fillmore campsite was fun for the groups staying there with all types of four-wheelers, riders gathered together to socialize and drink beer. For some reason, there were flies everywhere. I was able to wash my clothes at this site. Every campground has washing machines and clothes dryers, but this was my first time using their machines. I also went back to sleeping in the back bed with Willie; it was a better experience. [9/23-24/2021]

#47 Colorado - I finally got to Colorado. If I had a bucket list, Colorado, Detroit, Montana, and Pine Ridge, South Dakota, would have been on it. We had the opportunity to stay

Denver Colorado

in both the Colorado mountains and the city of Denver. The driving and seeing the mountains of Utah and Colorado were breathtaking.

Colorado River

We stayed at the Glenwood Springs West Colorado River KOA Holiday in Silt, Colorado. The campground is literally on the Colorado River. The description states that "you won't want to leave," and we did not want to leave because the atmosphere was so relaxing. This was another one of my favorite campsites. We were finally set up for camping by the water. We sat in our chairs on the riverbanks and enjoyed nature's serenity. We had cut up franks in beans for dinner. There was a time when franks and beans were part of our weekly rotation meal; now, we consider it a rare treat. [9/24-25/2021] #47state

After the campsite, we then stayed at the Hilton Garden Inn in Denver Colorado. There was a little drama and mix-up with the hotel reservations through the Booking.com travel site, but as always because of God it worked out… "acknowledge Him in all things. . ." But it was also a reminder of my brattiness with disappointments when I should trust that God got me. My mother used to always say that she is God's favorite and I have to remember that I am the child of God's favorite. God never failed me yet!

We were also able to park the RV in the hotel parking lot. There were several restaurants to choose from around the hotel. I had sushi, which is one of my favorite foods. It was also great to be in an actual real bed again. I must add that the Booking app is still my go-to booking site, even with a snafu. [9/25-26/2022] #47state

Kansas Glamping

#48 Kansas - The next great experience for me, but not necessarily for Willie, was Klamping, also called Glamping at Salina KOA Holiday in Salina, Kansas. We missed the Kansas Route 66 stop, so I was glad I could see Kansas this second time around. I loved the glamping experience, but for Willie, the bed was too short, and he did not feel secure out in the "wilderness" without walls and doors to lock. Although many moons ago, we would go camping each year and sleep in tents. They also delivered pizza to our campsite. I tried their delicious homemade cherries, pecan & cream ice cream with a color-changing spoon. Of course, I got extra spoons for my granddaughters and Szymon. We did not see Dorothy or Toto in Kansas, but they were represented at the Welcome Center and the campsite. [9/26-27/2021] #48state

We did stop in Missouri again, but this time further north at Kansas City East Oak Grove KOA Holiday in Oak Grove, Missouri. Willie was able to meet up with his cousin, James

Missouri Campground

'Jimmy' McDougle. This beautiful campsite had an oversized patio with a gas grill, a fire ring, a table with chairs, and a double swing. They had the cutest baby clothes in their office store. I got some pajamas for Legend, my newest grandnephew. Again, this campsite is on my list of favorite sites. This was the first campsite we stayed at during this trip with a gas grill. [9/27-28/2021]

The last two stops on our way home were supposed to be Illinois and Ohio off of Route 70. I made another mistake with my mapping. I do not know why I had us continuing on Route 70, but I put Route 80 KOAs in my phone. I lost money because I had to cancel the Illinois and Ohio KOA past the allotted time for cancellations. We did not get to go glamping again in Dayton, I am sure Willie was happy not to have another glamping experience. Instead of Casey Illinois and Dayton Ohio, we stayed in Rock Island and Toledo, Ohio.

We stayed at Rockland Quad Cities KOA Holiday in Rock Island, Illinois. Once again, we were near water. We were near the lake, and I decided that I would go for a walk around what I thought was a small lake. I found out later that it is a fifty-acre lake. It got dark, I was on the phone with my sister Shelley telling her about my error and I was not paying attention. I am not a dog person but I even stopped to talk to a dog owner about his adorable dogs that he was walking while I was talking to my sister which surprised her. I was not only very lost but I was scared too. It got very dark very quickly and I used the flashlight app on my cellphone to see where I was going. You know how you hear that it is so dark that you cannot see your hands in front of your face, that how it was in this abyss. Willie had to direct me via phone and flashlight back to our campsite. I must admit that this was a very terrifying experience. Thank God Willie now had a tracker on my phone

Illinois Campground

and was able to direct me back to our campsite. He would let me know that I was headed in the right direction and that I was getting closer. As I got closer to him in this pitch-black campsite he used his flashlight app to shine a light on my safe haven. I give a big thumbs up to the Life 360 tracker app and the foresight to those makers of these flashlight phone apps.

Toledo Ohio Campground

Last stop, Toledo East Stony Ridge KOA Journey in Perrysburg, Ohio. A nice site, but we were ready to go home. We met a nice couple who showed us their Mercedes Benz custom-made van with its king-size bed. We got up early because we had a 9+ hour ride back home to Teaneck, New Jersey. [9/29-30/2021]

I loved, loved, loved. . . did I say loved the Northern United States! It was not only beautiful, but I do not remember ever feeling so relaxed and free.

We have now been to #48states

As I end this chapter of my life I give a big shout-out first to my husband Willie, my partner, and my chauffeur. Shout-outs also to everyone who traveled to the States with me. Shout-out to Chrystal from Cruise America in Cliffwood, New Jersey, to all the KOA campsites and their owners, to every camper who befriended us and helped us, Booking.com, and to the hosts from the Airbnbs for their hospitality and beautiful equipped homes.

Panama Canal

2022
Panama Canal (Not A State)

The Panama Canal is not a state but it happened while I was doing my states. I like planning cruises for milestone birthdays. So, I cruised for my 60th and 65th. For my 65th Birthday celebration, Shelley and J joined Willie and me for my celebration. For the Holland American Panama Canal Zuiderdam cruise, we flew into Ft. Lauderdale. We met up with my niece, Shamanie, who lives in Florida. Willie, Shelley, Shamanie, and I stayed in Florida for two days, and J joined us and stayed one day. We stayed at the Hampton Inn & Suites Ft. Lauderdale Apartment South Cruise Port Florida. We had to find and make an appointment at CVS in Ft. Lauderdale for a Rapid COVID-19 Test. Thank God everyone tested negative! [1/14 -1/16/2022]

The cruise was an east coast to west coast 14-day cruise that left out of Florida and ended in California. January 16th

– January 30th, 2022. Because of COVID-19 restrictions, we did not get to go to the scheduled stops of Nicaragua or Guatemala, but we went to Panama instead which was a blessing because Panama was on my list of places to go to, and I was surprised that it was not included as one of the port stops. I was disappointed about not going to Nicaragua and Guatemala, but especially Guatemala because we booked an excursion that would take us to Antiqua too. I wanted to see Antigua because we have a church member from Antiqua, and she talks about her beautiful island. We also could not dock in Columbia, which was supposed to be our first stop.

Holland American Panama Canal Zuiderdam cruise ship is beautiful. Willie and I stayed in one large stateroom with a balcony, and J and Shelley had a connecting similar stateroom. The elevator carpets were changed each day with the day of the week on it. This was great because I think that everyone loses track of the days when vacationing. The ship was half its capacity, and the entertainment was outstanding. The Panama Canal itself is a must-see. The genius of this engineering is indescribable. Watching this huge cruise ship in the locks being raised above sea level, leaving the Atlantic Ocean, and going into The Pacific Ocean is incredible. [1/20/2022]

In Panama, we went to a native village and were entertained by members of the village of various ages with dance and songs. I bought a beautiful bright orange, magenta, and green colored shawl in this native village. We saw so many barges with cargo as we rode around Panama on our tour. [1/21/2022]

Our first stop was supposed to be Cartegena, Columbia but it was Costa Rica. Costa Rica was supposed to be our second destination. Shelley, J., and I went on a Costa Rica Nature & Cooking with Food & Wine Magazine excursion. During the tour, we saw alligators while driving to our destination.

We (I should say everyone else but me) cooked plantains, fresh spinach, and white rice with fresh turmeric and beets, and they also made a salad. All of the food and even the drink were all grown on this beautiful property. We hiked the land and saw exotic plants, a pineapple garden, and other fruits and vegetables being grown on the land, and there was a bee station. There was a yoga studio for guests who stayed at the Santuario De Macaw overnight. [1/23/2022]

Costa Rica

Next was supposed to be Nicaragua, Guatemala, and then Huatulco, Mexico. Huatulco, Mexico was next. We booked the Huatulco Beach & Snorkel excursion. We were supposed to go snorkeling, but Willie decided he was not going to snorkel, but he would go with us. I was unable to breathe or walk from the start with the snorkeling equipment, so I sat at a restaurant on the beach with Willie. Willie and I both snorkeled many years ago. Shelley tried snorkeling for a while and came back, but J stayed out there the longest. Shelley saw exotic fish and a lot of coral. She also said that her nephew/Godson saved her life by helping her back to

Huatulco Mexico

shore. It was difficult walking and breathing for us in the snorkel gear. [1/25/2022]

We also went to Puerta Vallarta, Mexico. We booked the Jeep Safari & Beach Adventure excursion. This was our second visit to Puerta Vallarta, Mexico, but it was J's first visit as an adult. We spent two weeks in Puerta Vallarta, Mexico when J was a child. The drive was a little (actually a lot) rugged. J thought that he could drive the manual jeep but Willie had to take over. I am glad that when Shelley and I went on a Jeep Safari in Arizona the Jeep was an automatic. We viewed the countryside and drove down the back roads. We saw two men riding on one horse in the street. We saw schools. We stopped at a small house that was a bathroom stop and the owner, an elderly lady, was selling refreshments.

We stopped at the Tequila Factory and tasted several types of tequila. We purchased tequila, coffee, vanilla spice, and souvenirs. We ate authentic Mexican food at the Tequila Factory, where they had beautiful murals on the walls. We also went to the beach, ate lunch, and saw people parasailing. We found a Walmart on our way back to the ship. They kiddingly called Walmart the American Embassy. We got snacks from Walmart and souvenirs, J also brought back snacks to his new crewmate friends. I said that I did not want any regrets, any wouldofs or shouldofs; but I should have gotten that gray leather bag at the leather shop before getting back on the ship. I am so ready to go back to Puerta Vallarta to get that unique bag. [1/27/2022]

Puerta Vallarta

Because the ship was probably half full/ half empty we met a lot of people and even remembered their names. We befriended the B. B. King Allstars band members and went to many of their shows. There was also a small group of young people from Mexico who were Cultural Ambassadors whom we also had the opportunity to spend time with. I think that J went to all of the shows of both groups and both Shelley and J still follow the members through Social Media. We also were on a first-name basis with the spa attendants, the gym instructor, and the dessert lady on the Lido deck. The staff on our Holland American cruise was beyond outstanding and accommodating. Everyone knew Willie aka J and his family. We went to the Thermal Suite and its therapy Pool every day. It was so relaxing and therapeutic each day. After a while, we got used to seeing and socializing with the same people at the thermal suite, the gym, and the Lido deck. Willie and I had a Couple's Deep Tissue Massage. By now you know that I have to have a massage everywhere I go.

The cruise ship docked in San Diego. Even though we took a van from the port to our hotel, we got a call that we had forgotten two of our seem-to-be million bags. J and I walked back to the pier to retrieve our two bags. Our hotel was conveniently within walking distance from the pier.

In San Diego, Shelley, J, and I rented a Lime Scooter. It was my first time on an electric scooter or probably any scooter. Willie, Shelley, and I again stayed for two days, and J stayed for one

San Diego

day at the Hampton Inn San Diego Downtown/Airport Area. We walked around San Diego and ate in Little Italy. We also walked down along the waterfront. The second day Willie and I were too exhausted to do anything, but Shelley aka Baby Girl continued to explore the city on her own. Shelley and I went for a walk and we explored restaurants later that evening. We flew home out of San Diego. It was good to be home. It was a spectacular experience; Florida, California, and the cruise (it was our longest cruise), but it was time to be home. [1/30 – 2/1/2022]

Alaska

Alaska Map

#49 Alaska - The plan was to revisit Hawaii in April 2022, but we had to put it on hold. We've been to Hawaii twice already, but I wanted to go to Hawaii for state #49. Our Alaskan cruise in August 2022 was supposed to be the last state. Actually, it was our 50th state because we had visited all 50

United States. We visited 49 states between 2019 and 2022 and Hawaii twice before.

We made it!

Alaska *The Last Frontier.* August 20 – 27, 2022 from Vancouver, Canada to Anchorage, Alaska. While I am writing right now, Willie and I are on our way to Vancouver to board Princess Cruise Line Royal Princess to Alaska, along with Marcia Morgan and her sisters Monica, Beverly, and Marva. This is our 50th state. I started this unbelievable feat with the notion that maybe in eight years, by age 70 I can visit the 50 United States. I started in March 2019 by meeting my daughter Shené in Indianapolis Indiana. From 2019 to today, August 20, 2022, at age 65 we have been to 49 states; There have been 6 states that we have been to many times, we went to 13 states in 2019, 15 states in 2020, 14 states in 2021, and now Alaska in 2022. Although we had to cancel Willie's 65th birthday Hawaiian cruise in April 2022, since Hawaii would have been a revisit we can officially state that we have been to all 50 states: 49 of them in the last three years.

When my mother went on an Alaskan cruise, I was wondering why anyone would want to pay to cruise in the cold. She told me about the beauty of this cruise. I do not think I would visit Alaska if I was not on this 50 states venture but I am so glad that I did witness the beauty of this 49th state. I also want everyone, especially young people, to experience Alaska.

I feel complete for now!

Traveling is difficult. I already mentioned what goes into packing and unpacking as well as the maintenance of an RV; remembering to turn off the generator at each gas station, at each campsite stop; dumping two waste tanks, and refilling fresh water. On this Alaskan cruise, again there is that preparation for the weather even though it is August, and we have a heatwave in New Jersey, you do not know what type of weather you will have in Canada again or in the various ports in Alaska even with checking the weather in advance, you still will not know what type of weather to expect while at sea on the ship. Packing for the weather can be challenging in both cases but with the RV or even our car which we always overpack, you do not have to worry about 50 pounds limitations on the weight of your luggage that you now have to pay for luggage checked bags.

The Panama Canal trip was the first time that I had to check two bags because of the length of the trip; two days in Fort Lauderdale, fourteen days on the cruise, and two days in San Diego California, leaving from Kennedy Airport in New York in the winter of January. This nineteen-day trip required two large suitcases, plus a roller carry-on bag and a large personal bag. Coming back Shelley and Willie's bags were over the weight requirements, which meant adjusting bags and even Shelley buying an extra suitcase at the airport. J also had to buy another suitcase from Target online and it was delivered to his hotel room before he left. Just between you and me J and Shelley bought too many bottles of souvenir tequila from Puerta Vallarta Mexico's Tequila distillery, that is why they needed the extra luggage.

Traveling by plane has been so difficult lately. I remember before 911 I would be running through the airport (I am getting ready to date myself with this old commercial) like O. J. Simpson trying to catch my plane. Now you have to wake up early in the morning, that is if you get to go to bed. You should try to book the earliest flight, especially after COVID-19. Also, after COVID-19 with the reduction in airport staffing; first, it is recommended that you get to the airport at least three hours ahead of time, then you have to navigate a kiosk, a lot of time means getting assistance before completing the task, especially if you are traveling internationally. Next, it takes at least an hour to go through TSA. If I am traveling without Willie going through TSA would take even longer. It only takes this amount of time for me when I am with my husband because he is in an airline-provided escorted wheelchair and sometimes we do not have to wait on all the lines (I am definitely not suggesting that you use an airport wheelchair if you do not need one). It is also the taking off of your shoes (remember to wear socks no matter what season), removing your hat and jacket, emptying your pockets, and putting everything in the designated bins, along with your phone, your carry-on bag, your personal carry-on item, also taking your laptop out of its case. Then make sure you do not forget anything in the numerous bins that you may use. I lost one of my favorite hats forgetting it in a bin and some TSA worker might be wearing it right now. You also must remember that you cannot bring your own beverage since 911 through TSA. You find yourself purchasing your beverage, even water, from one of the overpriced airport stores after going through TSA. You also need to remember not to have anything in your pockets, not even loose change. We have had issues with being detained because of back braces and knee braces that contained metal. The carry-on items can become a nightmare; size and packing requirements have changed over the years. I remember soon after 911 having my expensive (to me) Mac lipstick tossed away even though it is not a liquid. I also remember putting small items in Ziplock bags and being told that I had too many Ziplocked bag items. You are limited to one quart-size bag for your liquids, gels, and/or aerosols. I just had a conversation with a gym acquaintance Donna about this, on how we as women (some men too, like my son) want to bring our own shampoos and conditioners, lotions, oils, and creams, but now we are forced to pay to check our bags because we cannot go through TSA with too many of these 3.4-ounce items. I know that it sounds as if I am complaining but I actually appreciate all the safety precautions.

Being on this Alaskan cruise or any cruise you meet people from everywhere, and you hear so many accents and languages from the passengers and staff. The staff on the cruise are from all over the world and I am always intrigued by their stories. This time with the passengers on this cruise when we exchanged pleasantries of names and where you are from, I was ecstatic that I actually have been to the places that they were from, every state, and even passengers from Nova Scotia and New Brunswick Canada. When I finish the continents, I will connect with passengers and crew from various continents too.

We started out in Vancouver, but we had to rush from the airport to the pier. I wanted to get a Vancouver magnet, just because. I saw Tim Hortons and I wanted to get one of their delicious apple fritters and their French vanilla coffee, even though I am not a coffee drinker Soqui got me hooked on their coffee when we went on our Canadian road trip last month. We were basically the last group to check in, so we missed all the welcome-aboard festivities. I will always book my flights through the Cruiseline even if it is more expensive because they will wait for you. The same is true of their excursions. Today, because of the last-minute cancellations

Ketchikan Alaska

of flights and changes in flights, the Cruiseline staff waited to meet us and guided us aboard.

After a day at sea, Ketchikan was our first stop in Alaska. We went to the Totem Bight State Historical Park and heard stories about the culture of the Tlingit, Haida, and Tsimshian natives while we sat in a Clan House and stories about their distinctive art made into totem poles. At totem park, I also walked to their scenic beach. There were antique cars and antique firearms in their World-Famous Alaska Totem Trading Exciting Frontier Museum. We also went to The Great Alaskan Lumberjack Show being entertained with the chopping of wood, axe throwing, climbing wooden poles, and running on waterlogs. We were blessed with 63-degree weather and no rain. We passed by the famous Creek Street and the infamous Dolly's House on our tour. [8/22/2022]

Ketchikan Alaska Lumberjack Show

The second Alaskan stop was Juneau we took a beautiful scenic trolley ride to the Mendenhall Glacier and also went on the Goldbelt Tram. The tram took us up the mountain and there was

Juneau Alaska

Mendenhall in Alaska

entertainment and a gift shop. Willie and I went to a crab house and had crab bisque, mini crabcakes, and beer-battered huge shrimp. Walking back, I saw a white-headed bald eagle perched in a tree. It was our 42nd Anniversary and we went to one of the specialty restaurants and had steak and lobster tail for dinner. [8/23/2022]

The third stop was Skagway. This is what I expected an Alaskan town to look like based on pictures, movies, and television shows. Our excursion was the White Pass Scenic Railway. It was a narrated railway tour. The railway was on the edge of the mountain. We rode to the top of the mountain and the scenery was beyond breathtaking. After the railways

Skagway Alaska

tour, I walked around the quaint town making sure that I paid attention because GPS was not going to help me. I had to ask for directions twice because I got turned around when I went into shops for souvenirs. I know that I am supposed to always speak positivity into my spirit but I have such a (instead of saying bad) "not good" sense of direction. [8/24/2022]

Glacier Bay in Alaska

We spent two days at sea going through the glaciers. I was mesmerized by its beauty. We went through Glacier Bay National Park and College Fjord. The beauty of cruising through the glaciers (I am running out of descriptive words for these trips) was simply magnificent.

The pictures that I took of the glaciers look like paintings and not a Samsung cellphone photograph.

I was finally able to get some walks in on the ship while we cruised through the glaciers, we had a little rain but basically, the weather was good, and I only needed a light jacket. Some people saw whales and seals but I missed it because I was focused on my treks around the ship.

Willie and I also had our regular cruise couples' massages. But this time we had a vanilla scrub. We always book the thermal spas on cruises ever since our son introduced us to them after one of his cruises. The hot tubs, hotbeds, saunas, and steam rooms are amazing. This cruise also had water-beds. The thermal spa was definitely needed on this cruise because even though people did get in the water outside on this Alaskan cruise I do not do cold, the thermal suite water was perfectly warm even though we did not experience any real cold weather on the cruise. Also in these thermal spas, you end up meeting people whom you usually see every day and they become part of your cruise crew.

Upon debarking, Willie and I had another excursion because we had a late overnight flight. The excursion was the Portage Glazier Scenic Cruise & Drive. We sailed to an actual glacier, and I was able to go up top of the boat and take pictures.

If any of you remember what was going on in August 2022 with the airline staff shortages which resulted in delayed and canceled flights. Our flight to Vancouver through Air Canada was canceled the night before we left and we were placed on another flight through United Airlines with a layover and we lost our upgraded seats. We were so uncomfortable on the first leg of the trip with both of us in the middle seats. This was Willie's first time sitting in the middle of an airplane. I am the one who usually sits in the middle seat while Willie sits in an aisle seat but we usually opt for upgrading and paying for extra legroom. On the second leg of the trip, I was stuck in the middle again of these non-spacious seats. I thought the first flight was bad but the second flight's seating area had even less room. The return trip was just as bad if not worse even though we had the so-called roomier seats, we tried to sleep because it was an overnight long flight, but it was so uncomfortable. I have never been so happy to get off a plane. I will always sing praises for Jet Blue Airline. They are my favorite airline. They have the most comfortable seats.

Magnets on my refrigerator were collected from
49 of the 50 states

Magnets

I did it. . . It is completed!

How does it feel when you have completed something that
you were not even sure if it was even realistic? This is so sur-
real. 49 states in three years. TGBTG = To God Be The Glory!

"

I wanted to duplicate my father's Montreal, Quebec, and Toronto trip with my grands.

"

12

ArriveCan

Canada Sign

2022

Maine

Canada = Moncton New Brunswick – Margaree Nova
Scotia – Fredericton New Brunswick, Quebec, Montreal City,
Toronto, Niagara Falls

nother bright idea. I cannot remember if a Canada trip came up because Jayla was taking French in school in 6th grade and I mentioned that I would take her to Canada. However, she did not have a foreign language in 7th and 8th grades. Maybe it was because we needed to keep entertaining our granddaughters during their July visit. We went on this long Canada adventure one month before going to Alaska which was not being fiscally responsible.

My father and his cousin Leslie took their families on a Canada road trip to Montreal, Quebec, and Toronto when we were children. I did not get to do Canada with my children, even though we took my son to Canada on a bus ride before my daughter was born but he was too young to remember. I wanted to duplicate my father's Montreal, Quebec, and Toronto trip with my grands. My grandson is a working man now so he could not come. I heard about the historical aspect of Nova Scotia, so I suggested that we include Nova Scotia in our trip. I proposed it to all of my family because I heard about its rich African-American history, and I wanted to learn more by visiting it. Surprisingly Shavon, Jabari, Sharon, and Frank also wanted to go so I started planning. Sharon and Frank ended up not going with us. My sister Shelley is always ready to go, and I thank God that we have spouses who support our dreams of adventures. We traveled from July 17th to August 2nd, 2022, a 17-day trip.

Bangor, Maine - To break up the long drive to Canada we stopped in Maine at another KOA - Kampgrounds of America campground at Holden Bangor Maine KOA, for two nights. Shelley Soqui and Szymon went up a day before us and stopped in New Hampshire first. We both rented cabins. It was a really beautiful campground with a swimming pool, game room, an area for campers, and an area for tents, wigwams, and domes. The owner told us that his New York Style Pizza was just as good as the pizza that you buy in New York. The pizza was delicious

Maine

and their hot wings were even better. I also tried their lobster roll. Shelley and Soqui originally rented a dome but then decided they needed their own bathroom facilities, so they changed to a cabin. Darby and Szymon went swimming as soon as they got to the site. I do not think they care where we go traveling as long as they can go swimming. Jayla has grown out of the need to go swimming, now that she is 14 years old. The cabins were spacious and comfortable, with a full bathroom, living room space with a television, a kitchen with a table, a bedroom, and a loft. The girls were ecstatic about being able to sleep in the loft. Shelley, Soqui, and Szymon's cabin had two bedrooms, one bedroom had bump beds, so Szymon invited the girls to spend the first night with him. They had a campfire and made smores. The second night the girls slept in their loft. Shelley, Soqui, and the children went on a drive exploring the town of Bar Harbor. [7/17–7/19/2022]

Shavon and Jabari came a day later. Shavon met Jabari in Albany from Mount Vernon, New York (Shavon) and Utica, New York (Jabari) and they stayed in a hotel in Bangor, Maine. Shavon and Jabari were not interested in camping even though we took them camping when they were growing up.

Again, the KOA campground owner was very friendly and helpful. We left the campgrounds early to get on the road to Canada. To break up the drive to Nova Scotia, we stopped overnight in Moncton, New Brunswick.

I am very meticulous, and some may say anal, when we got to the Canadian border, they informed us that Willie's passport had expired. I inadvertently brought the wrong passport for him. But God always takes care of his own. They asked Willie for his driver's license instead and we were able to cross the border.

This Canada trip exposed us to all the various cultures of the different provinces of Canada. I found out that Canada has 10 providences and we visited four of them during this trip: Nova Scotia, New Brunswick, Quebec, and Toronto. We landed in another providence of Canada on our way to Alaska; (Vancouver) British Columbia.

Moncton, New Brunswick – We stayed at the Delta Hotel by Marriott Beausejour Moncton. Moncton, New Brunswick was Jayla's favorite place because at age 14 she is very sensitive to the need for inclusion. Jayla appreciated that they showed pride and acceptance of the LGBTQIA2S+ Community, with Pride flags on the lamppost and also painted on their crosswalks. Jayla introduced us to Tim Hortons Restaurant in Moncton but we revisited it everywhere we went in Canada.

New Brunswick Canada Pride

I ate apple fritters, but the children had Timbits and a variety of dream donuts throughout our stays in Canada; chocolate munchies, a smores, birthday cake, Reese's, and Boston Cream. Willie had their honey donut, Shelley had a Beyond breakfast sandwich, and Soqui enjoyed their coffee every chance she got.

This should not surprise me, but I am a native New Yorker, people did not J-walk in Moncton. They waited for the light even if cars were not coming. I conformed to their practice and patiently waited for the green light before crossing the street. Moncton is a clean, quiet, and quaint, eclectic town. Many of the stores and restaurants opened at 10 am and closed at 5 pm or 6 pm while we were in Moncton, New Brunswick. There was a plethora of ethnic restaurants to choose from and we chose an African restaurant but we did not realize that they would be closing so early. We, Shelley, Shavon, Jabari, Jayla, and I had Mexican food instead, while Soqui took Darby and Szymon to the pool to slide down their huge slide and swim in the swimming pool while Willie relaxed in the hotel room.

We met up with Shavon and Jabari again the next day and then we got on the road to Margaree, Nova Scotia. [7/19-20/2022]

Margaree, Nova Scotia - We rented an Airbnb house called the Yoganaut, a former yoga retreat, in Margaree, Nova Scotia. The part of Nova Scotia where we stayed showed the natural habitats of Canada with its countryside serenity. We ended up in Margaree, Nova Scotia because in my impulsiveness I do not always do my research. What I did not contemplate in my research is the size of Nova Scotia. Nova Scotia is 55,280 km² which equals 21343.7273 square miles; much larger than I thought. I should have looked for an Airbnb closer to Halifax

Margaree Nova Scotia Canada #1
Yoganaut

Margaree Nova Scotia Canada #2
Beach

to rent for the four days. Margaree was on the northern tip of Nova Scotia which is approximately a four-hour drive from Halifax. Now I will have to put Halifax on my list of places to visit. My friend Dulcie just went on a 5-day cruise that stopped in Halifax leaving from Bayonne, New Jersey. That is a doable future trip, and I will look into it after I finish digesting this July 17-day Canadian trip and the 7-day Alaskan cruise.

The house was difficult to locate but it was a beautiful spacious house, with a beautiful view. We stayed for four days. There was a beach on the property with a variety of colorful rocks. It was a bit of a trek to get to the beach and an even longer journey into town that closes down at 5 pm. We managed to catch the welcome center in town on our first day and an ice cream store. We found a beautiful beach while exploring the area. Nova Scotia became a more relaxing place than we anticipated. Shavon got a lot of reading done. Jabari caught up on sleep because he was always working. Shelley, Soqui, Jayla, Darby, and Szymon did a lot of exploring both beaches, finding unique rocks, and fishing (but did not catch anything). Shelley had the opportunity to fly her kite, and she also got in the water. Willie was able to relax and have his "me time." I was able to do yoga, do some writing, and listen to my latest audible book. I am so accustomed to air conditioning but at the Yoganaut our form of air was ceiling fans and open windows while we were inside. There were biting flies outside that ran us inside quite often. Jayla, Darby, and Szymon entertained us nightly with their original skits, songs, and dances. There was a projector that Jabari was able to hook up so that we could watch a movie one night. [7/21 - 24/2022]

After four days in Nova Scotia, we went on to Fredericton, New Brunswick while Shavon and Jabari left to go back home one day before we left. Fredericton, New Brunswick was another break stop before Quebec.

Fredericton, New Brunswick - We stayed at the Best Western Plus Fredericton Hotel & Suites for one night. While Willie rested from the 6+ hour drive, Soqui took Szymon and Darby to their favorite pastime again; swimming, Shelley, Jayla, and I went to pick up food but decided to eat in. We had pizza at Boston Pizza. "Boston Pizza is in a Canadian country with an American name founded by a Greek man who makes Italian food." We also found a Soye grocery store. This store was amazing, clean, bright, and organized, with all types of groceries; anything you might need. We ended up staying too long, I thought that Willie was sleeping but he was waiting for his dinner so that he could sleep. Where we stayed was on the outskirts and was a quick one-day stop on our way to Quebec City. [7/24 - 25/2022]

Quebec City – Quebec City exposed us to the preservation of French culture and language. In some stores, it became difficult to communicate because of the language. Everywhere we went and everything that we saw was written in French. When I told my dentist about our experience in Quebec City, he told me that he was from Canada and that in Quebec City, they frown upon Canadians who do not speak French.

The city was preparing for the Pope's visit. Shelley and Soqui went into the beautiful Catholic church that was probably a cathedral. We rented another Airbnb; this one was in a Ski Resort area. The house was very modern, spacious, very well organized, which I love, and simply beautiful. It had three floors with a kitchen, dining room, and living room on the top level. I even sent pictures of the Quebec City Airbnb to the owner of the Margaree Airbnb owner to show what I expected of his Airbnb because we became friendly through our texts back and forth.

A lot of the Quebec homes had bell roofs. There were several quaint little markets with fresh baked goods and a large

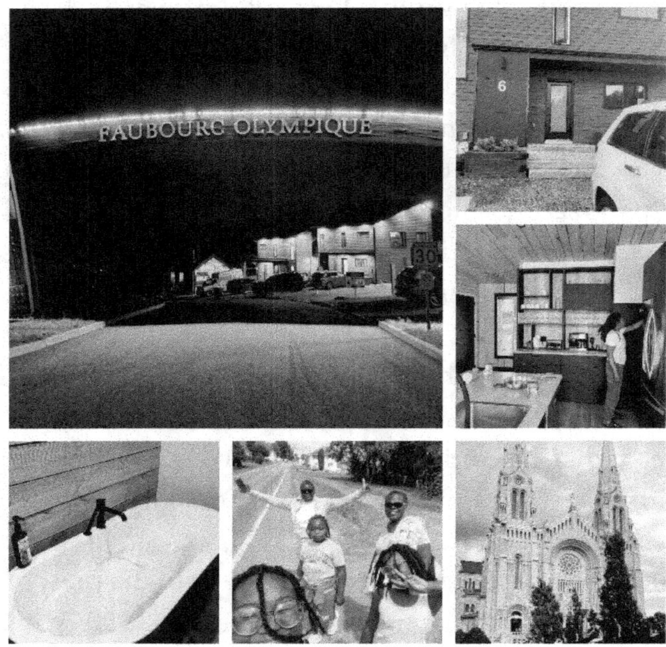

Quebec City Canada

selection of a variety of wines. The pastries were freshly baked and delicious. I have never been to Paris, but I feel like I was in Paris while in Quebec City. There were several types of foods in both the small markets and the grocery stores that we had no idea what they were. We went to two grocery stores. We were able to cook real meals when we stayed in the two Airbnb. We stayed in Quebec City for two days. We saw a beautiful waterfall with a rainbow while driving to the house. We saw a man ski skating up and down the steep hills. Shelley and I took Jayla, Darby, and Szymon for what they considered an exhausting walk. [7/25 - 27/2022]

The next stop is the city of Montreal.

Montreal – We stayed at the Double Tree in Montreal. I discovered that Montreal is the largest city in the Province of Quebec. I thought that they were each a separate Province. We found a Chinese restaurant for a sit-down dinner. After dinner the shopaholic in Shelley and me, which we inherited from our mother, had us going to Marshalls to shop until the store closed that evening. The next day Shelley and Soqui went back shopping. I took

Montreal Canada Pet Shop

Jayla, Darby, and Szymon (until he saw his grandmothers) to Walmart and to a pet shop in the shopping center. They were fascinated by the pet shop, and it did not cost me a dime. It was like taking them to an aquarium that also had cats. Then Jayla, Darby, and I stayed at the shopping center, while Szymon went with his grandmothers. We went to Marshalls and some other stores in that shopping center and then we went to the mall. Jayla and Darby also inherited the shopping gene. I got Jayla some unique jeans for going back to school at a store called the Garage. We also had scrumptious gelato. That evening we drove through Old Town Montreal with its cobblestone streets. There was a Ferris wheel and what looked like a fair, but there was nowhere to park, and we were in two cars. We went through a long underwater tunnel. The reason I mentioned the tunnel is that Shené started us playing this game with our grands; we played a game where we held our breath while going through a tunnel and I had to catch my breath at least three times through this long tunnel. We ate breakfast at the hotel restaurant with menus in French. I liked Montreal but I would have preferred being in the city instead of the outskirts. [7/27 - 29/2022]

Toronto – Every place we went to thus far in Canada was immaculate however as we approached Toronto, we started seeing trash on the side of the highway, while prior to that, throughout the drive we marveled at their well-kept highways. We began to see homeless people sleeping in tents. Toronto is a beautiful, active, multi-cultural, multi-ethnic city, with many skyscrapers. It reminds Willie of Chicago and reminds me of Seattle. It was Cabana time, and although we did not attend the Cabana celebrations, we saw a lot of the participants in the hotel and on the street made up in their elaborate festive garbs. We also watched some of the festivities on television.

We went to the Ripley Aquarium and to the CN Tower including the sky pod viewing the city of Toronto. The CN Towers lit up at night representing the occasion; the first night was the Chinese Year of the Tiger and the second night represented the colors for Cabana. Toronto is definitely a multicultural represented city. We stayed at the Residence Inn by Marriott Toronto Downtown/ Entertainment District on the 20th floor with connected two rooms and a great view of the city. The

Toronto Canada

parking lot at the hotel was full so we parked down the street and left the car parked for two days and walked around this downtown area of Toronto. We had dinner at Red Lobster the first night before parking the car because that is Willie's all-time go-to restaurant. We ate buffet breakfasts at the hotel. The Toronto Blue Jays had a game while we were there and it seemed like all of the people of Toronto were Blue Jays fans. [7/29 - 31/2022]

Niagara Falls – We stayed at the Embassy Suites in Niagara Falls. This was the last stop of our 17-day Canadian Trip. Our room was on the 32nd floor with a panoramic view of the falls and a magnificently relaxing massage chair. The falls lit up at night in various individual colors and also the colors of the rainbow. We went on a Whistle Horn boat ride to the

Niagara Falls Canada

falls. We were given red ponchos to wear, while on the United States side, we noticed that they had blue ponchos. We got drenched by water when we got close to the falls. There are three separate waterfalls: the American Falls and the Bridal Veil Falls on the United States side, and the largest waterfall is the Horseshoe Falls on the Canadian side. We had a great time. Shelley and Soqui took the children on the Falls Incline Railway where they also had ice cream. Niagara Falls is a very expensive tourist area aka a tourist trap. We could not get over the fact that the pancakes at IHOP were twenty dollars. With all the hotels and restaurants clustered together, it reminded me of Atlantic City or Las Vegas. [7/31-8/2/2022]

Before I leave this section on Canada Willie wants me to mention the taxes and how you are charged various taxes for everything you purchased. I actually saw a YouTube video recently by a Canadian woman explaining that their free health care is because of the abundant amount of taxes that they pay.

The total 17-day trip is over 3000 miles.

13

Foodie

This may be a why chapter. Being a foodie is a big part of my life. I hope that your mouth waters and your stomach rumbles as you read this chapter. I talk over and over about my obsession with food throughout this book. I was not going to put in a food chapter, but my daughter Shené reminded me that it is who I am. I also want to express my passion for the support of all small businesses including restaurants, especially since many restaurants that survived the pandemic, as well as new restaurants, are in need of our ongoing support. So I will also give shoutouts to my favorite types of ethnic foods and my favorite places to dine. So that is why this is a chapter!

I love eating. If it was not for the love of walking and being fixated on working out, I would be 300 pounds (no shade to those who are 300 pounds and who are not foodies). My mother used to say that she is on a see-food diet. I am a see-food eater. I eat all the food I see. Basically, when I am home, I primarily eat healthy. I do not buy snack food to have in the house except the individual .65 oz bag 100 calories Skinny Pop Popcorn which I limited myself to one bag a day, in addition to unsalted mix nuts for protein in which I eat ¼ cup per day. I mostly eat fish with veggies for dinner around 6 pm. I have yogurt with blueberries and walnuts, and flaxseeds and chia seeds most mornings. I was drinking smoothies in the summer. Now I added oatmeal to help lower my cholesterol now that the weather is getting cooler. To increase my protein intake, per J and Tasha's suggestions, I started including turkey sausage or turkey bacon, chicken or salmon, with eggs (mostly egg white) some days as part of my brunch intermittent fasting first meal after 12 noon. But when I am traveling, as I said before 'all bets are off', and whenever Shené comes to New Jersey from Virginia we make a food list. No, we do not cook, we go to restaurants.

Shout-outs to our favorite go-to restaurants; Greek To Me in Englewood for Gyros; lamb for me and shrimps for Né, as well as their delicious grilled octopus. Tani in Englewood with the best sushi ever; #44, Spicy Girl, and Precious Roll are our favorites along with at least the crispy duck and now steamed dumpling appetizers. We always indulge happily in some type of Spanish food, most of the time Elsa's Dominican food in Teaneck. Shené will not leave without having Veggie Heaven in Teaneck; either when she first arrives or on her way home to route 95. Breakfast is Golden Grill for a hobo (eggs, cheese, turkey bacon, or turkey sausage, and home fries on a bagel). Both of my children have been eating hobos since high school when the Met was down the hill from Teaneck High School on Teaneck Road. Golden Grill is Willies and most of the men, past, and present, at First Baptist Church of Teaneck's favorite diner. For my family, it is because of the sage sausages (turkey sausages for me are the best turkey sausages but Shené gets their turkey bacon), their creamy grits, and a very personable owner. (Just a sidebar: You will find the owner at some of the ole timers' funerals, wakes, or memorials paying his respects). Shené would stop at Hot Bagels in Teaneck, usually on her way out. She would have an everything bagel with either lox or veggie spread. If she picks up a bagel while she is visiting, for me, it would be a pumpernickel bagel with a little bit of cream cheese. Hot Bagels has the best bagels in Teaneck as well as the friendliest group of workers with a great system that has you in and out in no time, so do not be deterred by the line. Our new breakfast spot in addition to Golden Grill is in Bergenfield, it is the Brownstone Diner where we discovered our favorite turkey sausage with eggs wrapped in a pancake. We have not pinpointed our best Thai or Indian restaurant yet, but I have been ordering takeout (because of COVID-19) from Thai Shack on Cedar Lane in Teaneck. Empire Hunan, also on Cedar Lane, has been our longtime "real" Asian food restaurant. We can smell Reggae Kitchen's mouth-watering jerk chicken early in the morning as soon as we start driving or walking up the hill from our house. Shené introduced us to Vittorio's Pizzeria in Englewood many years ago and Willie and I still order half pepperoni and sausages and half mushroom and olives. Do I need to tell you which half is my half?

Am I making you hungry yet? There is still more to come…

Whenever and wherever Shené and I go we explore restaurants, especially ethnic foods. We try new dishes on menus. I am a foodie not only because I love to eat but also because I love trying new foods. I am always open to suggestions for good restaurants or good dishes to try. I remember Edith P. Green, from the church, introducing me to the Crab House in Edgewater so that I could try alligator bites. I am not a cook, I cook to eat, to survive, and to stay fit. Surprisingly, as a non-cook, I gave birth to a bonify chef. My son loves to cook. He creates all types of dishes. J and Denetra own a catering business, LoniV's Kitchen in North Carolina. The other professional chef in the family is my multi-talented cousin (I have to remind myself that he is from Willie's side of the family and not mine) Henri Bryan aka Henri Larrieux aka Chef Homeboirdee. He will leave Maryland in a heartbeat to cook for me, whip up a spread for an event, as well as help in any way that he can.

Whenever we are passing through Washington, D.C. on our way south, Willie and I have stopped at Ben's Chili Bowl for as long as I can remember. I always order Ben's classic turkey chili dogs, with vegetarian chili, onions, and mustard, while Willie has their chili half-smokes. Both dogs have to be split and cooked on the grill. If we are stopping in Virginia at my daughter's home we duplicate my order for Shené. We usually have Bojangles in Virginia and North Carolina. I always have their Cajun chicken biscuits with either their seasoned fries or Bo-rounds. I love their sweet tea as long as I am near a bathroom because teas go right through me. On our way back through Maryland, we usually stop and eat at Lidos Pizza in College Park Maryland. Our order is half mushrooms and black olives for me and half pepperoni and sausages for Willie. A half is actually the size of a tray. Their pizzas are rectangular shaped, thin, with a flaky crust. We've been eating Lidos pizzas for over 40 years. I remember putting J's baby carrier on the table while I ate their one-of-a-kind scrumptious pizza and J is now 39 years old. Willie has been eating at the famous Ben's Chili Bowl on U Street, for probably over 60 years. His father used to bring home Ben's half smokes, when Willie was a child, after picking up Willie's mother from work at the State Department in the evenings. President Barack Obama even tried the famous Ben's.

In Virginia, Shené would find new restaurants for me to try, Soul Food, Seafood, Sushi, Thai food, Indian food, and Mexican Restaurants. When she lived in Virginia Beach, which was the best location for me to walk, eat, and shop (but it's not about me)… our favorite foods and restaurants were Blue Fin Japanese Restaurant for Sushi (they knew her just like her current sushi restaurant Yamachen, they would start fixing her order when they saw her pull up to the parking lot). We also had to choose between Guadalajara and Plaza Azteca for Mexican food, we loved both places but we liked the guacamole better at one place and the entree better at the other restaurant. Most of the time we would dine at both restaurants during my stay. I have not found a Mexican restaurant near me to call my own. Shené just introduced me to a new Indian restaurant that she discovered in Williamsburg, Virginia; 'Spice Palace' which has what they call a mini buffet to your table, the food was so good we went back the following month during my visit and we also had a side order of samosas each time.

In North Carolina, J would create new dishes for me to try. If his children ask for Chinese food or pizza or any type of fast food, he will stop at the grocery store for the ingredients and make it himself. My son loves experimenting with foods and recipes. My grandchildren learned to ask their mother instead of their father for fast food or to eat out. My son instructed me on how to make pizza during the pandemic which I enjoyed but my husband prefers pizza from a pizzeria, even though I taste tested a variety of crust to find the one that he would like and topped his pizza with his favorite sausages and pepperoni.

My son is the gadget king and he even makes his own potato chips and cuts his french fries with what I call his new toys. Pancakes and waffles are made from scratch at his house as well as his cinnamon raisin pastry and my mother's biscuit recipe. When he lived in Raleigh, I would look forward to Tuesdays because he would take us to El Señior Mexican Restaurant for Arroz Tejano and Margaritas by the pitcher full. We would have breakfast at least one morning at the New York Diner in Knightdale, if he did not take me I would take the grands. We have tried various restaurants throughout the years while visiting J, Dee, and the grands in North Carolina but usually, we tend to have home-cooked meals.

I usually wait for Shené to come home to eat at our favorite restaurants. I told her that I feel like I am cheating on her if I have a gyro or sushi without her. But this year, 2022, I am trying to get Willie to try restaurants that are recommended. Teaneck Today has made some great suggestions. We have gone back to intentionally going on dates on the 23rd of each month. This is what we stress to other couples in the Married Couples Ministry at the church. But this time I plan on choosing the places where we will eat. If it is up to Willie, we would be dining at Red Lobster, Olive Garden, or White Castle. I will still have Thai, Sushi, Indian, and Greek food without him. Just like with trips, if it is up to him our vacations would be spent in what he calls the 'motherland' aka Washington, D.C. and Maryland so that Willie can spend time with his family and lifelong friends, or Virginia and North Carolina to visit with our children and grandchildren. He brags about being consistent, but I will not comment on that right now… I will just say this is another area in which we are different.

My must-tries wherever I go is to find the best chicken and waffles that taste as delicious as the back-in-the-day Wells' Restaurant signature entree located in the Village of Harlem. Right now, it is Melba's Restaurant in the Village of Harlem at 300 West 114 Street that wins my vote. Route 4 Diner had great chicken and waffles as well as turkey burgers, but now they closed their doors and an Assisted Living Facility is now in their location. If I am in a beach town I must find lobster rolls to try. I even tried lobster rolls in Maine. So far, my best lobster roll was in Cape May, New Jersey. I will try all types of raw sushi especially those with eel. Also, I will eat Thai foods; mainly Pad Thai, pineapple rice, and dumplings. With Soul Food, I prefer endorsements of restaurants. I find with soul food places I always compare the food to my mother's and mother-in-law's cooking. No one can touch my husband's fried chicken; Willie fries the best fried chicken and also fried chicken gizzards. I also love trying recommended Spanish restaurants and African restaurants. When my former (now retired) coworkers; Karen, Dulcie, and I meet up for our Sistahs Reunion Lunch, Karen usually has a Black-Owned restaurant in the Village of Harlem for us to dine in. Our last restaurant was The Edge on Edgecombe Avenue in the Village of Harlem. My newest dining delight is raw oysters with squeezed lemon, horseradish, and cocktail sauce. There was a post somewhere asking if you could eat one food for the rest of your life, what would it be? My answer is if it would not affect my borderline high cholesterol, my food would be shellfish. I love shrimp, mussels, clams, oysters, lobsters, and crabs. I do not know if it is because of my Johns Island, South Carolina roots but I can live off crustaceans and they are not good for my cholesterol levels. I remember going crabbing on Johns Island as a child. I also remember every time we left Johns Island, we were sent home with, I think mostly from our Cousin Roosevelt, a cooler full of crabs and shrimps, smelling up the car through our 14+ hours ride back home to New York, in addition to our Cousin Roosevelt sending us home with okra and pecans. I also remember eating crabs on newspapers on my grandmother's Sissie aka Georgetta Moten's fire escape in Harlem. We also used to eat watermelon on her fire escape at 53 West 131st Street in the Village of Harlem, New York.

As I sit here in my stateroom writing I am checking off what I love to eat because I just finished two sushi rolls and mango cheesecake. It is a good thing that I just discovered the variety of cheesecakes at the Princess Cruise line's International Café yesterday when I had lime cheesecake, and we are leaving tomorrow. I would have been eating cheesecake probably several times a day if I had known.

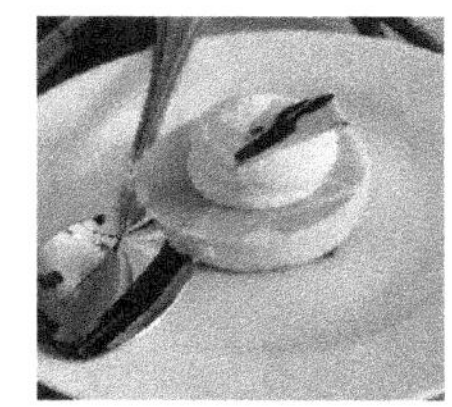

Mango Cheesecake

I am not a dessert person as far as buying desserts. I do not really buy desserts to have at home but whenever I get a chance while dining out I will order or eat a dessert. Occasionally, especially during snowstorms Willie and I will bring home Haagen-Dazs, his go-to is Butter Pecan and mine Vanilla Swiss Almond. Does anyone remember Frusen Glädjé ice-cream in the 80s? That was the best ice-cream ever; creamy, rich in flavor, and delicious! I used to envy my cousin Donnajean because my aunt always had desserts after dinner. I will eat any type of dessert, but I love cheesecakes and tiramisu. After a southern meal I am ready for peach cobbler or banana pudding. I mentioned before that I love Haggen-Dazs' Vanilla Swiss Almond ice cream and Ben and Jerry's Cherry Garcia. I will dabble in green tea or red bean ice cream after an Asian meal. I recently discovered a liking for coffee and also pistachio ice cream. While talking about ice-cream Bischoff's Ice-cream parlor in Teaneck is closing its doors soon after 88 years of selling delicious homemade ice-cream.

I like chocolate with nuts and will occasionally eat most candies. Willie will buy Almond Joy and Mounds candies around Halloween even though I do not celebrate Halloween and we have little to no children come to our door so we, mostly me, end up eating both bags of candies ourselves. Plus I tell Willie that Mounds and Almond Joy are old people's candies. For road trips I do not travel healthily. I often travel with Twizzlers Cherry Peel-Offs, and M&Ms with almonds. Chips are sometimes included on our road trips and chips can be addictive (if you remember the old Lays commercial ("no one can eat just one"). After my Panama Canal cruise stop to Costa Rica where we went on a cooking excursion, I now prefer plantain chips to potato chips. I had to stop myself from buying plantains every time I went to the vegetable market near Walgreens on Teaneck Road. I would use a slicer or a peeler to slice them elongated thin and fry them. Now that I have seen my son's new gadget that he uses to make potato chips I will invest in one for my home-made plantain chips. Prior to our Costa Rica Native Cooking excursion I would cut the plantains, fry them, take them out and smash them and then put them back in the pan to fry some more. Now I prefer the thin sliced elongated plantain strips. I love the Chifles Plantain Strips that they sell in Shoprite. But now I discovered Plantain Crisps Crispy Plantain Slices from Trader Joe's that I think that I like almost as much as Chifles Plantain Strips. But I still will eat any brand of Kettle Potato Chips including the 7-Eleven brand. Who knows, when I get my gadget like my son I might start making white potato chips and sweet potato chips. I also have to resist the urge to buy Pretzel Crisps when I see them in Shoprite.

Pumpkin Spice - it is fall which is pumpkin spice season. I am not a coffee drinker but I do have pumpkin spice lattes from Starbucks and Dunkin Donuts this time of the year. I try all types of pumpkin foods. Pumpkin bread from Starbucks, pumpkin donuts, and muffins from Dunkin Donuts. I heard somewhere (probably on a television show) that Black people eat sweet potato pie and not pumpkin pie but I am a card-carrying Black person that loves pumpkin pie as much as sweet potato pie. More and more stores now have so many pumpkin options, especially Trader Joe's. I think that Trader Joe's goal is to get you addicted to their seasonal products. It is now mid-October and they have their pumpkin products out but I'm still waiting for that pumpkin spread that I tried last year. I checked yesterday and it still says, "coming soon". I purchased their pumpkin cream cheese from Trader Joe's for an event but it was not eaten because everyone was enjoying my son's homemade honey apple cinnamon butter, so now I need to buy pumpkin bagels or my all-year-round favorite pumpernickel bagel even though I try to refrain from eating bread as much as possible but I cannot have the cream cheese go to waste. I do not and will not waste food. Now that I have tried the pumpkin cream cheese I will add it to my annual Trader Joe's pumpkin list. I am an annual consumer of their pumpkin pancake mix and their pumpkin bread muffin mix. I also tried Trader Joe's pumpkin ravioli, all I can say is I am sure vegans and vegetarians love it but I need meat or cheese in my ravioli. I should have put some marinara sauce on the ravioli but I tried it naked (the ravioli not me). Trader Joe's and Aldi's both have good pumpkin bagels. Last year I tried their pumpkin cheesecake and it was good but I cannot buy it again unless I have someone to eat it with me. I also tried their pumpkin ice cream last year but it was too sweet for me. While I am talking about Trader Joe's, their harvest salsa is already finished for the season so now I have to wait until next year to buy some more but I now know to stock up better than I have. I also keep going back for their root chips to be back in stock, they keep flying off the shelves. When they replenish them this week I am going to stock up. I am also trying some new pumpkin products; Trader Joe's Pumpkin Brioche twists which is beyond delicious. I also tried Dunkin' Pumpkin Spice Grahams Goldfish. The Pumpkin Brioche twists are especially delectable with pumpkin cream cheese spread on it. Now let me stop with my pumpkin fetish.

My friend and former college apartment-mate Gwen asked why all your sisters' get-togethers are around food? Now that I think about it all my meet-ups are around food. Not only with my sisters, but also, whenever my daughter and I get together we eat. With both gatherings, I try to get a walk-in, to or from the restaurant. I already mentioned that I try to meet up with my former teacher co-workers Karen and Dulcie a few times per year to catch up on each other's lives and to support a Black-owned restaurant. We ventured out of the

Village of Harlem to the only Black Owned restaurant on City Island; Seafood Kingz 2 Inc. My church daughter Andrea and I have met up to eat at the former East Japanese Restaurant for sushi in Teaneck, also to Englewood's Ramen Azuma for noodles, and we also went to Ft. Lee's Cap't Loui for seafood in a bag. Andrea and I did try to make a hiking date this summer but our schedules would not align. For the last two years our ministerial celebration for our Pastor for clergy appreciation month has also been at restaurants. I guess that all my fellowships are all about food.

Even right now, my son J and my daughter Shené are coming home for a week and Shené and I are planning our menus in order to introduce J to our food life. My husband Willie was never able to keep up with our eating ventures. Our plan is to 1. have sushi rolls for dinner from Tani in Englewood with Crispy Mango Duck Roll and probably some dumplings as appetizers. 2. Greek to Me in Englewood gyros for dinner and grilled octopus appetizer. Did I mention that I love appetizers? Most of the time I prefer appetizers more than the entrées. Shené and I used to go to Bahama Breeze in Paramus during happy hour and fill the table with just their appetizers. Bahama Breeze was not on our list but now I think that I will add it to our 'let expose J to our foods' list' (3). 4. A hobo at Golden Grill in Teaneck is on our list even though it is not an introduction for J. If we have time, we might go to Cap't Loui in Fort Lee for seafood in a bag dinner and the Brownstone Diner & Pancake Company in Bergenfield for breakfast.

As you can see throughout this book food is and always has been a huge part of my life. Yes, I am a bonafide card carrying Foodie for Real!

"

God has proven to me over and over again through abundant blessings on blessings that I can depend totally on Him.

"

14

I Surrender All!

I had to learn and I am still learning daily how to surrender all to God and not let Sheila get in the way of what God has for me. God has proven to me over and over again through abundant blessings on blessings that I can depend totally on Him. So it is definitely not because of doubt it is remembering always to let go of what I feel is control.

I already mentioned that I am a different kind of clergyperson. I am going to try to describe me, but I think that only a loner who has to turn themselves on at times will understand. When God called me to the ministry I knew that, even though we know that God does not make mistakes, that calling me into this office of service had to be a mistake. I felt and often feel that I am not clergy material. Some people will be surprised that I am an introvert and not really a people person. I am not a fan of small talk either. I love my church family but just like family, friends, and everyone else in my life, no offense but I can only take people in small doses. I think that I compartmentalize the people in life. I am not a shy person but I am easily withdrawn and often quiet but observant. I am a behind-the-scenes person. Surprisingly as a clergy person, I do not need to be seen. I do not have to be front and center. Like Moses, I am not a public speaker, it does not come naturally to me. But I can say that when it is time to be "on" I modestly shine. I know that it is with the aid of the Holy Spirit.

I have done some not so good things and have hung out with some not-so-good people in my life. I later found out that being good is not a prerequisite for God's call. We see that throughout the Bible. Two well-known examples of imperfect people being used by God; Moses was a murderer yet Moses was selected by God to lead God's chosen people to the Promised Land. David caused a death to occur to cover up his lust that led to adultery but David was called a 'man after God's own heart'. God calls those who are broken so that we can help God's broken people.

I used to question my calling because I thought that a minister who preaches God's Word to God's people should have extroverted tendencies, charisma, and the gift of gab. That was my perception of clergy until one of my preaching instructors and unofficial mentor at New Brunswick Theological Seminary informed me that she is an introvert. I know that she has been front and center in many visible leadership roles and large arenas. She is now a Pastor of a church. I also know that God has shown me through my relationships and interactions with people that God has placed in my life for ministry that I do belong. I see that God is placing me where God wants me to be when God wants me to be, in order to carry out God's will in God's way. (I know that there is a lot of God in this last sentence but I am working hard to be gender neutral, which is what I was taught in seminary and probably would be reminded by my "politically correct" "woke" daughter). I love God and I love God's people. Especially those who are trying to get to know their God. God has gifted me with the gifts of administration, teaching, intercession, and discernment, and (I was going to say that I try to but) I use these gifts to the glory of God. I also have the gift of Pastoring. It is not a gift to the office of a Pastor but it is a gift to be responsible for a certain group of people and this is a gift that I am using prayerfully to God's glory. I am responsible for doing new members sessions which allows me to use this gifting as well as lead the intercessory prayer ministry that we call Prayer Warriors.

I have to digress here because the Holy Spirit has gifted us all with Spiritual Gifts. We all need to know our gifts and use our gifts. There are Spiritual gifts inventories to determine your giftings, I personally use C. Peter Wagner's Spiritual Gifts questionnaire at my church.

As I am writing this chapter I am asking you to pray for all Pastors and ministers. Pray for all houses of worship and ministries that are doing God's will in God's way. Pray for ministry leaders and the leadership of churches. We are all called in Matthew 28:18-20 to "go therefore and make disciples of all nations, baptizing them in the name of the Father and the Son and the Holy Spirit, teaching them to obey all that I have commanded you." There is so much more than what you see on Sunday mornings. Ministry does not start on your sabbath mornings and it does not end on your sabbath evenings. Ministry is also not only within the church buildings. The sabbath morning classes, sermons, and the Bible studies take preparation and study, in addition to much prayer. I mentioned before about all the behind-the-scenes parts that make things happen, that includes the ministries that you observe or are a part of in any way. I am asking for prayer for your ministry too. We all have a ministry or ministries. We might not all be ministers but we all have been called to minister. Your ministry is the work that you do to serve God and to serve others. 1 Corinthians 10:31 says "Whatever you do, do it all for the glory of God".

I struggle with this chapter on ministry because it unearths layers of myself that are hard to articulate and probably comprehend. It also exposes me in a way that many do not see or choose to see. Not that I am hiding anything, it is more about people making assumptions of who I am or should be as a minister.

Proverbs 3:5&6 and Jeremiah 29:11 are two scriptures that keep me grounded and open to possibilities. "Trust in the Lord with all thine heart and lean not on your own understanding and He will direct your path." Proverbs 3:5&6, "I know the plans I have for you said the Lord, plans to prosper you and not fail." Jeremiah 29:11.

Even as a minister trusting in the Lord with all my heart is an almost daily struggle and a daily reminder to myself. It is not because I do not trust God, it's that I have learned through my trials and tribulations that the trust must be in God fully. It must be with all thine heart, mind, body, spirit, and soul, no matter the situation and no matter how long it might take. I need the daily reminder to keep Sheila out of it, to let go and let God. I do not know if it's the January Capricorn in me, or if it's the middle child syndrome, those who know me know that letting go and surrendering is difficult for me. It is a constant battle for me to let go of control. I will never ever be able to completely understand God's will in my life, but I have learned to trust God enough that I can allow God to lead, guide, and direct my path more and more of the time.

I thank God daily for the plans that God has for me, my life, and the lives of those I love. I thank God for prospering every aspect of my life and those around me. I trust and believe that God will never ever let me or mine fail. Those areas that I once thought were failures, I realized were opportunities for growth or redirection. I thank you for those too, God!

I sat first in the second row of the annex of the old First Baptist Church of Teaneck with my family, right behind the Hannibal family, before sitting in the right-hand side, fifth row, end seat of the new sanctuary alone, minding my business, sitting right behind Sister Mayo, when God started whispering in my ear, and then eventually tugging at me. It was like a mosquito that kept buzzing around me that I could not squash. But like I said it had to be a mistake until it was not…

I was not a willing participant. I ran from this next step of ministry for a while before I surrendered. I literally was knocked over the head unconscious by a VCR while cleaning when I realized that God was serious and was not taking no for an answer.

I became a licensed minister in January 2002 and was ordained in September 2009. I have been a minister for twenty years now. I was the first licensed and ordained female associate minister at the First Baptist Church of Teaneck in Teaneck, New Jersey. I was licensed under the Pastorate of Reverend Kevin Jones and ordained under my current Pastor Reverend Dr. Marilyn Monroe Harris. My husband and I became members of the First Baptist Church of Teaneck in Teaneck, New Jersey in 1990, thirty-two years ago. My family and I have been actively involved in the church since Willie and I became members. My husband and I were asked to be a Deacon and a Deaconess in 1992. Willie accepted his call to be a Deacon but for some reason (that I did not understand then) I knew that being a Deaconess was not my calling and I declined. We each need to allow God to let us know what God has called each one of us to do and be.

Willie is now the chairperson of the Deacon Board at First Baptist Church of Teaneck. Prior to me becoming a minister, I was involved with the women's ministry, youth ministry, church school, and Bible study. I was even a part of the choir for a very short while. My husband and I were youth advisors for many years at the church. Both of my children were junior ushers, they were in the youth choir, and youth group. My children held leadership positions and held speaking roles during holiday events and on youth Sundays. I will say it here and I have often said publicly that First Baptist Church of Teaneck is part of the village that helped to raise my children. First Baptist Church even grew up Willie and me. Willie and I were 33 years old when we came to First Baptist Church of Teaneck with a 7-year-old son and a 4-year-old daughter. We are now blessed to be 65 with thank God two amazingly blessed children: a 39-year-old son and a 36-year-old daughter.

I think that I am approachable and relatable as a person, a woman of God, and as a minister to all people. I believe that being part of being Christ-like is accepting other people's lifestyles as long as they are not hurting themselves, not hurting you, or hurting others. I accept all people for who they are and who they are trying to be. I do not shun people because of society's or denominational standards of sin, because I too am a sinner just like you. Truth be told we are all sinners saved by grace. I am unlike a lot of ministers that I have come in contact with when I occasionally attend church related events and conferences. I pride myself on being welcoming to all people without having some type of holier-than-thou demeanor. I do not need to be the center of attention. I am not a know-it-all or even a Bible scholar, in fact, I am always a receptive learner who is always ready and willing to learn more. I am not in the world but I try to be knowledgeable of what is going on in the world and how it is impacting others. Being in tune with the latest slang, music, and even dances are long gone since I have not been working closely with young people in years, but I am open, receptive and acceptive. Reverend Dr. Vernon C. Walton stressed the ministry of presence when I was doing my supervised ministry at Mount Calvary Baptist Church in Englewood, New Jersey. I know that the ministry of presence is crucial and that the harvest is plentiful but the workers are few. I am here for you but I am also aware that I have to pace myself and moreover be mindful of balance in every aspect of my life including ministry. I also realized after being with my current Pastor for seventeen years that I will never be able to keep up with her because she has a vigor that could only be from God, for her ministry. I know that I do not have the energy that my Pastor has and knowing that I know that I have to manage what I take on because I tend to be more tired than not tired each day. I thank God for bringing additional ministers to help with the harvest. But I pray that through prayer and relationships that my presence is always felt even if I am not physically in the room.

My life, my ministry, and all of my preaching of sermons are through God and come from my need to help and encourage people along their journey. I have preached many sermons throughout these twenty years of ministry. I have titles such as: "P.U.S.H." pray until something happens. GPS about allowing God to direct every turn you make. "Don't Look Back" is a reminder to not let your past define your presence. I think that my all-time favorite and most memorable sermons early on might be about dry bones from the book of Isaiah (which is my husband's favorite). Another one of my most memorable sermons was asking "May I" fashioned from the childhood game "Mother May I" where we either move forward or backward with baby steps or giant steps based on God's permission. I truly believe that God has called me into ministry to be myself, genuine; plain talk, straight no chaser, quirky humor, to bring others closer to God through God's Word delivered through me, in my high-pitched voice.

When I retired, I said that now I would be able to spend more time in ministry. I mentioned earlier that that plan did not really become as much of a reality as I thought. Ministry is part of who I am. I could not help but minister at work, in the schools unofficially. There was always a student, teacher, staff member, administrator, or parent that needed to be ministered to and prayed for. I could not walk into a school building without praying first, as well as ending my day with a Thank You Jesus. In fact, in more than one of the schools that I worked in, there were morning prayer groups. Wherever I am my ministry is with me. I might not be spending more time in the church building or in church activities but I have expanded my territory of ministry by being available and being present when needed as well as being in constant prayer. A day cannot go by without me praying for you.

I spent a long 5 ½ years at New Brunswick Theological Seminary as a part-time Master of Divinity student with all of my electives in counseling. It was an exactly 50-minute drive from New Brunswick to my front door in Teaneck after leaving a 9 pm class while working a full-time job as an assistant principal in Southern Westchester, which was 1½ hours to New Brunswick Theological Seminary. I am adding these details because the commute was brutal and it was a struggle two and sometimes three days per week (no exaggeration) being an administrator, a wife, a mother, a minister in my church, a student, and so much more. I thank God "sometimes" that my call to ministry came late in life; with one child away in college and the other child would be going away to college soon. I surmised that with the mothering part, being an absentee mother at this stage of my children's' life at the time would not be too much of a concern. I do not know if my son who was away at college and especially my daughter who was at home would agree although Shené at age 16 was probably relieved for the break from me being around being a helicopter mom. I have been in school throughout my children's entire childhood. From using my son as a test subject when I was getting my master's degree in reading, as he was learning how to read in pre-school, as well as strapping my daughter to my chest while studying in the library when I was finishing up my degree.

Maybe that is why my son was reading in pre-school and was always 2 to 3 years above grade level throughout elementary school and my daughter has not stopped going to school and will be Dr. Owens soon. They will tell you that I always had some type of textbook or doing assignments at their games and activities. I remember reading on the bleachers at football and basketball games. There were never enough hours in a day and I was burning the candle at both ends.

I digress. Having three tuitions to pay at the same time was not in my carefully made college payment plan. I cannot stop thanking God for the husband that he placed in my life because my being a minister and also going to seminary at the same time as our two children being in college was never anything that any of us ever anticipated. We were paying monthly, bi-monthly, and quarterly tuition payments at the same time. Having a bachelor's and two master's degrees were enough, why would I need a third, especially at my age was my question. I graduated from seminary in 2007 at age 50. I think that every family member and close childhood friends, or even friends from my 20s and 30s are constantly shocked about my call to ministry and how God has shaped me. My testimony of who I used to be would shock many people but I am an open book about my past. "I know the plans I have for you saith the Lord. . ." (Jeremiah 29:11) and God has and is prospering me in every aspect of my life. My Pastor often preaches from the pulpit, "If we knew the stories of the people in our pew we would change our seats." I have one of those testimonies. I am a witness

Seminary Graduation

of Dorothy Norwood's song "Somebody Prayed For Me". I thank God for the prayers of others...

As a woman in ministry, even being the first licensed and ordained woman minister by First Baptist Church of Teaneck, I do not have the experiences that other women in ministry might have. I think that because of God putting women in the ministry in place to come before me to pave the way, I always felt accepted by both men and women in both the ministry and congregations. My family: my parents and grandparents were raised in the African Methodist Episcopal church, where women were ministers preaching in the pulpit, it was not something that I was inspired to do, but it was not uncommon to me. It never dawned on me that Catholic Priests were a men's only position as I spent many years in the Roman Catholic church.. Unfortunately, in the Baptist Church, it took longer for the Baptist denomination, especially African American Baptist, to accept women in ministry. The testimonies of my sisters in ministry who came before me were not positive. God blessed me by placing my former Pastor Reverend Kevin Jones in my life. He accepted my calling, but before that, he brought in many women ministers to preach and teach. I still thank him to this day for bringing in Reverend Sheila Riley, whom I consider my first female clergy mentor. Reverend Riley facilitated Bible Studies, and occasionally preached God's word at First Baptist Church of Teaneck, way before I knew of my calling. Reverend Kevin Jones also brought in a female seminary student from New Brunswick Theological Seminary to do her supervised ministry. I truly believe that first, Deacon Mae Francis Jones having the audacity to accept her calling as the first female Deacon not only in our church but also in our area, then later the church was introduced to the Reverend Sheila Riley's ongoing teaching and preaching, as well as the now Reverend Diana Brown in her ministry, these three were the forerunners preparing First Baptist for first, my calling into ministry, and then the acceptance of the first female Pastor, Reverend Dr. Marilyn Monroe Harris.

Being raised in the Catholic church, I was not fully introduced to the Bible until college when I started exploring other religions. I do not have the experience of attending Sunday School growing up. I attended religious instructions through the Catholic church as a child, but it did not include learning about the Bible, it was more about learning how to be a good Catholic (learning their prayers and rituals). In high school, I dappled in the Muslim tradition because of the teachings of and my admiration of Minister Farrakhan. My parents were both raised in the African Methodist Episcopal church. My father's father was an AME minister. Therefore, I was baptized as a baby in Bethel AME Church on 132nd Street in the Village of Harlem. At school age, to attend Catholic School in the 60s, you and at least one of your parents had to be Catholic. So, in addition to my mother becoming a baptized Catholic, my older siblings and I were all baptized again. This is an example of the sacrifices parents make for their children because my mother loved the church in which she was raised but she wanted her children to have the best possible education more. My mother wanted her children to attend Catholic school while we were living in the Village of Harlem, so she temporarily left Bethel African Methodist Episcopal Church and became a member of Our Lady Queen of Angels Church on 113th Street when we lived in the Village of Harlem and continued at Holy Spirit Church on University Avenue when we lived in the Bronx.

When I initially left home to go to college I had no intention of going to church on a regular basis, after all who was going to make me get up on a Sunday morning to attend a church service. But I soon realized that I needed that covering that I did not realize that I had while at home. At home, if you did not go to church/Mass then you were not going to go or do anything else on Sundays. In fact we had to go to confession on Saturdays and I remember some Saturdays getting off the bus with my siblings on our way to my grandmother's house to stop to confession in a Catholic church near my grandmother's house. While I was at Howard University for college in Washington, D.C. I started searching churches for the perfect fit. My friends Gwen Wells and Ronda Robinson from Howard University freshman dorm "the Quad" were Baptist and I explored churches with them and found that the Baptist tradition was my fit. I needed (for a lack of a better word) noise in my worship. I needed movement other than the standing and kneeling in my worship. I needed to express myself in my worship. I needed outward as well as inward signs of praise. I found myself being loosened in the Baptist church. I was baptized by emersion in my senior year of college in 1979 at St. Marks Baptist Church in NW Washington, D.C., by the then Pastor Reverend Wilborn Gilmore. I joined and was baptized at my soon-to-be husband's church that he grew up in. At the time, I had no idea that learning about various traditions and denominations would be part of my ministry as I now facilitate the new members sessions at my church and I am well versed and acceptant of all religions. I was and still am like a sponge in learning God's Word. Bible Studies, Sunday School classes, and various Bible-based classes intrigue me. Unfortunately, while in seminary, I did not take the opportunity to immerse myself in my love of learning with my theological studies. I focused more on memorizing facts for assignments and exams instead of engaging fully in the academia. I still struggle to be in the moment. In seminary, my focus was more on completing the work and classes, as well as mustering up enough energy for the long commute to and fro, instead of appreciating the journey.

When Pastor Harris came to the church I was assigned to be the Minister of Christian Education which gave me leadership responsibilities of our church school, new members classes, our Back 2 School ministry, and tutoring ministry. This became too overwhelming because I tend to overwhelm myself with ideas and adapting structures. My ministry became more manageable as I continued with the New Member's Ministry. I was later given the Intercessory Prayer Ministry, the Prison Ministry, and later the Marriage Ministry. I still facilitate the New Member's Ministry, the Intercessory Prayer Ministry, and the Married Couples Ministry. As a minister at First Baptist Church of Teaneck, I had other leadership responsibilities throughout the years; I was the leader of a new ministry that we called the Follow-Up ministry for a brief time. The Follow-Up Ministry was designed to keep track of and stay connected with new members so that they would not fall through the cracks. It overlapped with the Deacon's responsibilities so it was discontinued. Being responsible for new members classes keeps me connected to the new members as they find their footing on this part of their journey and oftentimes when they go on to their next. I inherited the Prison Ministry for a while when Deaconess Phillips moved back to Jamaica. It is now the Redeeming Hope Ministry. I also inherited the Intercessory Prayer Ministry when the now Minister, Dr. Shirley McDougald relocated to Philadelphia. I resumed the duties of the Intercessory Prayer Ministry and continued with Prayer Service before Bible Study, and a version of Summer in the Son, the ministry also solicited prayer requests. I tried to revamp and improve attendance in the prayer services by involving the Mother's Board and the seniors of the church. Hymns were an intricate part of the Prayer Service and I came to rely on two soulful singers Deacon Willie Jones and Sister Annie Jamison, who both went home to be with the Lord. I tried to get our Prayer Intercessors ministry involved and more visually committed. We as intercessors collectively stop and pray each day at 12noon wherever we are. The members of the intercessory ministry have been given prayer assignments to be responsible for as we cover our church with prayers. We all are responsible for praying for the Pastor. The other prayer 17+1 assignments are for 1) babies, 2) bereaved, 3) caregivers, 4) families, 5) intercessors, 6) leadership, 7) marriages, 8) men, 9) ministerial team, 10) ministries 11) mother's board, 12) seniors, 13) sickness, 14) social justice, 15) women, 16) young adults, and 17) the youth. We also have a disciple of the mother's board that I call our "Closer" who covers us all and our assignments. Then COVID-19 hit and our ministry heightened and my prayer was answered. My prayer was not answered the way that I thought that it would be answered but the intercessors became to this date very busy. We were adding names to our prayer list and bereaved list. We became Prayer Warriors because we were in the middle of a battle on behalf of others through prayer. Our Pastor had Reverend Diethra Postle lead a 12 noon and 6 pm prayer line when the pandemic began. When Reverend Postle had to return to work virtually in the fall, Pastor asked me to do the noon prayer and Reverend Postle continued with the 6 pm Prayer until recently. I can say that 19 months later God has reintroduced me to my purpose for this season as a Prayer Warrior. It often breaks my heart, from texting the Prayer Warriors the numerous names and situations in need of prayers. But I also delight and I am strengthened by the trust in the Lord's plans for people's lives. In addition to being lifted up and also blessed with praise reports and testimonies. Won't He do it! Those on the prayer line exalt my week. Those who lift up prayers on the phone line aloud and even those who pray silently give me the strength to minister to others. I call our time together on this prayer line, our mid-week, mid-day prayer and worship service. It is more than a prayer call!

There was a time, that I call the old Sheila; I would fall completely apart with bad news. I had what I call a heightened sense of empathy. I still empathize with people's hurts, pains, and losses but I have a stronger sense of trusting in God's plan "that all things work together for good to them that love God, to them who are called according to His purpose." (Romans 8:28). I finally (I must confess eventually) use my favorite scripture in all situations (Proverbs 3:5-6) – Trusting and acknowledging God, while stifling my own understanding.

God has and continues to strengthen me to strengthen those in need. This is my ministry for this season. I pray without ceasing from when I wake up, at noon with my daily cellphone alarm reminder, and as I end my day. Even when praying over meals I am lifting up someone in prayer. I keep a prayer journal as names come to mind or when names are mentioned.

I am still currently responsible for the New Member's classes. This ministry was always the ministry that I felt that I was most "satisfied" and most effective with. With the New Members' Ministry I get to know Disciples at the beginning of their journey at First Baptist Church of Teaneck. Because of my multi-denominational experiences and studies, I can relate to those who are changing their denomination as well as being able to explain the differences in various traditions for those who were born and raised Baptist. I think that my unpretentious open view on life and people helps to make these new members feel comfortable and they sense that I am approachable to those who were recently led to this church for just a time as this. As I mentioned before I often establish relationships with the new members and follow them as they connect to others and other ministries in the church as well as after they leave this church for whatever reason.

I will always have a special place in my heart for the young people in the church even though I am no longer the Minister of Christian Education. I still have a great relationship with those now young adults, both those who are still in the church and those who moved on, those that were in the Youth Ministry when I was the advisor. I have seen them through finishing school, getting engaged and married, having children, and/or starting their careers. I am so proud of each one of them and the paths that they are on.

The Married Couples Ministry is a ministry that I reluctantly accepted for the second time. The ministry ended up on hiatus for a while because of the death of some of its members the first time around including the passing of the First Gentleman of the Church James E. Harris; Reverend Harris' husband. Years later my Pastor announced to the congregation that Willie and I would be doing the ministry again unbeknownst to my husband and I. We, both my husband and I, are transparent in every aspect of our lives. We, I must say, are a great teaching team, we even did a book study together. As far as marriage is concerned, after 42 years of marriage, we can write a book about 'what not to do'. We married before we should have at age 23 with no job and no money. We had our first child without having a clue about life almost 3 years later. We purchased a house at age 30 before we could afford a house. We were oblivious about homeownership and thought that budgeting was only for the cost of the mortgage and not all of the house; the monthly expenses in the form of bills for gas and electric, water, and trash pick-ups, as well as the repairs of both this house that was built in 1932 and our two blue not so new cars; a Ford Tempo and a Hyundai. Thinking back now we always had a high monthly telephone bill because calls to family in

New York and Washington, D.C. were considered long-distance calls and we were not going to make our calls to family members after 11pm weekdays or wait until the weekend for the lower rates. Getting a little off topic: I know that young people would not know anything about Ma Bell and 0 for the operator or 411 for information or even the Yellow and White telephone book pages. I know that they do not know anything about a rotary telephone and using a rotary dial. Anyway, we did not expect the unexpected expenses, not to mention the unforeseen in life itself. Even with living in two apartments in Maryland prior to moving to New York and then New Jersey, I do not think that we fully understood the concept of spending needs with grocery shopping that also included toiletries, toilet paper and household needs and not just food for our meals. We have made numerous financial mishaps throughout the years and that is an understatement. Through it all, God took care of us! They said God takes care of babies and fools, and we were not babies. We bring these transparencies to couples as well as the fact that marriage is work, and prayer is necessary. God loves marriages and the enemy is constantly trying to destroy marriages and our families. In this ministry, we all share and exchange experiences with others. We have fun playing games and doing activities too. We play our form of the Newlywed Game which is our all-time favorite in addition to other games. We have couples dinners in the church's fellowship hall and at restaurants. We had a paint and sip. We did karaoke at a restaurant and again with love songs karaoke at the church. We bowled and went to the movies and an Off-Broadway play. We have an annual date night dinner for valentine's day at the church and during COVID-19 the date was virtually. We always stressed the importance of having God be in the forefront in all marriages. Willie and my marriage have taken on many dings. We have had many ups and many downs, many breaking points but we believe that "what God has joined together, let no man put asunder" and we express that in this married couples ministry. I must add as long as you are not in any type of abusive relationship.

I realized that as ministers, we set aside our vulnerabilities while ministering to others, but ministry during 2020 and afterward was a very difficult time for all. I must admit that it was not easy for me at all during the pandemic as a minister and as the wife of the Chairperson of the Deacon Board. Mostly because of Willie's extreme sense of obligations as the Chairperson of the Deacon Board, his love and his dedication to God's work, and his devotion to our Pastor and his church, I feel sometimes as though he seems to put the church very close to first after God. It was not only me, but the people who loved Willie (especially me) did not want him out there on a different type of front lines' essential worker, with a disease that we knew little to nothing about that was annihilating individuals.

First Baptist Church of Teaneck did not miss a beat during the pandemic. First Baptist Church of Teaneck never stopped their ministry. Sunday morning services in the sanctuary never stopped which was a blessing for all those that the church ministered to from all over the country and including the Caribbean and South Africa. If you remember, little was known about this disease and the facts, precautions, and regulations were constantly changing. I commend my Pastor for being a trooper but her second-in-command had to come home to me. Willie, to me, is not as conscientious as he should be about the germs around him. I might have been overly cautious but I was and still am a germaphobe and a little bit of a hypochondriac. I had a supply of disinfectant wipes, Lysol spray and liquid, and hand sanitizer (even though I prefer soap and water) before people were stocking up on them because of the pandemic. Washing hands, wearing a face mask, and socially distancing was not enough for me. People, healthy people were dying all around us. The phone calls kept on coming. It got so bad that when the phone rang or a text came in, I knew that someone was either sick, in the hospital, was dying, or died. It broke my heart for those who were unable to see their loved ones in the hospital, nursing homes, and those who could not have farewell homegoing services for their loved-ones. I attended or presided over a few funerals and burials. I was constantly praying for families. I tried to keep in touch with the seniors of our church during the pandemic checking on their wellbeing. I would pass by Volk Leber Funeral Home in Teaneck with the freezer trucks in their parking lot and pray. I prayed for all health care workers and other essential workers including those working daily who might have been overlooked as essential workers like those working in waste management, public transportation, police and fire fighters, those factory workers and warehouses workers, truck drivers and those delivery personnel, as well as restaurant and grocery store workers, and those helping to keep the worship services going. If I did not mention you believe me you were in my prayers. I prayed for all those who went out to work to provide for other peoples' needs. Mental and physical wellness took a toll on a lot of people during the pandemic especially the elderly. It will be years before we will know how the pandemic has impacted on our young people's psyche. Concerns about medical care, isolation, loneliness, and fear, as well as finan-cial upheavals of others inundated my mind while staying at home during the pandemic as I was in constant prayer. I was and still am in the high-risk category because I am over sixty with breathing issues, among other things such as high blood pressure and according to BMI overweight. I did not want to leave my house and my husband had difficulties staying in the house. All ministries were done virtually for most of us, but our church doors were open but adhering to the Governor's ever-changing mandates. I do thank God for those who made sure that we had service virtually from the church. The Pastor, the leadership of the church, the musicians, and the media ministry. Those who were in the church building from day one all deserve our thanks!

My brothers and sisters in the ministry returned to the church before I went back. Even though I cautiously traveled during COVID-19 I was not prepared to be around others who went into the real world to go to work and be around people. I salute my fellow ministers who are essential workers and worked during the unknown days of the pandemic; those who work in hospitals or have family members working in the hospitals or driving New Jersey transit buses. I returned to church after getting my COVID-19 shot as the church slowly went through phases of reopening. Two years later we now have hybrid services.

I thank God for all of those throughout these many years who were and those who are a part of my ministerial journey. Even those who were with me before I became Sister, Minister, or Reverend Sheila R. Burns-Owens.

15

My 2022 Vision Board #65

Chapter 65! It is January 2022, marking my 65th year on this earth. I wore a t-shirt saying Chapter 65 EST 1957. This is the 65th Chapter of my life and I was established on January 16th, 1957. I am determined to live my best life while having no regrets. God has blessed me with the means, the opportunities, and the family to do me and do the new me whatever that may entail. I already mentioned the perks of being an official senior. I thought that the perks

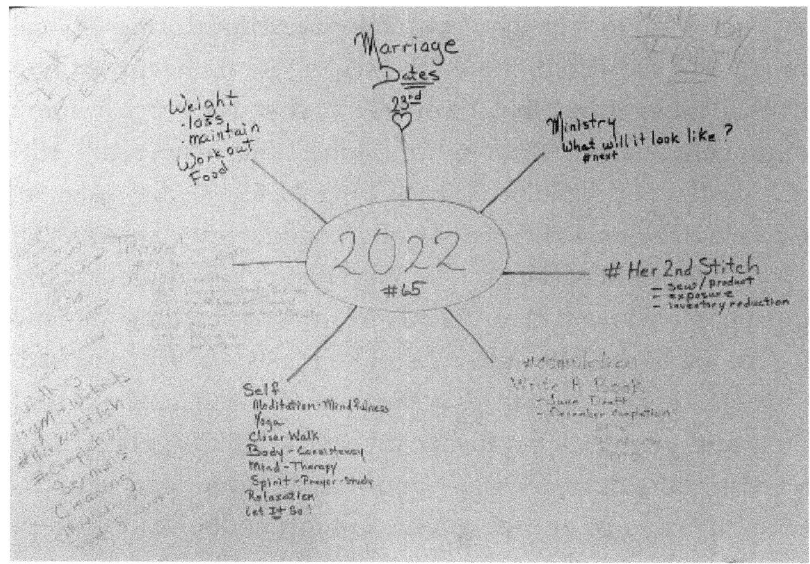

2022 Vision Board

would begin at 50 when AARP started sending me membership information, but it did not. I quickly realized that I was considered a baby senior. I could not join the senior center and I still was not eligible for a lot of the senior discounts. At age 55, I was able to join my neighborhood senior center. I was also hoping for an incentive so that I could retire at 55 but that did not happen either. At age 60 I was able to get movie discounts. But all senior discounts at places and flights came at age 65. Medicare started at 65, even though I had to jump through hoops to finally get my supplemental insurance straight. I might have a higher co-pay for specialists but I have a lower co-pay for my primary doctor's visits. All of my generic brand prescriptions are free at age 65. Also at age 65, I am eligible for silver sneakers and my gym membership is now free, which for me is the best perk of them all!

I still do not understand why so many people are shying away from revealing their age when it is such a blessing. We are living longer than ever before (except during biblical times). We are also living better; we are living healthier long lives. I must admit that I am seeing changes because more older people are celebrating milestones. I have been to birthday parties of people proudly turning 70, 75, 80, and even 90. God bless their souls. Sister Rosalie Springer out-danced us all at her 90th birthday celebration. With people's attitudes changing, people who are older than I am are now showing me how to live life to the fullest instead of being sedentary, achy, sad, tired, and just waiting to go home to be with the Lord. I do not put limits on myself because of my age. I think I am becoming more mindful of wearing age-appropriate clothing most of the time. But my age-appropriateness might not be your perception of what a 65-year-old minister, grandmother should wear. But that's okay, to each its own.

I will bust a move in a minute to any music often embarrassing my grandchildren because sometimes I might be a little off beat.

At age 65 I feel that I am trying to do all the right preventative things even though my sister Shelley who is a vegetarian and my sister Sharon who is a pescetarian feel as though I can do better. Even though my diet basically consists mostly of fish during the week, I do occasionally eat chicken, ground turkey, and I went back to eating beef with Parks Hot Beef Sausages especially cut up in my red salmon with grits for Sunday's breakfast. I will occasionally indulge in a steak, lamb chops, or BBQ lamb ribs.

It is important to see physicians for every part of our bodies regularly at any age for preventive, maintenance, as well as concerns at any age but especially as we get older. I see both a cardiologist on regularly scheduled appointments every year because of my family history as well as a neurologist annually. I have my yearly mammogram and gynecological exams. I have my regular scheduled eye, ENT, colonoscopy, and bone density exams. I have seen an orthopedic for my back, knee, shoulder, ankle, and now my hip. I see my primary physician every four months. I take prescription medication daily for high blood pressure, hypothyroidism, and allergies. I have a box full of supplements that I take 1 to 2 times per day for the prevention and maintenance of my health. I take 1. Ginkgo Biloba and 2. Phosphatidylserine or Ginkgo Biloba for memory, 3. Kyolic garlic to keep my blood pressure and cholesterol stable, 4. I take Magnesium Citrate to prevent cramping, but it is also used for energy production and promotes regularity, 5. Calcium for bone health which is a must for all women, 6. I take Krill fish oil for brain health, 7. Women's 50+ Daily Vitamin - Trader Joe's had a great brand that has been discontinued but my doctor suggested the Vitamin Shoppe brand, 8. Turmeric for inflammation I also season my food with turmeric while cooking, 8. D3 because I and probably everyone else lack vitamin D because of our slowly destroying ozone and we are not getting enough sun, 9. Psyllium for regularity, 10. Collagen for hair and nails with the hopes that it will tighten up my flabby skin, 11. Low Dose Aspirin for heart health, 12. a generic Pepcid (acid controller) that was recommended to accompany the prescribed Cetirizine for allergies and allergic reaction protection, and 13. B12 for energy. I just found a B6/B12 with folic acid from Trader Joe's that I am going to try. I did not realize that I am taking 13 supplements until just now but I did ask my doctor if there are any of the supplements that I am taking that I could eliminate. My dermatologist informed me recently that taking collagen is only giving me expensive urine. So I will take collagen off my daily supplements intake. I take a total of 4 prescription medications (two high blood pressure, hypothyroidism, and for allergies) and 13 (now 12) supplements to stay as healthy as possible. I also eat citrus daily to help keep my cholesterol numbers down. I try to stay away from foods that cause my cholesterol and glucose levels to elevate. Unfortunately some of these foods are considered healthy. I basically order my prescription medication through CVS mail-order pharmacy. I get my prescription allergy medication Cetirizine from Walgreens pharmacy. Most of my supplements are from The Vitamin Shoppe's Auto Delivery (with a 10% discount). Low Dose Bayer Aspirin, D3, and some type of Collagen I usually pick up from any of the following: Harmons, Walmart, Walgreens, or CVS. Now I am trying the B6/B12 with folic acid from Trader Joe's. I included these specifics because preventive measures are so important as well as health maintenance. That is why I attend a gym for various workout classes now three days per week, and a senior center for yoga once a week. Also taking advantage of classes and workshops will improve both my mind and body. I pray that my children or grandchildren will not be part of the growing number of adults who have to take care of their parents while raising their own families aka the Sandwich Generation. What is the saying? "An ounce of prevention is worth a pound of cure." It's easier to stop something from happening in the first place than to repair the damage after that has happened. With escalating healthcare costs, I pray that you will all reevaluate your methods of prevention.

In my own introverted life and my intentional reclusive lifestyle, I give honor to my space and my selective ways of venturing out. I still find it difficult to say all the nos, and all the no thank yous, or even the I do not want to, that I want to proclaim in some areas of my life but that too is improving. Oftentimes, I am surprisingly glad that I ventured out, even though I reluctantly initially accepted the invitation, especially when it involved having the opportunity to dance. But I also give myself permission to say no!

Chapter 65 means to travel, uphold healthy living, and take advantage of new things/new adventures. My vision board for 2022 #65 lays out my plans. My plans include making improvements in my marriage. Includes being deliberate about dating at least once per month, working on improving our two-way communication and intimacy, as well as finding a marriage therapist. Reevaluating my ministry and my relationship with God. Be more deliberate in improving the marketing of my business #Her2ndStitch. Complete this book and have it published (if you are reading this book I have accomplished this task). Work on self (meditation, mindfulness, yoga, having a closer walk with God, consistency with workouts, praying & studying more, relaxing, and letting it go…). Travel to all 50 states and plan for the 6 continents. Weight loss and maintenance (workout & food). Do the work! Speak it into existence! Walk by faith!

My chapter 65 is to be a better me and celebrate me!

16

Be Whole

I added this chapter because of our First Baptist Church of Teaneck Bible Study topic; "Do You Want To Be Made Whole." This topic came from John 5:6 "When Jesus saw an invalid man near the Sheep Gate pool lying there and learned that he had been in this condition for a long time, he asked him, Do you want to get well?" I was asked, by my Pastor to facilitate the teaching of the second session regarding wellness. My focus was on the Mind, Body, and Spirit. Based on the man by the pool being disabled for 38 years waiting for someone to help him in the pool so that he can be healed. Therefore, I ask the question; Do you really want to be made whole? Are you waiting for someone to help you? Are you comfortable in your illness, in your bondage? This chapter is included because it is my passion to improve my mind, body, and my ministry to have others re-evaluate and improve their mind, body, and their spirit. Proverbs 14:30a written by King Solomon states "A heart at peace gives life to the body." Our heart needs to be at peace so that we can give life and wholeness to our entire body.

There are many forms of mental health that go undiagnosed as well as not addressed or treated throughout the world. There might be some overlapping with other chapters, but I know that it is important for all of us to self-reflect on the wholeness of our minds, bodies, spirits, and emotional health. As well as discovering ways to make improvements, in addition to getting help.

LL Cool J was on Hoda and Jena's NBC Morning Show and he sent out a message that I too am sending to me and to you "Never Limit Yourself".

My November 2022 Bob Gass Daily Devotion said that there was a sign on someone's office wall that read: "You are not what you think you are. But what you think – you are!" I need you to check your thinking right now…

Also in my daily devotion it had that Marcus Aurelius said, "Our life is what our thoughts make it" which is so true. It went on to say that you can "set your mind". "The most basic control you have when it comes to your mind is your ability to choose what you pay attention to. At any given moment, it is within your capacity to turn your thoughts in one direction or another." Let us turn our thoughts towards positivity, good health, growth, and wholeness.

Tasha Turnbull from T-2 Fitness wrote an inscription in her book to me "The Last 10 Pounds" several years ago that I hope will inspire your wholeness also. She wrote "Please remember to continue to put yourself at the top of your priority list because YOU MATTER. In order to take care of others and keep that infectious spirit of yours, you must take care of yourself. Also, the more you move, the more travel & impact you will have on this world." Yes! Tasha I am listening, doing, and sharing…

My daughter, Shené V. Owens has two quotes that she just shared as a panelist at Mighty Dream Forum "Bright Sparks Live Powered By The Community: A Conversation About Reclaiming Spaces, Belonging, and Building Community." She shares these two quotes as the Associate Director, Center for Student Diversity at William & Mary University in Williamsburg, Virginia with first-year students during their orientation on their first weekend at the college, she also has these quotes displayed in her office to motivate young people and her students that I feel that we all need to embrace "I Dare You To Believe In Yourself – You Are Amazing" and "Be You UNAPOLOGETICALLY."

My son Willie J. Curlee Owens, if I should say so myself is an amazing "daddy's-girl" father. He has his daughters Jayla (14) and Darby (9) initially saying each morning before they enter their school building "Push To Be The Best And Nothing Less" but now he realized that it might not be being internalized so they now declare, "I Will Push To Be The Best And Nothing Less". We need to not only instill in our young people but also in ourselves mantras that will reinforce our wholeness.

'Good Better Best Never Let It Rest Until Your Good Gets Better and Your Better Is Best" – this is one of my mother's sayings that she lived by and recited (even when she could not remember anything else) until she went home to be with the Lord. She also wrote it in her children's graduation autograph books, as a teacher she taught her first and second-grade students, then she taught her grandchildren, and I think everyone she came in contact with. This saying can also help with focusing on wholeness. I plan to have "Good Better Best" tattooed on my left forearm soon (just a side note I originally wanted the tattoo on my inner left bicep but my triceps are determined to continue to change from muscle into flab even with targeted weight training).

Please take the time right now to ask yourself these ten questions based on these quotes because we all need to be made whole:

1. Are you limiting yourself?
2. If you are what you think, what are you thinking?
3. What direction are you turning your mind/life?
4. Are you making you a priority?

5. Do you know that you matter?
6. Can you dare to believe in yourself?
7. Do you know that you are amazing?
8. Can you be you unapologetically?
9. Are you pushing to be the best and nothing less?
10. Are you determined to strive to be good, better, and best and never let it rest until your good gets better and your better is best?

Self-care and wholeness are so important. Wholeness of our mind, the wholeness of our body, and the wholeness of our spirit:

Mind

I am so focused on identifying weaknesses and addressing ways to improve my mind because both my mother and her mother suffered from dementia from blocked carotid arteries. My concerns have caused unnecessary anxiety. I began talking to Dr. Michael Denker, my primary doctor about this probably when I turned 50. When I retired at age 58 my unease was heightened because I knew that I would not be using my brain as much since I would not be working. I now have a neurologist, Dr. Marissa Oller-Cramsie at Holy Name Hospital, who understands both my self-imposed anxiety and my memory concerns, in addition to my Type-A personality. Through Dr. Oller-Cramsie I have had both an MRI to rule out any physical condition or abnormalities, and a battery of psychological testing to determine cognitive decline, as well as to ease my mind. To be completely transparent in this book, I have had two MRIs of the brain. They found that I have a meningioma that is being monitored but it is not in a location to affect my memory. The second MRI a year or two later showed no growth of the meningioma. I mentioned this because it is important that we check every part of our bodies from head to toe and keep pursuing any of our concerns. A perfect example is my hip stiffness over the years, I was told to continue doing yoga to loosen it. I was never very flexible, not even as a child in dance classes but I realize a difference between the flexibility in the left hip versus the right hip. There has been slow improvement in my right hip because of stretching and yoga but today I finally went to my orthopedic at the North Jersey Orthopedic Specialist which has offices in both Teaneck and Englewood New Jersey and had an x-ray done of the hip. Thank God that it is bursitis and not arthritis. Dr. Owens (no relations) said that arthritis is not reversible but bursitis is. I am to rub Voltaren gel on my hip three times a day and also use heat. I was also given a referral for physical therapy. My right hip problem is caused by my left lower back discomfort. I am overcompensating on the right side of my body because of my left side lower back reoccurring pain. I already start my day with a heating pad on my back, using this great weighted massage heating pad by Sharper Image. Now I will use it on my hip too two to three times per day. I try to do whatever is necessary to improve every part of my body inside and outside. I am a big fan of Dr. Teal's Epson salt, their foaming bath, and their body wash. My go-to Dr. Teal is Relax & Relief with Eucalyptus & Spearmint for my after-workout soaks or Sleep Blend with Melatonin & Essential Oils for my nighttime bath. The physical therapy with Karen at North Jersey Orthopedic Specialists twice a week is now loosening my hip and helping with my lower back pain. Through physical therapy, I now purchased a Theragun massager and Zynex NexWave medical electrodes to duplicate the treatment that I receive in physical therapy. I also purchased a balance board to strengthen my core and improve my balance because it was part of my physical therapy exercise.

I occupy my retired mind with believe it or not by following instructions in exercise classes; it keeps my focus and my listening and my cognitive skills alert until I remember the routines and unfortunately I become less focused. I love puzzles, which you saw in a previous chapter. I am a self-proclaim #puzzlehead. The patience, intricacy, and details of putting puzzles together also improve my cognitive skills as well as problem-solving skills. Being still, being focused, and being present is so difficult (I want to say impossible) for me. My sister Sharon suggested meditation, which is part of her daily routine. She knows that I cannot sit still for a minute (yes, I timed myself). I eventually started trying on focusing on being present after talking to my brother in the ministry, Reverend Kenneth Jones about not being able to stay present. I think it became more apparent and seemingly uncontrollable in 2020 during the isolation of the pandemic. First with no in-person contact, and then when I had to participate in zoom meetings, virtual events, and virtual services.

I started doing mindful meditation through Ramapo College for 30 minutes per week on Thursdays until it interfered with my yoga class schedule which was changed from Tuesdays to Thursdays. I am now taking a six-week Health Body Healthy Mind workshop at the Rodda Center with Teaneck's Social Worker Alex Cerbone MSW, LSW. This course includes various types of meditation at the start of the class. The course includes topics on being healthy through living a healthy life, a healthy diet, and exercise, cognitive behavior therapy, the basic function of the human mind, emotions versus feelings, coping with grief and loss, coping skills, motivations, goal setting, and self-care. My therapist Lorna recommended an 8-Week Mindfulness-Based Stress Reduction Course with the Krame Center of Mindful Living on Thursday evenings that is really helping me with meditation and being present through weekly body scans, and meditation techniques, including yoga meditation. This course also has us re-evaluating our perceptions. I highly recommend both the workshop at the Rodda Center and the course at the Krame Center. The workshop at the Rodda Center is for seniors in Teaneck, New Jersey. The mindfulness courses at the Krame Center offers partial scholarships. Both facilitators Alex Cerbone at the Rodda Center and Ken A Verni stated what we all need to remember "there are more things right with us than wrong with us." I need to say that again "there are more things right with us than wrong with us." Like our blessings will always outweigh our troubles.

I can be considered the 'post-it queen.' Daily affirmations of encouragement are so necessary and they should be placed in your view, on your mirror, on your closet, on your refrigerator, on your bulletin board or cubical at work, or as a screen saver on your computer. Surround yourself with positivity.

In my transparency, I have mentioned my need for assistance with my mental health. My current therapist is helping me with my obsessive-compulsive-disorder tendencies, my obsessive needs for completion, my ADHD, being overwhelmed by trying to balance all the balls that I choose to juggle, as well as anxiety, depression, and life itself. She has given me many tools that I can take out of my toolbox when needed such as stopping; I have a pause sign in my room on my television as a reminder that I can stop. I can go nonstop from the time I wake up and my mind starts speeding, to me being in constant movement until I force my body and mind to stop when I go to bed. I also need a reminder to breathe! Remind myself that it is okay "not to" when I become too obsessive. My OCD, I recently realized, can get so bad that if I go someplace; someone's house, a restaurant, or even my dentist's office, anywhere, and if I see toilet paper or paper towels with the roll down instead of over, I am so tempted to change it or should I say fix it. Please tell me that I am not the only one, besides my daughter, who also feels this way. There have been "Great Toilet Paper Debates." I recently told my husband how irritating it is for me if our concomitant light switches for upstairs and downstairs are not up when the light is on and down when the light is off or if they are not all in the same direction. He actually surveyed other family members and found out that others felt the same way. I tend to fixate on things if they seem to be out of place, unbalanced, uneven, and/or crooked. My therapist even challenged me as a homework assignment not to unpack, wash or put everything away after one of my trips until I saw her again in two weeks. It was a difficult assignment but now I am not obsessed with unpacking and rushing to wash my clothes after returning home from a trip. I am learning to force myself not to obsess about other people's lack of neatness and order if it is causing me anxiety. I recently had another homework assignment to make a list of things that bring me joy or that I enjoy doing because I expressed that other than food and traveling to new places everything else seems like a necessity. I am also looking at my needs versus my wants. I need to go to the gym, I need to include weights in my workouts, I need to stretch and do yoga, I need to walk and do cardio, I need to eat healthy and drink plenty of water because I want to be healthy. I want to travel and see new places. I want to eat tasty foods as well as try experimenting with new, especially what I consider exotic types of foods.

Thinking about all these needs verses wants; children rush to grow up because they think grownups do not have to answer to anyone. Even grown and working there was always someone that I was accountable to. I am thinking about the things I enjoy. I am also thinking about the things I want to do, as opposed to those things that I have to do, or the things that I am expected to do with either my family or my church. Even with being intentional with being able to say no, with the help of my official therapist Lorna and my unofficial hair-stylist therapist Jeannette, there are still a lot of expectations that I cannot seem to have complete control of no matter how adult, how retired, and how free that I consider myself.

As I sit here in Englewood Hospital and Medical Center in Englewood, New Jersey after my husband's second major surgery, I am adding trauma to our wholeness. I am definitely no expert on trauma but I do know that it does not just go away without being addressed. So many people suffer from known and unknown Post Traumatic Stress Disorder - PTSD. My PTSD and also my daughters have been triggered just being in this hospital because of surgery complications my husband had in February 2018, and it is now October 2022, over four and a half years later. Previous trauma when triggered (and you never know what the triggers might be) can cause elevated stress and unexpected and sometimes uncontrollable emotional feelings, as well as (in our case) an overly heightened need to protect.

Let me end this section with something that I discovered. I mention the half-empty versus half-full mindset. Your mindset is so important in how you live your life. Even though I am generally a half-empty type of person, I have forced myself to change my mindset in situations to Romans 8:28 "And we know that all things work together for good to them that love God, to them who are the called according to *His* purpose." What I might consider good or bad, I now see it as God at work. A perfect example of me changing my mindset; I am not a fan of sitting in traffic but I now see this sitting time as God slowing me down to spend time in God's presence and spending time listening to God or God keeping me from some unseen danger. God also has me praying for those who I pass by whose car may be disabled or may be in a car accident.

Body

I am going to start with the need to rest before I get into relaxation. In looking into why sleep is so important I found that through my internet search that "most cells of the body show increased production and reduced breakdown of proteins during deep sleep. Sleep helps humans maintain optimal emotional and social functioning while we are awake by giving rest during sleep to the parts of the brain that control emotions and social interactions." "Sleep plays an essential role in stress management and good mental health." "Sleep makes you feel better. Adequate sleep is a key part of a healthy lifestyle and can benefit your heart, weight, mind, and more. Insufficient sleep is linked to a host of health problems, from depression to cardiovascular disease." I do all that I can to have a restful night's sleep. I wear my Samsung fitness tracker watch while sleeping and I am able to check the app on my phone for my sleep patterns. It indicates what time I fell asleep and when I woke up, the number of hours I slept, my sleep score with the actual sleep time, and even my REM sleep, light sleep, deep sleep, and awake time during my slumber. According to this app I am considered a Penguin Sleeper. A Penguin Sleeper wakes up too often at night. This app also offers sleep coaching so that I can have a better night sleep. Such as, building habits to relax before bed. Calming the body and mind helps you stay asleep and sleep deeply. Another suggestion is making your bed your sleeping place. It's easier to sleep soundly when your brain connects your bed with sleep and not other activities. This technology of this Samsung Health Fitness Tracker App fascinates me because it can tell you how many calories you burned while sleeping, your snoring data if you put your phone near your head while sleeping (it recorded my snoring, now I cannot deny that I snore anymore), your oxygen level while sleeping, as well as a chart with your ongoing sleep consistency. In addition, the stats on your body composition, stress level, your heart rate, and daily activities. I am not a Samsung spokesperson but I should be compensated for my constant promotion of their watch and my love of my Z-Fold Samsung cellphone to everyone. I usually get at least 8 hours of sleep. I wish that I had higher numbers of REM and deep sleep. The only days that I schedule a wake time are Sundays for church, and Monday, Tuesdays, and Fridays for my 9:30 am or 9:15 gym classes. Unfortunately, because of my inattentiveness I have to wake up one to two hours before I need to be some place.

I occasionally take Goli Nutrition Ashwagandha Gummies, it is known to relax, restore and unwind. I have Olly Sleep which contains melatonin, L-Theanine, and Botanicals on hand if I need it. Herbal tea works for some people but I am not really a tea drinker. My niece Shavon just gave me some Yogi Kava Stress Relief tea that eases tension and promotes relaxation that I am enjoying and drinking when needed. My child (not naming any names) introduced me to gummies. I tried it once after an event but I was so exhausted when I tried it that I do not know if it was the laced gummies or fatigue that caused my sound sleep. Another confession: I was never a fan of marijuana or any other mind-altering drug. In my late teens and early twenties, which was the 70s and 80s. I think that I smoked marijuana and smoked cigarettes out of my self-imposed peer pressure or a need to belong or fit in. But with marijuana or even alcohol, I did not like ever feeling that

I was not in complete control of myself so I did not continue. The occasional smoking of cigarettes ended when I was pregnant with my first child in 1982 at age 25. I started smoking cigarettes when I went away to college just because, in addition to a couple of swear words, both made me feel grown and independent. Now I detest both smoking and cussing. I am a social cocktail fruity drinker or wine drinker (even though I do not know how to order wine). I basically only drink with family members or if I am cruising or vacationing on a Caribbean island.

Water definitely contributes to body wholeness. It is suggested that you drink half of your body weight. My go-to water is Trader Joe's Alkaline water + Electrolytes, my daughter and I call it "Jesus Water" because it revitalizes our bodies and seems to help with joint pains. I also drink Poland Springs water. My husband feels that water is water but there are some waters that I do not like its taste. I try to drink at least 50 ounces of water per day, but my goal is 100 ounces daily. Staying hydrated is so important to every part of your body including your brain and heart health, in addition to your skin. I read that our bodies need water to lubricate the joints, drinking water forms saliva and mucus, water delivers oxygen throughout the body, and water boosts skin health and beauty. I definitely need a daily supply of water because for me any other drinks are empty unnecessary calories.

Massages are so needed for your wholeness. Massages trigger the release of endorphins and serotonin. These are natural chemicals produced by your body that improve your mood, reduce pain, and ease stress and anxiety. I started with massages because we, including me, feel that massages are for special occasions or a way to treat yourself when they should be part of your regular body routine. Tasha from T-2 Fitness suggests monthly massages because we deserve it. I am going to practice what I preach because I usually get a massage on special occasions or when I travel. I need to do better and schedule quarterly massages like I schedule everything else in my life.

I do not know how many times I am going to promote yoga in this book. Yoga is and still is difficult for me, but I see and feel improvements in my limberness, endurance, strength, balance, and breathing. Since doing yoga regularly my breathing/shortness of breath has improved tremendously. Every woman and every person should use weights in their exercise routine for both bone health and strength. I was advised to use weights three times per week. I prefer weight classes such as Body Pump in order to challenge myself. Cardio is also important to your exercise regimen. I love walking, it is recommended that we walk 10,000 steps per day. If you do not have some type of tracker app on your cellphone, or a fitness tracker please make the investment. Walking, Zumba, dancing, bike riding and/or other aerobic-type exercises should be incorporated into your exercise plan. I tend to overdo my walking therefore I am trying to limit my extensive walking to three times per week.

Since I am talking about the body, I want to include looking good and feeling good. I think that when we look good, we usually feel good. Many of us during the pandemic lived in things like sweats and pajamas. When virtual work began people started dressing from the waist up. I am not a make-up person in fact my hair stylist and friend Jeanette insist that I do my eyebrows and wear lipstick daily, but she knows that is not going to happen. I used to start each day wearing lipstick when I was working. Now I do my eyes (eyebrows, eyeliner, mascara, eye shadow) and wear lipstick on Sundays for church or if I go to an event. Full-face make-up has only happened maybe three times in my life; my wedding, seminary graduation pictures, and a photo shoot for ministerial head-shots. Now the fourth time is for this book. Make-up makes some people feel good so if that is you, do it. Getting your 'hair did' or getting a mani-pedi is your feel-good thing do it. Clothes and certain colors make some people feel good so if that is you do it. Losing weight makes some people feel good so if that is you do it. Whatever makes you look good and feel good please do it!

Whatever you feel is wrong with your body, keep pushing until you get to the root cause. I told you about my hip when I suffered from fatigue many years ago. When I was fatigued, it felt like I was walking through knee-high mud. I might have been in my late 20s when I complained to my previous doctor in the Bronx. It was during the beginning of HIV Aids, and she asked me questions about my and my husband's sex life insinuating, that we might have contracted Aids. Maybe 10 years later, another doctor's physician assistant in New Jersey decided to test my blood for Epstein-Barr Disease. Epstein Barr is a disease that is found mostly in Jewish women. This disease causes fatigue and joint pains, and it usually flares up because of stress and also seasonal changes. Recently, my sister Sharon complained about still being fatigued after retiring, and I suggested that she insist that her physician test her for Epstein-Barr Disease too, and she too has this disease. Because this disease is not usually found in Black women most physicians will not test you for it, especially because it is a more expensive test. I am glad that I finally had a health professional that listened to me and went the extra mile to help me. I tire easily and I am more tired than not tired each day but now I understand why and how to pace myself, (even though my husband does not think that I am slowing down or pacing myself). I take multivitamins and supplements daily to promote energy. I do all of my activities early because I know I have little to no energy by three o'clock. I am also now taking designated "rest" days.

Spirit

Much prayer! Spending alone time with God. I found that surrounding myself with a community of positive, faithful believers helps with my spiritual health, my spiritual growth, and my spiritual journey. I tend to lean towards the negative, so God has placed positive people in my life to cause me to do a U-turn back to positivity, to see things half full instead of half empty, which results in me giving reassurance to others. My mother would say "hand go - hand come." We often do not think about how words can affect our spirit. Words that we say, and words that people say to us, or say about us, can both positively or negatively affect you internally and externally. I mentioned before that the word 'cannot' cannot be in my family's vocabulary. I am asking you now to eliminate words that can limit you. I was talking to someone, and she told me that she has always been slow and takes her longer to comprehend things. She also said that people also told her that she was slow. I asked her to promise that she will never say that about herself again because I believe that you are speaking that into your spirit. Do not speak negativity into your spirit, and do not allow other people's negative words to enter your spirit.

I grew up in an era where I was called all type of black in a negative way because of my dark skin. I was teased for wearing not only eyeglasses but thick glasses. I went through stages of feeling overweight because of the thickness in my body and what society has emphasized as what beauty looks like. Having a flat nose was always mentioned in a harmful way. Believe it or not when I later in life embraced my natural hair in the 70s, I heard nappy hair comments. In the 80's people insisted that I cut my son's hair instead of corn-rolling it and wanted me to hot comb aka straighten my daughter's hair. I still promote being natural as I went from locs to a short natural cut. I am blessed to have a father who assured his wife and daughters of the beauty in their darkness, but it probably was when I went to an HBCU - Howard University in Washington, D.C. that I accepted me completely. I strongly encourage loving who you are and what you are on my own children. You can do all things through Christ that strengthens you (Philippians 4:13). You are more than a conqueror through Him that loves us (Romans 8:37). Words may not break our bones, but they do harm us. Words harm our spirit! Do not say harmful words to yourself, including 'I can't'. Do not say it, do not accept harmful words, and just as importantly do not speak harmful words to others.

Mindfulness and yoga are helpful in improving our spirit. Mindfulness and yoga encapsulate the mind, body, and spirit. In my sessions in meditation, I am learning that mindful yoga is so necessary for my wholeness as it releases my self-imposed stress. My spirit improves when my mind and body are balanced. Improvements in my physical, mental, and spiritual well-being are what I am striving for. I need to be faithful and diligent with doing these practices since they can help improve the serenity of my life, improve my circulation, trim, and firm up my body, reduce illness, give me better flexibility, strength, and balance, as well as learn to be mindful aka being present.

Wholeness

On April 26, 2022, I began wearing a hearing aid. Even though my hearing loss has been the butt of my family's playful taunts for many years. My audiologist Alex Malyarovich, SC. D. told me that you do not know what you do not hear until you hear it, and that is so true. I realized all the things that I did not hear until I started wearing my hearing aids. I was told that I did not hear certain sounds and I now realize that too as I utilize spell check, Alexa, and Google voice to help me spell words that I was hearing and saying words incorrectly while writing this book. I realized after my hearing aids that I relied on hearing by seeing. Now that people are wearing masks it gives me another reason for being thankful for the hearing aids. So many people who need to wear hearing aids refuse to wear them. Some will not wear them because they find them uncomfortable. My hearing aids are so comfortable that I have forgotten that I had them on while entering the tub or shower, as well as going to bed. Some people will not wear them because they are vain. I hope that this testimonial will help someone to be whole even in one of their import-ant senses. I heard on News Radio today that hearing loss is the third-highest chronic illness in older adults. Hearing aids are becoming more affordable and available in more places. I do not know what these other places offer with their hear-ing aids, but I am paying five hundred dollars a month for twelve months to pay for my hearing aids, which I did not think that I could afford, but God made a way. I wanted to purchase my hearing aids from a licensed audiologist who will continue the follow-up with me on my hearing improve-ment journey. My television and music are always loud, and I do not realize it unless someone points it out. I miss out on a lot of parts of conversations and pretend that I heard them. People talk loudly around me and repeat themselves so that I can hear them. Now with my hearing aids on high volume and loud voices are irritating to me. When I finally decided to pull the plug on giving in to wearing hearing aids it was a mental and emotional adjustment. Several years earlier I did go for an in-depth hearing test because of my hearing loss but I was also having inner ear issues so hearing aids were not a priority. This time when I was told by my ENT that I will need to wear a hearing aid she said that I would probably only have to wear one inside my left ear. It took me days to wrap myself around the fact that I would be wearing one hearing aid while convincing myself that it was okay because it would not be visible inside my ear. I was thinking that now I will be able to hear my Pastor during service because I sit to her right, and when she talks to me, I usually have to turn slightly to hear her through my right ear because my left ear has severe hearing loss. I realized my vanity during this process but when I was told that hearing loss also affects your brain and memory. My memory concerns started about fifteen years ago, around age 50 even though I never had a great memory, not even as a child when I needed to memorize poems or parts in a play. I have a mental process for remembering names and things that I am unable to explain but my recollection seems to be similar to my visual and tactile learning process. I have difficulty remembering things like names of well-recognizable artists and even well-known songs from my era. Writing things down, repeating things mentally, and associating new people's names with people that I know has also helped in remembering things and names. I also have a tendency of not completely paying attention to things and people or listening fully. My hearing started deteriorating about fifteen years ago, getting noticeably worst over the last ten years. I do puzzles, take classes, and take supplements (Krill fish oil, Ginkgo Biloba, and Phosphatidylserine) for brain health, if a hearing aid will help with my memory, I can do it. I recently heard that hearing loss can cause three things that I can promptly check off as pertaining to me: 1. Cognitive decline, 2. Depression, and 3. Social Isolation.

If you noticed I keep saying one hearing aid inside one ear but when I met with the audiologist, he explained to me that first I would have two hearing aids even though only my left ear has severe hearing loss while the right ear has moder-

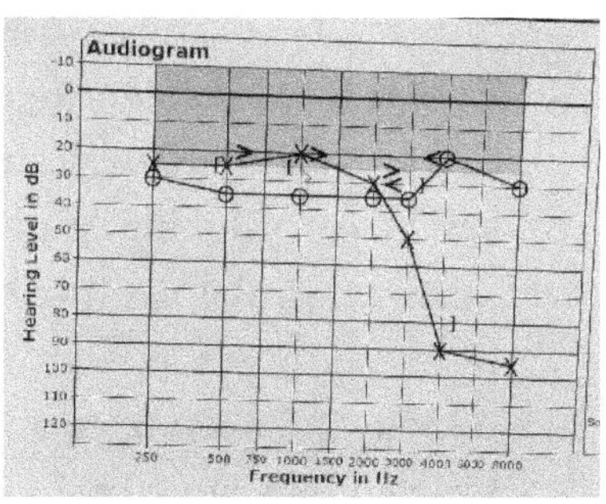

Hearing Test Results

ate hearing loss. He informed me that if I wore one hearing aid it would be in my right ear and not my left ear because of the right-ear left-brain connection (no I do not understand) but I was ready to start hearing better in both ears. The second shoe dropped when my audiologist also told me that with my hearing loss, I could not wear the inner ear hearing aids, I would have to wear the outer-ear hearing aids. I was not ready for this… I had to remind myself that although I work hard on looking good to the point of sometimes being a shopaholic and being coordinated wherever I go. I am also one who preaches to 'do you', do not worry about what others think, I am not my hair, embrace being different, and I always applaud uniqueness. It was time to turn the tables on me (even though I thought the tables were always turned. . . I did not realize that I had some vainness in me, now I know that it was not completely turned). All that to say I could not imagine 'me' wearing visible hearing aids. I told the audiologist that I had to think about it. When I got home and told my husband, he said what is there to think about? I called back and told the audiologist that I wanted gold color hearing aids. When I went back to the audiologist with Willie to be fitted for my hearing aids the audiologist had brown flesh-tone hearing aids ready for me assuming that is what I wanted. I explained to him that I was going to wear my hearing aids as accessories and not camouflaged, in fact, I went and had two additional sets of ear piercing to go with my new accessories. Coincidentally, or probably intentionally, Jeanette my hair stylist has lightened the top of my hair more and more until now to me it looks gold too. Hearing aids are supposed to be worn all the time so that your brain can adjust to them. You can adjust the volume, adjust the sound balance, and adjust the directional hearing. My hearing aid also has a masking-wearing feature to better hear people when they are wearing a mask. My son actually envies the Bluetooth feature because now I do not need earbuds to listen to music, listen to my audio books, or talk on the phone. Now I am just waiting for Signia to make this Bluetooth feature compatible with my read aloud feature on my computer. I currently wear my hearing aids proudly as another accessory, now I can really hear you.

When I told my Pastor that I was apprehensive about wearing noticeable hearing aids, she connected me to an extremely talented musician that we know, and whom I did not know that she wore hearing aids. We talked, and she told me about her journey. My Pastor also said that my wearing these hearing aids might inspire others to seek help to improve their hearing and/or wear their hearing aids. If I can help someone in this way, so be it!

17

I Still Do

I Still Do

I thought this book was finished until when I sat down to break bread with a small group of people, and someone was talking about how celebrity couples write books on marriage and then end up getting divorced. I am not an expert on marriage I got married on Saturday, August 23, 1980, and even after 42 years of marriage and co-chairing the Married Couples Ministry with my husband Willie, at my church First Baptist Church of Teaneck, I am finding out that I am still evolving. A lot of us are fascinated with the idea of marriage. I added this chapter just to say that marriage no matter what your dreams or fantasies of marriage since childhood might be; marriage is WORK!

To have an I Still Do attitude means to have a determination that I (actually we – it takes two – like

Wedding Pictures

hop duo Rob Base and DJ E-Z Rock sings, "it takes two to make the thing go right") I am going to make this work no matter what and it starts with having God in every aspect of each of your life individually and collectively in your marriage. The devil hates marriage and family. The devil's mission is to destroy both marriages and families, but we cannot let that happen. Let the devil know that you cannot have our marriages, and you cannot have our families. In Jesus' name, I pray!

It seems to me that couples are not getting married in their twenties anymore. Which I think is great. I even asked my twenty-year-old grandson Dasaiah to promise me that he will not get married before age thirty. Looking back on my marriage journey; when I was in my twenties like most twenty-somethings, I thought that I was grown, that I knew it all, and that no one could school me on anything in life. When in truth, I did not even know myself yet. I met Willie when I was twenty and he was nineteen in March of 1977. We met at the National Institute of Health - NIH Library in their Photo-duplication Department. We were both in a Stay in School program for high school and college students. We were both sophomores in college; me at Howard University in Washington, D.C., and him at Bowie State University in Bowie, Maryland. No, I was not robbing the cradle; my birthday was in January, and he turned twenty the next month after we met, in April. Even though I thought that he was too young because I was used to dating people older than me (my sister Sharon said that was the rule in dating because girls/women mature faster than boys/men). Willie tells everyone that I am older than him but technically I am older than my husband by only 103 days (three months and thirteen days). I kissed so many frogs before meeting Willie and Willie was different, and it was time for different.

I do pre-marital counseling for couples preparing to get married. I am very real with the couples that I counsel, but I know that nothing I say would change their minds, because lust or maybe even love has couples spelled bound, just like I was when I was planning to get married. Instead of pre-marital counseling, there should be pre-engagement counseling because once you get to the pre-marital counseling stage; the acceptance of marriage, and the planning of the upcoming nuptials there is usually no turning back.

I use Dennis Rainey's book 'Preparing for Marriage – Discovering God's Plan for a Lifetime of Love' in my pre-marital sessions. In the sessions, we discuss the eight chapters of the book that include questionnaires that each person must complete concerning their personal history and marriage expectations. Do we really think about how marrying your expected spouse most likely means marrying their entire family even though the bible says, "Therefore a man shall leave his father and mother, and shall cleave unto his wife: and they shall be one flesh"? Do we consider how our childhood, family dynamics, and family influences might impact a marriage? Do we even consider how our parents' relationship can impact our marriage expectations? There was a story that the father always turned off the bedroom light at night, so the bride expects that her husband should turn off their bedroom light before going to bed at night. We all go into marriage with past experiences and beliefs. We often think that our finances are our business, but many marriages end because of finances. Often, mothers tell their daughters to have their separate savings or checking accounts or a stash in their underwear drawer. It was like when we were told to keep a dime and then a quarter in our shoes if we had to use a payphone in case of an emergency. Now it is to make sure that you have your cellphone and a backup battery or make sure you keep five dollars in the glove compartment of your car just in case you run out of gas (now gas is almost five dollars a gallon); now it is twenty dollars or a gas or credit card in your wallet. I digress again… Finances are also discussed in my sessions. You should be able to discuss your finances and your expected spouse's finances and debts, strengths and weakness, and both of your pathologies on spending, saving, bill paying, and distributing money. Student loan repayment, car notes, and sometimes child support payments are real in addition to what goes into putting a roof over your head. I can go down a laundry list of things that put a ding in marriages besides relationships with in-laws, both of yours family dynamics, and finances, such as friendships, household expectations, sexual expectations, children (how many children / when to have children / raising children), employment and careers, previous traumas, religious and spiritual upbringing, and beliefs, as well as thoughts and dreams about vacations, leisure time and your futures individually and as a couple.

I do not have the statistics on any of these things, but more and more people of all ages seem to prefer shacking –up, a.k.a. living together, over legally saying I do. Some couples want to test the waters first and decide to start living together before marriage, with the intent that they will get married eventually. Some have no plans of getting married at all while they are living together. I am not sure about people's intentions with common law marriages. I am sure there are many, but I also do not know the legality in each jurisdiction. Either way, my father would say, "Why buy the cow when you can get the milk for free?". There are also many unwed parents raising children. I am not judging anyone's situation or relationship, but marriages seem to be diminishing, and divorces seem to be increasing.

I recently read in my daily devotion that these days many divorces are based on grounds of incompatibility, that couples complain that they have nothing in common. "If you were exactly the same, one of you would be unnecessary! The very reason you need each other is because you are different!" The reading goes on further to say, "the real issue isn't your differences - it's making those God-given differences work for you instead of against you." "It also says to start looking for what God is trying to teach you through your mate; you stop griping and start growing."

When I think about my marriage journey; at the beginning, I did not think about the fact that we will not be the same people forty years later. When Willie and I met we were both in school with plans that I would be a teacher and Willie's major was sociology. Willie was an athlete, he played football in both high school and college. We married at age twenty-three, which was too young. Willie proposed to me seven months after I graduated from Howard University so romantically (not!!!) in December in his parent's basement the night before I was going home for Christmas. We got married eight months after his proposal and wed seven months after Willie lost his father to colon cancer, which in hindsight getting engaged and married was probably too soon. My original plans after graduation were to move to Atlanta and attend Emory University for graduate school but I thought that marriage was a better offer, so I started graduate school at the University of Maryland. I think that I was conditioned, even though it was expressed to my mother in the 50s and not to me in the mid-'70s, that you go to meet your husband in college, marry and start a family. I heard the old-time question "are you going to college for a BS or a MRS.?"

Willie and I lived and worked in Maryland about four years after we got married. We had our first child three days after I turned twenty-six (Willie was twenty-five) in Maryland and our second child at age twenty-nine in the Bronx, New York. We moved to the Boogie Down Bronx so that I could start teaching. For five years I could not find a full-time teaching job in Washington, D.C. or Maryland and the inconsistency of being a substitute teacher in Washington, D.C. was not working for me, so I started working at Electronic Data Systems for a steady paycheck. This adulting, which consists of being responsible and paying bills, was not fun. Plus, I did not go to school for four years to answer phones for EDS for inquiries about Flood Insurance and then Black Lung Insurance. Speaking to individuals after the devastation of losing their belongings after a flood or others finding out that their conditions from working in coal mines have caused other illnesses like heart disease and their black lung insurance will not cover the cost of these expensive medications was a daily mental and emotional drain. I urgently needed to get on my career path.

We lived in the Bronx for three years with my parents in what was renovated for us as our "garden apartment," aka their basement, supposedly to save money to buy a house while I taught third grade. Even though I became a teacher, life happened, and Willie's career plans changed; he worked at Paid Prescription and Federal Express, aka FedEx, and eventually became a manager at FedEx.

Becoming a parent changes the dynamics of a marriage with each addition to your family. Relocating from my husband's birthplace to my hometown changed facets of our marriage especially when both of us have strong family circles and strong family influences. Purchasing a home that we were not financially ready for also put a strain on our marriage. Both of us working two jobs, me continuing in school, and transporting children to and from schools as well as to their various activities, while maintaining and balancing a household, a family, and a marriage, in itself was challenging.

In our **twenties,** everything was new, lust-filled, and exploratory, marriage and parenting were not always easy, but it was new, and we were young. Marriage was illuminating because neither of us knew what was involved in this thing called marriage. I mentioned before that God takes care of babies and fools, and we were not babies anymore. Our idea of marriage came from our vision of our parents' marriages, which was the outside-looking-in scenario. We were raised similarly but differently so our perceptions of a good marriage and raising children were also similar but different.

In our **thirties** life was more of a struggle, to be honest, it was not good at all. We purchased a new old house, a mortgage, and expected as well as unexpected bills. In our thirties we now have two children. I was commuting from New Jersey to New York dropping off children and then going to work. Both of us worked two jobs, and I was in school getting my second and third master's degrees. Our children began getting involved in town activities and sports. We joined a church in New Jersey and the whole family got involved in church services and activities. We both can honestly say that we have reached our breaking points many times in this decade. We thank God for the family members and church members that helped with the juggling of our schedules and being the village that helped raise our children. I do not know if I was moodier in my thirties or my forties, but I know that my moods also put a strain on our marriage. I was more mellow in my fifties and sixties, but now Willie, in his sixties, is very sensitive.

In our **forties**, the children were more self-sufficient. They were now going to school in New Jersey. In our almost mid to late forties, our children went away to college. The first adjustment was our son leaving, and then three years later, our daughter left to attend college. We traveled back and forth to North Carolina and Virginia to visit my son at North Carolina Agriculture and Technology and my daughter at Hampton University every chance we got. I was in seminary, and we struggled to pay three tuitions. Willie went into management, and I was an administrator which is another type of stress.

In our **fifties**, we had an empty nest and had to readjust to it being just the two of us again. We also had to find ways to adapt to being together and also finding our own space. We always said that we had a four-legged stool, and now we had to balance on a two-legged stool which is not as easy to stabilize. Many times, throughout the difficult years we jokingly, but not jokingly, said that when our children went away to school, we would go our separate ways. Our last child left the nest in 2004.

We also became grandparents and began traveling to Florida when our son moved to Florida to work after he graduated and then to North Carolina when our son and his family moved to North Carolina.

Now in our **sixties**, we are retired and have to figure out who we are as a couple without children or jobs as distractions. We had to reevaluate our plans for our life and our future. In fact, we are constantly re-assessing both. We had to decide what we wanted, liked, and disliked as individuals and as a couple living in this new reality.

This timeline paragraphs seem simplistic, but there were a lot of ups and downs, many peaks and valleys, and a lot of stretching almost to our breaking point, but through the Grace of God, we made it through.

Who we are at sixty-five is not who we were at twenty-three. Willie did not marry a minister, in fact, he married someone who was just discovering her religious identity. He did not marry someone with a severe allergy to one of the few fruits he would eat, which causes our social outings to be limited and cautious. We are unable to go to cozy entertainment places like jazz clubs and dinner cruises because of the possibility of strawberries on the menu. Willie did not expect a woman with monthly PMS mood swings and the hormonal changes of menopause. Willie did not know because I did not know about the inconsistent behaviors that OCD and ADHD entails. I remember my sister Sharon telling me right before I got married that everyone would not be as neat as you. I think that I put off being a real nag about it until we retired and were spending more time at home together.

On the other hand, I married an active athlete who now because of sports and his type of physical employment has limited mobility with bad knees, shoulder dislocation, and surgeries on his wrists, back, and neck. Even after college football he would go out and join pickup games and play basketball every chance he got. He also loved playing racquetball. Willie would play softball with our church competing against other houses of worship. Willie now has a sedentary lifestyle. Swimming is now his sport, mainly for therapeutic and fitness reasons. I may weigh over fifty pounds more since we got married, and he claims credit for filling me out in all the right places, although there is some extra filling out that I can do without. But Willie weighs more than one hundred pounds since we got married and that athletic physique is long gone, there are a lot of extras that he can do without also.

I can be very impulsive, and sometimes Willie will feed into it, but most of the time he brings me back with his practicality. My dream vacations are seeing the entire world and exploring each destination. While my husband's dream vacations are visiting family and friends in his hometown in Washington, D.C., and Maryland, visiting his daughter in Virginia and visiting his son and grands in North Carolina and being inactive or relaxing during his visits. Willie cannot be couped up in a house, and I have to literally force myself to leave the house. Willie loves driving, and I wasn't a fan of driving or being a passenger on his drives until we started traveling to the fifty states three years ago.

My daughter expressed her thoughts about something that she observed that I never thought about. She said that Willie and I, from being together for so long, enable each other, but I said that we each have our own established roles. But she pointed out that when one becomes incapacitated, the other does not know how to do the other specified tasks. She has me thinking.

Willie and I are so different. I am an introvert, and he is more of an extrovert, but we both have a quiet spirit, and we can both turn it on or turn it off when we need to. We have totally different ways of socializing and communicating. Willie welcomes company (he has the gift of hospitality) and I love the quiet of being alone. When it comes to cellphone use, Willie prefers talking over texting while I prefer texting over talking to anyone on the phone. Willie is mild-mannered, and I can be feisty. Willie is a natural-born coach and encourager a cheerleader to and for everyone and I tend to be critical, straight no chaser. I am organized and obsessive-compulsive, and Willie, for lack of a better word, is more carefree. What many might consider a small thing, but I have to make my bed when I get up and have to go to bed at night in a made bed, while Willie takes a daily nap and will not pull up the covers to remake the bed. I eat dinner early (around 5 p.m. - 6 p.m.) and Willie eats dinner late because he worked nights for 20 years at FedEx (he eats around 9 pm – 10 pm). We, more Willie than me, compromise on Sundays and eat dinner together at 6:30 pm. Sunday breakfasts and dinners together are non-negotiable. I go to bed early, and Willie goes to bed late. Willie is an early riser and wants to meet in the morning, he loves sunrises. While I am fine with meeting in the afternoon, and I am fine with sunsets. Willie loves sports, mainly football and basketball and I can care less about any sport. I love to dance, and Willie does not dance. I tend to see things half empty, while Willie sees things half full. I can be a little hyper, and Willie is very laid back. Willie is flexible and will accept change, while I am more inflexible and rigid. I struggle with accepting change. Willie's retirement plan is to sit back and relax and take daily naps while my plan is to do, see, and do everything that I can and see the world. But with all of our differences, We Still Do!

So based on this chapter in this book and my journey, you should understand that compromising (the work of both parties) is the key to a healthy marriage. There is no fifty-fifty percent in marriages. Both of you need to give one hundred percent with the knowledge that the percentages may change as the need arises. Willie's and my input percentages changed for different aspects of our lives throughout the years. Sometimes he gave more to our relationship, more to raising our children, and more to the home, and then other times the tables changed, and I gave more. Throughout our marriage, like most marriages, the giving and the taking have and will change. It is accepting the role changes that keep a marriage strong enough not to break. I am pretty sure that Willie agrees with my analogy. Willie just told his daughter that marriage is what you accept. He said, "if you accept thirty percent in the beginning, then you will have that thirty percent throughout your marriage". I do agree that if you start out unbalanced in your marriage, balance in the giving and taking, it will probably be next to impossible to become balanced later before there is a shifting of role percentages.

Dating is so important in a marriage. We suggest that you date at least once per month. Setting a monthly date on your anniversary day or weekend will help with dating consistency. We were married on the 23rd, so there is a reminder on our phones that the 23rd is date night, but it could be any time of the day. It does not have to be an expensive or elaborate date. One day a month, you need to set aside time for each other. It could be meeting somewhere for breakfast or lunch. It could be fixing a special candle lights dinner with some low jazz or R&B love songs playing in the background. It could be taking time out from your busy schedule to make love. If you think about it little things can be special like a foot massage or even a scalp massage. I got us a massage table during the pandemic because I am always ready for a lavender-scented baby oil or lotion, head-to-toe or toe-to-head – back-to-front or front-to-back massage from my husband. If the two of you can fit in the tub together, a couple's bubble bath or even a couple's shower can be a date night foreplay delight. Watching a movie together and actually sitting closely next to each other instead of one person on the chair and the other on the couch. Going for a walk together. Going for a mani-pedi together. Holding hands. Touching each other. Dance together. Do something different from the everyday routine together at least once per month to refresh your relationship.

Communication is another important aspect of a marriage, and that important factor has always been missing in my marriage no matter how much I try to promote it in our marriage. It has been said that women marry their fathers and men marry their mothers. Like my mother, I, too, have one-sided conversations, but my mother-in-law also shared a lack of matrimonial communication too. All three of us married similar men when it comes to communication.

In the Married Couples Ministry that we facilitate at First Baptist Church of Teaneck, we are always open and honest about our marriage and that we did and probably continue to do all the things that you should not do in a marriage. We have the 'do as we say and not as we did' scenario. I guess that we have made the mistakes and have all of the bumps and bruises of a marriage, and we can tell our survival stories so that you do not have to make those same mistakes.

Sometimes I feel like rethinking telling prospective married couples that it is great that they complete each other with their differences. It is not that I do not think that it is true, I truly believe that God placing two different people together is like the Bible describes in 1 Corinthians 12, how our body parts and Spiritual gifting each has its own function coming together to make us whole. The only reason I am reconsidering my perspective is because I now know through experience that I need to elaborate about the long run. The differences will not always seem as though it is working for the betterment of marriages. God does put two unalike people together to complete each other. What you are not, the other one is. I found that many years later, these differences can become annoying, especially when the distractions are removed, and the routines change; once your nest is empty and/or you are a retiree. But now I am finding, as my husband is recuperating from surgery, that I miss and appreciate those contributing differences. I believe if you stick it out for the long game, everything in your lives together comes full circle.

I do not think that anybody really takes seriously the traditional vows and what they involve "In sickness and in health." We do not expect it, but what are our limits on sickness? As well as the vow "Until death do we part" again, I do not know the statistics on how many marriages end before death. Marriage is of God, and I pray daily, and I pray that you will too, pray for all marriages.

"We are never too old to become better versions of ourselves."

18

Aging

When you are young and you hear people say that time flies you know that is not true for you because you wait what seems like forever for your birthday to come, you wait for Christmas, you wait for school to start, and you wait for summer to begin. I vividly remember dressing up to take this picture in our apartment in 21 West 116th Street in the Village of Harlem, prior to moving to 1695 Madison Avenue in the Village of Harlem at age 5 - 60 years ago.

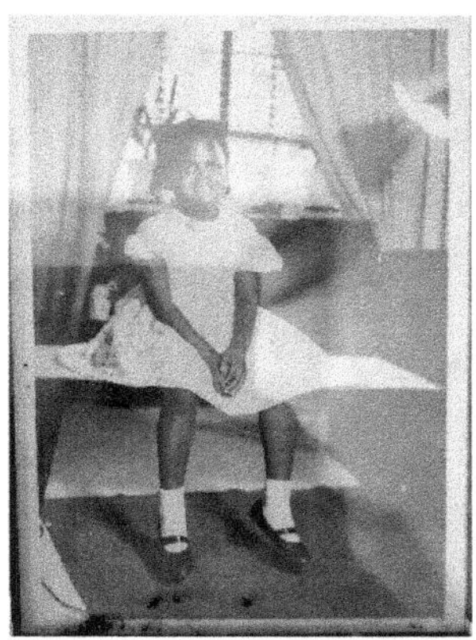

Age 5

This chapter on aging was one of the last chapters that I added to this book. It may look like a laundry list on my outlook on aging. I was in the middle of my Body Pump class, lifting about 13.5+13.5+5.5 on the bar = 32.5-pound weights on my shoulder and doing squats, looking around through the wall-to-wall mirrors at the variant ages of those in the class and thinking about how much weight I can squat now and how much weight I used to be able to squat, lift, and pump. Even though I am consistent with my weight classes it seems as though I am losing strength.

This aging chapter is not only about my aging process but it consists of a mishmash of perspectives on aging as well as stages of adulting. My sister Sharon sent me a text this morning that "We are never too old to become better versions of ourselves". I am constantly working on becoming the best possible version of Sheila.

I think that we all can say what we could do or used to do or feel at a certain age. I was at a baby shower listening to 36 and 37-year old's talking about their aging. I keep reminding my daughter who just turned 36 and my son who will be turning 40 that they sound so old. Even though I was married with two children at their age I feel as though I had more stamina and fewer ailments than they have.

So many things in our life change as we get older. From head to toe for me, my hair is thinning. They talk about dimming eyesight. I wore glasses almost all my life. I think that I wore my first pair of glasses at age five. I started wearing contacts when I got married at age 23. I stopped wearing contacts as I got older because I could not see clearly with them anymore. When I got a certain age, I was told that I needed reading glasses with my contacts. I tried wearing a suggested nearsighted lens in one eye and a farsighted lens in the other eye. I also tried bifocal contacts. I even tried wearing contacts with reading glasses as a last resort. I was almost blind as a bat without eyeglasses growing up but now, I am taking off my glasses to see better, especially to read. I could not understand that when my mother used to go around without glasses when she got older after they were a fixture on her face most of her life. Now, this is another way that I am my mother and I too keep misplacing my glasses from taking my glasses off and leaving them in various forgetful places. It is so true what they say that you turn into your mother as you get older.

Continuing with from head-to-toe aging. I have been losing my hearing in my left ear throughout the years and now I wear hearing aids. I hurt my left shoulder walking our Akita puppy that kept pulling the leash several years ago and I still have re-ocurring discomfort. I hurt my lower back twice, breaking up fights at work and it does not take much to remind me of the injury. I have bursitis in my right hip. There seems to always be fluid on my knees. I had carpal tunnel in my left wrist from driving and typing during the 5 ½ years at seminary. I hurt my ankle while working out. My feet have been hurting on and off since I started teaching in 1984. This is not a woe-is-me I am feeling bad scenario, it is a quick synopsis of my head-to-toe aging narrative.

When you get to a certain age you realize that it is true that time flies. It seems like the older you get the faster time moves. I tell parents to enjoy every minute of their child's life because even though it does not always seem like it but children grow so fast. I tell teenagers and twenty-somethings to not rush their life. I always hurried my life preparing myself for the next. As a child I rushed my life navigating towards older people including my older brother and sister and their friends. In high school, I spent part of my afternoons in an elementary school assisting teachers and students as well as I took classes at Bronx Community College for college credits when I should have enjoyed the high school experience. Again, in college, I did not take the opportunity to experience campus life at Howard University. I convinced my parents to allow me to get a car during my sophomore year, so I started working at the National Institute of Health to pay for my car note and gas. I also persuaded my parents that it would be just as feasible to let me move off campus and get an apartment in my junior year of college as it was to pay for a dorm room on campus (the math still does not make sense to me but I allowed both of my children to convince me of the same thing when they were in college). I missed out on almost three years of the college campus experience rushing into being grown. I wish I could say that I was speeding-up my life until I hit 65, but I cannot because I am now preparing for 70. I too still rush my life away.

As you look back over your life you wish you would have taken more time to do certain things, taken the time to try certain things, and taken the time to enjoy certain things. I do have that feeling sometimes but through God's grace and mercy, and if it is God's will, I will be able to use my time wisely to do, try and enjoy new things for a long time to come.

As you age you discover new components of every part of your body mostly through pain and/or discomfort. You can predict the impending inclement weather through aches and stiffness in your body. Certain movements can cause discomfort, pain, and/or dislocation of various parts of your body.

Different parts of my body take turns aching. I have been to the orthopedic and physical therapy for my lower back more than once, my shoulder, my knee, my ankle (no PT), and now my lower back again and hip. My orthopedists and most of my physical therapy are done at North Jersey Orthopedic Specialty in Teaneck. I remember getting a cortisone shot in my knee after a slow knee injury recovery so that I could walk in my first 5K Race in Norfolk, Virginia, on June 1, 2019, with my son through Tasha and T2-Fitness. It ended up pouring down rain right before the race, and the race had to be canceled. My doctor advised against me doing the race, and I did not listen, so I guess it was from his mouth to God's ears. Did I also mention before that unexpected weather seems to follow me? I still have to do a 5K Race because it is on my must-do list.

I am now one of those seniors that smell like garlic, and some type of rub, not Bengay but Sombra Warm Therapy natural pain-relieving gel, Salonpas Pain Patches, or Max Freeze roll-on for my back, and now Voltaren Arthritis Gel for my bursitis. I season all my foods with garlic, turmeric, and black pepper, even my Sunday morning grits. I would always comment about the old people's smell now I am that old person with old people's smells.

As I am aging, surprisingly, I am just learning how to, what I call; "real cooking". My mother did all the cooking when I was growing up. My father would only eat my mother's cooking. My apartment-mate Gwen taught me how to cook some things when we had an apartment together in my junior year at Howard University, but she did most of the cooking for Ronda and me. Gwen complained that I did not know how to use a knife to peel potatoes so that she could make potato salad. I just recently became a sharp knife user. At that time the only knife that I used was a butter knife, for my buttered cinnamon toast and for my peanut butter sandwiches. I would use a steak knife to cut meat, but I had a fear of sharp knives since I was in Junior High School when a friend of mine was playing around with an open pocketknife throwing it up in the air and catching it until one time it landed in my thigh. I still have that scar over 50 years later. Now I can use sharp knives and even dice onions, without cutting, not my finger as often, but sometimes I end up cutting my fingernail.

My niece Shannon just taught me how to make gravy so that I could make her Uncle some smothered porkchop even though I do not eat pork. I make and can make every vegetable and meat.

I have brine turkey breast for the last two years for the last two Thanksgivings with instructions from my son and my cousin Bryan. I have been making Thanksgiving meals since my mother went home to be with the Lord four years ago, using box stuffing and jar gravy. I can make most Italian foods but using jar sauces, aka gravies. I tried making my own sauce using an Italian co-worker's recipe but prefer jar sauces. My husband fries the best fried chicken (do not tell my son, but my husband's fried chicken is better than his), so I do not even bother trying to fry chicken, but I can fry mouth watering fish and shrimps. I am a Geechee, but I cannot make rice and do not want to either. I probably ate rice every day for the first eighteen years of my life, so I really do not have a craving for that carbohydrate, but I love rice at a Jamaican, Spanish, or Thai restaurant. I will eat good red rice anytime especially if it tastes like my grandmother's or my mother's down-home cooking red rice. Being a Geechee, I must confess that I cannot make hoppin' johns, but I keep saying that I will try to learn how (which means learning how to make "real" rice) for my traditional New Year's dish.

When turning 65 you are eligible for Medicare, which is great, but the transition is not always great. I am typing this after year two of Medicare and making sure that Willie and I have the correct supplemental plan and coverage. I advise you to start your research on supplemental insurance before age 65. I thought that once you select a plan that unless you decide to change it the plan will remain the same. This is year three for Willie because of his disability and for some reason, in year two his supplemental plan dropped his dental and vision coverage. Now, right this moment, we are going through the "can you hold" scenario as well as speaking to several agents and supervisors to make sure that we receive the coverage that we want and need. My experience last year with getting supplemental insurance coverage was a complete nightmare, which resulted in me going two months without supplemental health insurance coverage, even though I started the process in October, and you know by now that patience is not a virtue that I possess. My daughter-in-law brought me back to earth and reminded me that there are many people who only have Medicare coverage without supplemental options. Again, I thank God as I pray for others!

I am actually finding it not as difficult, not easy, but not as difficult to lose weight as I am getting older maybe because working is not getting in my way. Work stress is known to prevent weight loss. I still struggle with the last 10 pounds and sometimes 15 pounds, but it was always more than 15 pounds that needed to come off prior to retirement. Now my knees feel better, and I have more mobility.

Most people complain about menopause, but I will take the occasional hot flashes over monthly heavy menstruations and cramps any time. I used to watch people sweating and fanning for years before I joined the club, I was a late bloomer. I still have had only an occasional unexpected flash. When I eat spicy foods, which I love, I know to expect a drenching. I am warmer now but not flashing. With menopause, my sexual desires have increased. My husband asks where this Sheila was when we were in our thirties. My reply is raising children and helping with trying to make ends meet. We both worked multiple jobs throughout our younger years to pay our mortgage, car notes, and all the other bills that come with adulthood, parenthood, and home ownership in Bergen County New Jersey at age 30. The lust in our 20's turned to tiredness in our 30s and 40s. I think that menopause symptoms are linked to your diet. I observed that those with the worst dietary eating plans have the worst menopause symptoms. I might have bugged my gynecologist for about 8 years about why I have not gone into menopause. My mother did not remember when she started, and I went through menopause before my older sister Sharon, so I did not have a gage. It finally happened at age 58. Everything happened at age 58. I shed my monthly and my job at age 58.

I used to have a nervous head twitch in my late teens and in my early twenties around the same time that I was losing the sides of my hair because of the stress of my undergraduate studies. Now I am beginning to notice a shaking of my left hand, my left leg, and sometimes my head that my sister Shelley had me ask my doctor about Parkinson's disease.

I have a very high pitch voice but when I began preaching it became an indescribable noticeable nervous shrill which I thank God has gone away (the shrill not the high pitch voice). But sometimes when speaking in public it sounds like I am getting ready to cry. As I am aging, I do not know if my voice is changing or that I am paying more attention to my voice, especially with hearing aids.

This is very personal, but I said that I will be open and honest about everything, including my aging process as I recall or notice things. I suffered with hemorrhoids during and after my two pregnancies. Now as I am aging, I go through bouts of constipation. I take psyllium capsules twice a day to stay regular, as well as flaxseeds and chia seeds, but sometimes the irregularity causes hemorrhoids even with drinking plenty of water daily. But I also get anal tearing or cracking called anal fissures. I use Preparation-H for hemorrhoids and Neosporin for anal tears. I used to have occasional anal cramping. I pray that I have outgrown that type of cramping because I have not figured out how to remedy those cramps.

While I am being embarrassingly honest as I am aging, flatulence from more foods is becoming more evident and less controllable. Beans, cabbage, and collard greens were always a given but now onions, tomato (my favorites), and tomato sauces as well as anything with mayonnaise causes me gas. I am not a mayonnaise person, but I do like tuna, turkey, and potato salads, as well as coleslaw and broccoli slaw. As I am growing older, I realize that my body does not allow me to do a lot of the things I used to do or eat a lot of the things I used to eat without suffering the consequences later.

As I am aging foods have been causing a variety of reactions; cheese causes me to become nasal and congested. Sodium causes me to become bloated, especially my hands and knees as well as headaches and becoming dizzy. Sodium also causes extra fluid in my knees. Lack of water causes constipation. Spicy food causes me to have hot flashes. Dairy products such as ice cream are like Russian Roulette; sometimes I am fine and sometimes I am not, but flatulence is a given. I do not even try to drink cow's milk. I love Califia Almond Coconut Milk, I do not drink cups of milk, but I do add this milk to everything including scrambled eggs, grits, and oatmeal.

My body has become so sensitive to food. I can not let lemons sit in my water for long periods of time without causing me to break out into a rash. I am highly allergic to strawberries. It has been getting worse as I got older. I ate strawberries as a child but as an adult, the allergy is now airborne and has become deadly. I was wearing a mask in grocery stores before COVID-19 mandates. I now take daily: Cetrizine; an allergy medication and Pepcid to prevent a possible severe episode. I feel that these preventive medications that I take daily are desensitizing my reaction to strawberries, but I am not going to test it to find out if it is true. I have been in the emergency room twice because of allergies. Once because someone brought strawberries to the church, and I passed by the church kitchen on my way upstairs to the church's sanctuary. The second time even though the venue was given strict instructions that there were to be no strawberries for an engagement shower, like so many other places they garnished the desserts with strawberries and figured that my dessert would be without the garnish. Once the waiter passed by me, I was done! I had to run out of many events and restaurants because of strawberries. I am going into these specific details about the severity of food allergies because some people think that by taking a Benadryl or sticking yourself with an EpiPen then you are good and that is all to it because of what we see on television. Using my EpiPen is my absolute last resort. I will drink a ton of water, take my Pepcid and Cetirizine tablets that I keep with me always, then if necessary, a Benadryl tablet knowing that it will make me drowsy. After all that, if I do not feel my throat opening back up, I will have no other choice but to stick myself or have someone stick me with my EpiPen and either head to the emergency department or call 911. All of this is done in a split-second time. I have graduated from flushing my system with water, to popping an allergy medication, to taking Benadryl and sleeping it off, to my throat closing – using an EpiPen – and then oxygen in an ambulance or emergency room – staying in the hospital until my oxygen levels are good – then being sent home with a corticosteroids pack of a stepdown steroid regiment for seven days. Then eventually, after about two weeks, my lungs would get back to normal after seeing my allergist and paying a co-pay for two to three weekly visits. I carry an EpiPen at all times. I try to remember to RSVP to events with stipulations about my allergies. I am cautious when eating out; staying observant of breakfast foods and desserts because it seems as though strawberries have become increasingly more popular. I am strategic when going into grocery stores and fruit markets to avoid strawberries aisles. The thinking is that manufacturers are using something to enhance the smell of fruits like strawberries. If you have not noticed you will notice now that a lot of stores are placing their large, lush strawberries in the front of their stores with a noticeably strong aroma. Many people are aware of the severity of peanut allergies, that same cautious mindset should be taken for all allergies. I am thanking God that there have not been any more allergic reaction incidents.

I do not know what is happening with my nails. My husband's fingernails and toenails grow long and hard as nails (pun intended), but my fingernails are always breaking, and like my mother, one of my nails split down the middle from the cuticles to the tip. I take calcium and collagen with biotin daily to help with the strengthening of my nails. I mentioned that my dermatologist recently informed me that I can stop wasting money on collagen. Because of my impatience, I am not a regular at the nail salon. A nail attendant found it odd how my fingernails are layered and will split.

As long as I can remember I always purchased hard bristle toothbrushes until my doctor told me maybe ten years ago that it is not good for the enamel on your teeth. I have sensitive teeth, so I brush with Sensodyne toothpaste. I also switched to Oral B electric toothbrushes. But I am losing the enamel on my teeth. I started brushing with Sensodyne Enamel Protection toothpaste, but it is probably too late. I do not want to lose my smile.

I used to have undiagnosed dizziness and went through a lot of unbearable tests and useless medication until my now retired ENT Dr. Katz informed me that it was from too much sodium. I now know if I intake too much sodium I can expect dizziness, a headache, and stiff puffy fingers. Now I also feel the extra fluid in my knees. I have manageable high blood pressure through medication that Dr. Denker and I think that it is hereditary because I was raised not using salt and I do not add salt to my food even while cooking. Yes, many people complain that my food is bland. My cholesterol level is either borderline or a little above which may also be hereditary. Because of my intentional lifestyle, diet, and exercise both my high blood pressure, high cholesterol, and even sometimes glucose level sums up to heredity and aging. It is important that you know your numbers, that you are mindful of the foods you ingest, and that you read labels, especially in processed food and even the so-called healthy foods. When trying to lose or maintain weight a weight journal could be helpful as well as a fitness app like My Fitness Pal.

Another example of me becoming more sensitive to things as I age; I do not like taking medication, I prefer finding alternatives such as herbs or teas, but I remember that I was having either severe back or knee pains, so I started taking pain relief medicines that contained ibuprofen. I started getting dark blotches on my back and the back of my knees, and I had to switch to acetaminophen because I found out after the fact that ibuprofen can cause hyper-pigmentation. I also had to stop taking the recommended daily Bayer aspirins that helps prevent blood clots from forming. I now take them every other day.

There are things that I cannot explain as I age that are happening to my body. Three examples are that sometimes I get this stiffness cramping in my fingers where I cannot move them. My doctor changed my hydrochlorothiazide - water pill from every day to every other day to alleviate that from happening too often. I went through a phase of my legs cramping when driving and working out. I increased my water intake, I started taking magnesium citrate twice a day, and I used to bring coconut water with me on road trips to drink to relieve the cramps. Sometimes the cramps are so bad that all I can do is pull over on the side of the road and try to rub and stretch it out. The third aging phenomenon is my brain-freeze or when my brain cannot switch over or comprehend the next thought usually when I am asked a question that I know the answer but for some reason, I cannot get it out. I find myself mentally processing questions and conversations as though I am dual lingo.

I find that I also cramp when I stretch or during yoga. I was getting a pain in my stomach as though a muscle was protruding. I checked it out with my doctor, and he informed me that it was gas. It is like a ball that I can actually touch but I thank God that it is nothing serious and I started massaging it out. . . aging!

I mentioned that I take 4 prescription medications and 13 supplements each day. To remember to take all of my medication I use a medicine case that is set up for 7 days a week with 4 sections each day divided for morning, noon, evening, and bed. I take medication 3 times per day with the noon and evening being taken at the same time after I eat my first meal. I take my morning medication in the morning as soon as I wake up and my bedtime medication before going to bed at night. Because my medicine is set up in this medicine case, I now remember to take all of my medication each day. I mention this because so many people have told me that they forget to take their medication or they cannot remember to take vitamins. I do know that preparation and consistency can form new daily habits. You can also set reminder timers on various devices (cellphones, smart watches, Alexa/ Google/Siri).

My sister Sharon warned me that at age 65 you start losing the fullness in your breast. I got a similar warning about breastfeeding. I guess time will tell but I hope that my weight-lifting class will help keep my breast from atrophying and becoming like pancakes. But I found out through Google that "with age woman's breasts lose fat, tissues, and mammary glands, due to the decrease in the body's production of estrogen that occurs at menopause. Without estrogen, the gland tissue shrinks, making the breasts smaller and less full."

Hair stopped growing under my arms which is great for my Saturday evening underarm shaving but there is always a new fresh strand popping up under my chin at least every two to three weeks. I constantly inspect for mustache hairs to pluck.

I used to think that I was cold-natured, and Willie was hot-natured now I am always hot (without the hot flashes) and Willie is often cold. It becomes an interesting turn of events with covers and ceiling fan on and covers and ceiling fan off in our bedroom.

While working I had regular appointments with my podiatrist because my work as both a teacher and an administrator required me to be on my feet all day. Since retiring I rarely have to see my podiatrist. But a few years ago, my ankle started hurting for no apparent reason, which orthotics helped relieve the pain. Recently my foot in the toe area started hurting and cramping while just leisurely walking without my New Balance 860 sneakers.

I had to give up my cute and fashionable Nike, Adidas, and Puma sneakers for New Balance sneakers. I was having knee and lower back reoccurring pain, and someone recommended that I try New Balance sneakers especially because I have slightly wide feet. I always considered New Balance sneakers for older people, and I had to admit that with me aging maybe that it was time for a change. Now the New Balance company are making fashionable sneakers and clothing for all ages. When I went to the New Balance store in Hasbrouck Heights, New Jersey they analyzed and scanned my feet, measured my feet, and then recommended their 860-style sneakers based on my sneaker usage. Since wearing these sneakers there has been a noticeable difference in my body aches.

Some of this forgetfulness that I am pointing out I also hear from people of all ages: Going to get something and forgetting what you were going to get. Forgetting to turn your keyless car off while leaving the car. Misplacing your car/house keys.

Trying to get out the car without unbuckling your seatbelt. Mixing up the names of your children or siblings.

As I am writing this I often become concerned about my mind. What is going on in my mind is indescribable, sometimes it feels like a fog, and it seems as though things are behind this veil of fog, and I am constantly trying to push them forward. Even with writing this book when something comes to mind, I have to quickly jot it down or type it unless I lose it. With retirement, I wanted to finally relax my mind, but I did not want my mind to start deteriorating. In conversations now, I struggle with remembering words and names or getting them out as well as the pronunciation of words. I often struggle with remembering how to spell even the simplest words. I usually have to think longer than I used to. I second guess myself, if I put on deodorant, turned off the light and/or stove, turned on the dishwasher, washing machine, or dryer, and if I put things away or where I placed things. In writing this book I thank God for Google, Alexa, and the thesaurus to help me with the wording that is behind that veil that I mentioned. If this is the beginning of dementia, I am glad that I am expressing it in this book. I often wonder when my mother started noticing her forgetfulness. She always joked that she needed to double up on her Ginkgo biloba. We, as a family, started noticing her changes more after she turned 80 and she started getting lost while driving. It could have been much earlier because now I see that there are ways to camouflage the deterioration of your mind. I need my family to know what is going on as it is going on. I try to keep my mind occupied with classes, books, and puzzles. I used to be a reader but now I am more of a listener of audio books. I used to be a multitask but now I have to be intentional with focusing on one or two things at a time because my mind is not able to do the juggling anymore. With any change in routine, I seem to be confused. I am still trying to recover almost three years later from being forced to adjust my lifestyle during the pandemic.

My neurologist Dr. Oller-Cramise has told me not to be too concerned about my memory, especially after taking a battery of tests which results indicates above average in memory. I feel that I am doing all the right things to have a healthy body and also a healthy mind, but I still feel limited in the mind. I still almost literally kick myself when I forget things that I feel that I should not forget, especially because I am so anal with everything that I do. I write down just about everything. I make lists. I have notes in my room, in my car, on my phone notes, and on my phone calendar notes, so that I can remember things, so I will not forget things. If there is anything that I have to ask a physician I have it in my phone calendar notes under my appointment date. I basically wake up and go to bed jotting down things that I need to remember. It seems as though once I note it, I seem to remember it better. But I am still often forgetful. I also set alarms on my phone for events that sometimes include a second earlier alarm as either a reminder or a preparation for the event. My Alexa device has also been helpful with reminders. Not that any of these practices will deter memory loss but I do not want to be the fourth generation of mothers being taken care of. My great-grandmother was taken care of by her daughter Sissie, my grandmother because her legs had to be amputated because of diabetes. My grandmother Sissie and my mother had to be taken care of by their daughters because of dementia and then deteriorating health. They say that we are in the sandwich generation because we are living longer. I do not want my children or even my grandchildren (we tease that we have to be nice to our grands because one of our grandchildren will have to take care of us) to have to change their lives to take care of either one of us or that we have to become caregivers for each other.

But I pray that my husband and I have a long mentally and physically healthy independent life together.

I wish my mother was more open about her aging process. Now I want to talk more to my husband about his aging process as we age and change but it does not seem like something that he wants to discuss. This is another one of our lack of communication topics. I am so proactive in everything including my health, which I am trying to get him to be also.

As I am aging, I am finding it difficult to figure out my own identity outside of being a daughter, a sister, a wife, a mother a grandmother, and a minister. Who is Sheila without the labels, influences, and expectations of others?

This aging process is so interesting… but I will take observing my aging process over the alternative!

"

I pray that this part of my journey will help you make sense of your loss(es). We all have experienced some type of loss.

"

19

RIPower

I did not even think about having a chapter on loss - Rest In Power until Willie and I was discussing parts of the chapter on marriage, which was supposed to be the last chapter, when he pointed out that my loss(es) was another intricate part of my journey. I pray that this part of my journey will help you make sense of your loss(es). We all have experienced some type of loss. A loss of a pet, a loss of a friendship, a loss of a relationship, a loss of a job, a loss of health, and also a loss of a person.

After my husband's recent surgery, he said that I'm obsessed with death. To be honest I tend to fixate on waiting for the next shoe to drop. I remember every death notification that I received, and I guess in the back of my mind I'm almost always preparing for the next notification. I also know that you are never prepared for that notification. If truth be told I start to get concerned (because I try not to worry because you cannot pray and worry so I choose to pray) when my family travels and I do not hear from them right away. Also, when Willie is late getting home from anything based on my timetable of his ETA.

I used to be the most emotional one in my family. I am stronger now but do not get me wrong I am stronger, but I am ready to cry, and I will cry if you cry. Willie strongly advised me early in my ministry not to cry in the pulpit because he used to think that crying showed weakness, and as a woman in this ministerial role, the congregation needed to witness strength until Willie began to have difficulty holding in his own emotions as he got older. I also think that he has come to realize now that both strong women and strong men should not hold in their feelings. We in church leadership should be our authentic selves regardless of gender as we serve God's people.

I was in my studio apartment on November 19, 1978, almost three months into my senior year of college when I was notified that my maternal grandmother passed away. She was in the hospital scheduled to have her leg amputated from diabetes just like her mother. I was devastated because I could not imagine my life without Sissie. I grew up with Sissie being a constant presence in my life. She fried fish and red rice on Fridays for our family dinners, we ate watermelon and crabs on newspapers on her fire escape, and she took us to Coney Island, and once to Johns Island South Carolina by train, she had Easter Egg Hunts in her apartment, she let me comb and roll up her hair with those wire leather rollers, and Sissie also let me play with her pop pearl beads that I still have today. I wanted Sissie to see me graduate from college. This was probably my closest family member's funeral, and I was an emotional mess; with full-blown crying, hollering, and screaming. To add to the misery Sissie was funeralized in her church First Bethel AME Church on 132nd Street in the Village of Harlem and then we traveled to South Carolina for a second funeral and then buried at her home church, in our families' cemetery behind the church, on Johns Island at St. Stephens AME Church in South Carolina.

I lost my paternal grandfather Reverend Martin Burns in 1971 when I was 14 years old. I thought that my grandfather was so old, but he was only 78 years old when he passed. My paternal grandmother lived eight years after her husband's death. My paternal grandmother Carrie Burns went home to be with the Lord in 1979 on October 30th at age 84 when I was 22 years old. My paternal grandfather died before Sissie and my paternal grandmother after Sissie. My maternal grandfather passed away when my mother was a child. I lost both of my grandmothers a little more than one year apart. Both of my parents lost their mothers almost a year apart. I remember my grandmother Carrie giving me words of comfort when Sissie died because I was taking it so hard. The two losses of my paternal grandparents were different. I loved both of them and would miss them, but I would only see my grandparents once a year at the end of the summer and in my young mind I thought that they were old and sickly. What was interesting, I thought they were sickly because they had so many medications to take. Now I look at my shoe box full of medications and supplements and I think about my grandparents. The ache of the loss of my grandparents was more of my feeling my father's pain of losing his father and then his mother than me losing granddaddy and grandma. It was probably like that feeling that my father must have felt every time it was time to get back on the road to come back home after spending two weeks with his parents every August but heighten because you will not talk to them throughout the year or see them anymore each summer. I now know that losing your parents changes your life forever. I also felt for my aunts, uncles, and my South Carolina cousins for their loss. I did not realize how much I would miss my grandparents and our visits until they were gone. After my grandparents were gone the visits became very infrequent. We went down mostly for funerals, but we did go down for two family reunions. We went to one family reunion on each side of the family with the promise that we would do better with communicating and visiting.

I have witnessed the loss of loved ones; both my parents, my only brother, grandparents, aunts, uncles, cousins, my father-in-law-to-be and in-laws, my oldest niece, friends, friends' relatives, and coworkers. I experienced these losses and I strongly both sympathized and empathized with those who were more closely personally affected by the deaths especially if it was their parent(s), sibling(s), spouse, and/or their children. It broke and still breaks my heart that my now husband lost his father at age twenty-two and his mother at age thirty-five. My husband's mother was his world. My husband talked to his mother every day even when we moved to New Jersey. He visited her in Washington, D.C. as often as he could. You do not realize that you still need parenting in your twenties and thirties until either your parents are gone, or you are parenting your own twenty-something and thirty-something young adult children.

I believe that God orchestrated that I moved back home right before my mother lost her only sister Auntie, my aunt, and my Godmother, Thelma Moten. This was another notification that I cannot forget. My mother was at work when my father came to her school to inform her of her sister's death. I was in my classroom when my parents came to my school to inform me that my aunt was gone. If you have someone who is like a second mother to you, you will understand how I felt about this loss. We used to tease my mother and aunt that they were like Siamese twins. When you saw one you saw the other. They did everything together. This loss was more disconcerting to me for my mother than my mother losing her mother. When my mother lost Sissie I knew that she had her sister, Auntie. But when she lost Auntie I felt as though she lost half of her. My Aunt/my Godmother always contributed to my brattiness. When my parents said no, I would go to Auntie, who I cannot remember her ever saying no to me. My cousin Donnajean was pregnant when her mother passed which is devastating in itself. Auntie was scheduled to be moved to hospice the next day because of cancer but God took her home instead.

My next life-altering loss was in 1990 when my father was taken from us. I am a daddy's girl! It took me a long time for me to forgive God for taking my father. I will always feel the hole of my father not being with us. My heart broke for my mother because to me she lost the three most important adults in her life; her mother, her sister/best friend, and now her husband. Although my mother had a plethora of friends it seemed as though she had no one left. My father was sick from July 1989 to March 1990, and I was always with him as well as the rest of my family being by his bedside. But the one time I was convinced to go to Washington, D.C. with my husband and children for the weekend, I was the last one to kiss my father good night the day before I left. As soon as I got to my mother-in-law's house the call came in informing me that my father is gone. I was convinced that my father would not have let go if I was not away. I also realize now that I was being selfish wanting him to live as a shell of himself after an unsuccessful brain aneurysm surgery. I remember right before my father went for his surgery (that he contemplated not having), he told everyone else in our family that he loved them but with me, he told me to be good. My parents know me so well. It took me years to rectify with God.

Ten years later, in 2000, when I lost my only brother, I think that I was and still am numbed with unbelief. It was the Saturday after Thanksgiving. We were all together on Thanksgiving and my brother and I had our first disagreement that I can remember as adults that day. I was home when the phone call came in saying that my brother was in a car accident in the Poconos. My husband drove my children and me to my mother's house to be with my mother while Willie and my two sisters Sharon and Shelley went to investigate and bring my brother back home. We figured that his car was probably totaled, and he needed a ride home. My thinking was that my brother has always been daring; trying to run to Washington, D.C. with our dog Dinogetta to visit me at Howard University, riding his motorcycle to South Carolina to see family members, falling off his motorcycle on his way to his own wedding at a campground in Ellenville, New York, or flying to places like Arizona to camp-out, ride his bicycle, and/or run. This accident in his van will be just another story to add to his adventuresome resume. But the gut-wrenching unimaginable call was that my brother was gone. Leaving a wife and five children at age forty-five. My brother left us! Again, I say my heart breaks for his family. My brother loved his family. He was a great son, brother, husband, father, and uncle. After having four sons which my brother cherished, he finally had his baby girl. My brother shared the middle place in the family with me and was a partner in mischief and dance. RIPower my brother!

This next loss is the reason for this chapter being suggested. My mother is the true matriarch of our family. Mother of four, grandmother of ten, at the time of her death seven great-grandchildren, two sons-in-law, two daughters-in-law, a stepmother to Louise, four-granddaughters-in-laws, and beloved Godmother and second mother to Donnajean as well as an aunt, and grand-aunt to many nieces, nephews, grand-nieces, and grand-nephews. Also, many lifelong friends, "the group", Delta Sigma Theta, Inc. sorority sisters, and her Bethel family. My mother is my everything! I thought that this was just a metaphor but my heart literally broke when my mother went home to be with the Lord. I thought that I was ready for her death until she died. My mother was ninety years old with congested heart failure and dementia. Her cardiologist told us for years that it would not be long as he was amazed each visit that she was still with us; weak but as witty as ever. The last two hospital visits left her with bed sores that would not heal. We thank God that my mother was financially sufficient and we were able to hire an amazing caregiver and her niece to take care of my mother during the day while loving family members took turns in the evenings to feed her, give her night medication and get her ready for bed. My mother lived with Shelley and Soqui for the last six months of her life when she was not in the hospital. They both gave up their lives to care for our mother. I thank God for them and the other caregivers. My mother always said that she was God's favorite and it was evident in the caregiving that she received. My mother was definitely rewarded because she poured out so much love in her lifetime. This is truly hand-go-hand come.

I feel as though we definitely gave my mother her flowers while she was with us, but it can never measure up to how much she poured into each one of us. We probably spent every Mother's Day with her as a family as well as celebrating her birthdays with her in some way. We continued to celebrate the recognition of her union on August 22nd even after my father's passing. We had a tribute for her at her church for one of her birthdays. We celebrated another birthday by renting out Sylvia's 2 in the Village of Harlem. We even celebrated her half-birthday on July 14, 2017, when she turned 89.5. Once again, we celebrated her 90th Birthday at Sylvia's Restaurant because she and the legendary Sylvia knew each other and grew up together in The Village of Harlem.

I already mentioned that my mother always proclaimed to be "God's favorite" and she was blessed abundantly. Wednesdays was her designated "Be Good To Loni Day", My mother went home to be with the Lord on Wednesday, March 21, 2018. Because she is definitely God's favorite there was a snowstorm, and the schools were closed; even New York City Schools which rarely closes, were closed. Shelley and Soqui could not go to work. My mother's morning home attendant and now family friend, Movelette, could not make it to my mother because of the weather. It was like my mother orchestrated that her family would be around her as she transitioned. Because of the slick icy roads, it took Benta's Funeral Home several hours to get from the Village of Harlem to Yonkers, New York, which gave us as a family time to be at her bedside, as Alexa played Mahalia Jackson's gospel songs, and we said our farewells. Fridays have always been family Fridays with fried fish, red rice, potato salad, and collard greens. My former neighbor Mamie Gailes catered for my mother's half birthday, and she also catered our traditional family Friday meal for my mother's wake after her Homegoing Service on this Good Friday. Yes, God's Favorite was funeralized on one of the holiest of days on our Christian calendar in her church since childhood First African Methodist Episcopal Bethel Church by her beloved Pastor Reverend Henry Allen Belin III. Good Friday is as recognizable as Resurrection Sunday which took place in two days and Christmas. My mother was laid to rest on the following day at Calverton National Cemetery next to my father in Long Island.

My mother being gone has indescribably affected every member of our family and everyone that has known and loved her. My mother had close personal relationships with every family member and her friends individually and collectively. She has a unique bond with each of her children, her grand

and great grandchildren, her daughters-in-law, and her sons-in-law. It should be in-love instead of in-law! She took on the mothering role for my husband when he lost his mother. In fact, she would take my husband's side over mine because she would say "I know my daughter" and she did, probably better than I knew myself.

My mother was my mother, my forever friend, my confidant, and my role model. Her words of wisdom are still guiding me every day of my life. A former co-worker of mine who is a school psychologist explained to me that losing my mother at age sixty-one is harder than a child losing their mother because I had my mother through every phase of my life. When I testified in church based on a post that I read that "my mother taught me everything except how to live without her." Deacon Willie B. Thornton, my sister-friend and my mother's Soror, said that I am not living without my mother because she is in me. That has brought me comfort because now I see my mother when I look in the mirror sometimes. I hear my mother when I or someone else is quoting one of her many sayings. Sharon, Shelley, and I are starting to look more and more alike, and we are starting to look just like our mother. Shelley looks, walks, stands, acts, and often sounds just like our mother. I feel my mother as I now cook thanksgiving dinner. Her presence was with me when I visited Central State University in Xenia, Ohio in October 2019 and when I stepped foot on the grounds of Pine Ridge, South Dakota in September 2021. So as much as I miss her physical presence, my mother is always with me, and I feel her spiritual presence. I thank God for such a mother! Rest In Power Ma-ee!!!

For those of you who are grieving any type of loss and are having difficulty moving on, I pray that you allow, yes allow, God, to give you the needed strength each day. I pray that there are good memories that will bring you joy. If there are not-so-good memories, I pray that you will be led toward an understanding of why you were impacted, and that you will find forgiveness in your heart if forgiveness is also needed. I also pray that you seek and find help that will assist you through this difficult time. In Jesus' Name, I Pray!

20

Stigmas

Why is being different frowned upon, instead of embraced in our society?

I started thinking about the aftermath, after two years out from COVID-19, not saying that it is over but that we are recovering. Because of this recovery stage, I had to add a chapter on mental health. This chapter is titled Stigmas because I pray that we will continue to advance in removing the stigma of mental health. We do not know all the various symptoms and effects of Long COVID-19. We do not even know all of the countless effects of the pandemic on each person's psyche, especially our children and our babies born near or during the pandemic. Thinking about isolation alone can have a long-term impact on those of all ages but especially babies, young people, and our senior population. I have been an outspoken advocate for therapy before 2020. Now I believe that therapy is a must for all children, adults, and couples even if we just start with a mental wellness check. Do not use the excuse that you cannot find a good therapist or that you cannot afford one. We make other things that we need or want possible so make this need possible.

Unfortunately, we will refer people to every one of our extraordinary medical doctors and dentists, but we have difficulty admitting that we have a therapist. I must admit that it may be difficult to find a therapist of color in your area, but now sessions can be done virtually. Also, mental health care is being made more affordable and accessible.

It's a shame, even today that so many cultures feel that mental health help is taboo. When we look at what is taught in the culture of people of color; African American, Hispanic, Caribbean and I must add the African communities it confirms the recent commercial by BetterHelp saying that it is alright to ask for help and the person's response was "you don't know my family." Cultures and genders too are often taught to push-through, man-up…

Often Christians struggle with feeling that seeking help from a specialist for mental or emotional help can be considered a lack of faith, we are so often told to "pray about it". I agree, we need to pray for a good therapist that fits you. Every part of our body can be in need of professional help. No one questions you about going to a cardiologist or a podiatrist. Why is going to a therapist any different? I want to have a therapist be part of our everyday life. Let it be chic to say in everyday life "my therapist said. . ." I know I do it all the time because it is in my nature to share information that might help someone else. Everyday stress, whether because of work, school, parenting, or just navigating life can cause many physical ailments as well as mental disorders. Many of us have buried childhood trauma that have affected us also. The pandemic has caused many stressful moments. Other mental and physical conditions have come to the forefront such as depression, anxiety, fear, loneliness, sadness, bereavement, post-traumatic conditions, and now adjustment disorder.

During my seminary days, I felt the need for a therapist for balance. It was strongly suggested that all clergy have a therapist. If you are truly connected to your congregation as clergy; empathizing and sympathizing with other's journeys, struggles, and even accepting their blessings, you need a therapist for your own outlet even while praying. I probably needed a therapist while growing up as a middle child (any birth order but I have this middle child hang up), a therapist while raising my children, or even a therapist while going through undergraduate and graduate school. I know that I need, and I am seeking an older, probably male, experienced, Black, marriage therapist.

I already mentioned how my current therapist is helping me with my OCD = obsessive-compulsive-disorder tendencies, my obsessive needs for completion, my ADHD = attention-deficit-hyperactivity-disorder, being (self-imposed) overwhelmed, and the need for balance, as well as anxiety, depression, my relationships with others, and life itself. I will say it again and again no matter who you are it is okay to ask for and to get help.

I usually think about stigmas in terms of mental health, but recently I thought about colorism. The definition of stigma is a mark of disgrace associated with a particular circumstance, quality, or person. I realized through listening to the book by Ibram X. Kendi 'How To Be An Antiracist', that we are all racist. We all possess subliminal and/or overt pre-judgements of people and things. I am learning more and more about colorism and classism in different cultures from friends from Puerto Rico, Cuba, Haiti, Dominican Republic, and Jamaica, but my point of reference is my own African American community. I just saw a Disney Jr Cartoon "Rise Up Sing Out" with animated children about micro aggression that included the darker and lighter skinned micro aggression and also the touching of Black hair (which is a definite no-no). Racism and biases are also stigmas. We each unfortunately have our own perception of a certain race of people and groups of people and we tend to generalize these groups. I will leave it at that with the hopes that we will self-examine ourselves.

I know that I personally tend to live in a self-imposed bubble but for this book, I am trying to look at the outside world. With that said, I struggle with the acceptance of racial slurs and what I consider negative descriptions of people and maybe things. I still cringe when I hear the "N-word" in both adults whom I feel should know better and our young people who should have been taught to know better (not to mention from people of other races). To me, it seems as though our young people are eradicating its negativity through their music and talk. I am learning to desensitize (trying to) myself as this new society who is making changes to how we view the word but I still need them (all of them) to know its ugly history. It might seem that I digressed again, but words too are also stigmas.

I have to include in this section that I have been blessed with a father who always told me of my beauty. I pray that we all have someone to help build our own self-confidence. I am a very dark woman with natural hair that I now keep cut short and colored (listen to India Arie's song "I Am Not My Hair") I was never my hair – I guess like India Arie sang in her song; my hair is part of my creativity. With that being said I must also add that I always lighted parts or all of my hair. My hair being colored is not to hide gray hair because I seem to be a late bloomer with graying, but it is to highlight my skin tones. I went through life being called all types of negative dark-skinned names in school and in my Bronx neighborhood. My last name Burns added to my torment. I was also teased about wearing thick glasses and having a flat nose. I had and still have a postnasal drip and seasonal allergies that often caused me to be called booger nose. So-called peers can be so unkind because now that I think about the name calling was mostly from who I thought was my closest male friend growing up. He also teased my younger sister Shelley. I also thought that I was overweight until I went away to school and there were so many people at college from everywhere that were my size or larger. I loced and had locs in my hair as a teacher before it became fashionable. Looking at Hair Tales right now on Hulu it reminds me that a fellow teacher who also had locs, said that I will never be accepted or move up the ladder with my Afrocentric style of clothing and my hair in locs. I did become a school administrator and prayerfully a role model for others who looked like me and for those who did not want to fit in the societal box. I have witnessed the acceptance and successes of my lighter-skinned sisters in brothers. It is obvious in our historical success stories that the lightest people of color were more acceptable to the Caucasian workforce and even our historically Black colleges. The Paper Bag Test is not a myth (please visit the African American Museum in Washington, D.C.). My mother who grew up in the Village of Harlem, New York said that she did not experience racism until she went to a Historical Black College in the early 50s. My mother was too dark to even consider participating in the paper bag test. It was my father, who was a tailor, who convinced my mother that she did not have to wear dark clothing, That bright colors enhance her skin tones, that she probably did not know she had. I thank God that changed when I too went to a Historical Black College in the mid-70s where the name-calling that I received in the Bronx, New York was embraced. I relished the name 'Chocolate' as I strutted across Howard University's campus in my dark skin and my fro. I feel as though society is slowly changing, I am reluctant to say in our community, as well as other communities. We are now seeing beauty in the blackest of our brothers as well as now our sisters. There was a time that you would hear that you are cute for a dark girl (which is the same thing that was said for my next stigma case). We are now seeing people of all shades of the spectrum being represented, embraced, and celebrated just about everywhere we look and slowly in the minds of others, even of the same race. I must also include the acceptance of natural hair.

Sizes have been a stigma for so many years when certain communities used to embrace the voluptuousness of their women. I love that now we see full-size models on runways, the manikins in stores, and in magazines as well as full-size performers and actresses in various roles including romantic characters and not just housekeepers.

I cannot end this chapter on stigmas without including the LGBTQIA2S+ = lesbian, gay, bisexual, transgender, queer and/or questioning, intersex, asexual, and two-spirit community. It is so important that we accept all people for who they are, including our government with equality, and our Christian community with love. I gave students from this community in both my elementary schools and middle schools a safe haven with a listening ear, and acceptance when I was an administrator. In addition to friendships without judgement, all my life. The acceptance of this community of people has continued to widen publicly, but I pray that the acceptance of this and all people will continue to expand for all externally and internally. God knows our hearts!

21

Next

As I bring this book to an end, "God willing, and the creek don't rise," taken from Deacon Leary Puryear. I would have been to all 50 states and the eastern and western parts of Canada. As of August 2022, this has come true. TGBTG - To God Be the Glory!!!

I am surprised and not surprised about how I feel now that I have accomplished what I consider a huge feat. I guess it is called mixed emotions. Now that it is done, I feel like I did after preparing and getting married, finishing seminary, being ordained. . . I feel now what? It is like preparing for or anticipating an event and when it is over (at least for me) I feel like it is time to prepare for my next. To me, it is like with all the preparation and buying of Christmas presents then watching the receivers open their gifts with excitement and maybe in less than an hour later there is this sense of deflation going back to normalcy.

Now I am getting photo memories reminders from Google of our fall 2020 and fall 2021 cross-country RV road trips that have me wondering, other than financially if I am ready for a do-over.

My next is first, to stop spending every waken moment and sometimes in my dreams thinking about this book with changes and more content to add to specific chapters when thoughts occur.

Before I get into travel, I have personal next:

- Always to improve my relationship with God, to serve and to be used for God's people.
- Maintain my weight at 165-170 pounds and strengthen my core through the gym and yoga, and now the balance board. Continue walks, weights for strength, and yoga to improve my flexibility and balance. I might as well throw in a flattened stomach and firm triceps.
- Continue to improve my mind and memory by still being active, mindful, and relaxed.
- #Her2ndStitch – whatever is needed to keep it profitable without stress.
- Let me throw in home improvements including open concept modernization, renovating our kitchen, and installing an outdoor kitchen.
- This should be done if you are reading this book – but finish this book and God willing sell more than I can ask or think an unexpected number of copies of Completion with rave reviews but more importantly that this book will help many somebodies.
- Write a second book with beautiful pictures of my visits to the six continents.
- I have to include a 5K do over but this time with better weather – Tasha I am ready!

I do not have a bucket list because to me it means that there are things that I need to or want to do before kicking the bucket. My outlook on life is that I thank God for each and every day because tomorrow is not promised to any one of us, so with this day that God has blessed me with there are some things that I want to do and places that I want to see all to the glory of God.

I have been ziplining in the Poconos, Costa Rica, and in Honduras. I did I-Fly on Norwegian Cruise Line on my way to Bermuda. Now I want to go skydiving. I want to ride in a helicopter over a scenic area during my travels. I am mentally debating if I want to fly in a hot air balloon. My daughter wants to ride an elephant in Thailand, but we are now aware of its cruelty and will visit an elephant sanctuary, so I am ready for that too.

My travel Next will be first, to visit the other six continents, even though some revisits of states and parts of Canada will happen while planning my continental visits.

- Europe in June 2023 with my sisters Sharon and Shelley and South America in August 2023 with my husband as we celebrate 43 years of marriage. Both trips have already been booked
- The only two states that I have never spent the night in are Iowa and New Hampshire so I will be doing a getaway to New Hampshire and maybe another RV trip that includes an overnight stay in Iowa, if not a flight to Iowa might be more doable.
- I need to revisit South Carolina and Georgia; even though we went through these two states on the way to Florida, I have not spent the night in either place in years. So, in addition to Hawaii, I have these four states to revisit also.
- In 2024, I plan to go to Asia with my daughter to celebrate her doctorate.
- In 2025, I plan to go to Africa. My plan was to go to West Africa to Ghana and Senegal first, but my sister Shelley wants to go on a safari in East Africa. I am not planning on visiting all 54 countries of Africa, but I do want to eventually visit all parts (west, south, east, north, as well as some of the inner countries) of Africa so I will wait for opportunities to arise.

- My granddaughter Jayla informed me that she is graduating high school in 2026, since I plan to go to Australia in 2026, I can take her too. My granddaughters have been to 34 states with me and their Big Daddy aka grandfather, and Alabama without us, they also went to Nova Scotia, New Brunswick, Quebec, Montreal, Toronto, and Niagara Falls, Canada with us too. Jayla went to Italy with her school during Holy Week in the spring of 2022 and will go again with her school to Greece in the fall of 2023.

- My plan is to end the travels to continents with Antarctica in 2027 to celebrate my 70th year that God has allowed me to be on the land of the living. You are welcome to join me!

- I will continue to take advantage of every opportunity to travel to different parts of the United States.

- I want to go back to Nova Scotia, to Halifax, Nova Scotia to visit the Black Loyalist Heritage Centre. This time I am considering going by cruise ship with my grands.

- There are some states that I would not mind returning to in order to spend time in these cities:
    - Charleston and Johns Island, South Carolina – with my children and grandchildren as a reminder of their roots.
    - Houston, Texas - Because of the show Top Chef, I want to experience Houston Texas' delicious cuisines, historic Freedmen's Town, Bethel Church, and Jack Gates.
    - Savannah, Georgia – to see its antebellum architecture and cobblestone streets, the Spanish moss trees like John's Island, and of course shop their boutiques and eat their southern cuisines. I think that I became interested in Savannah after seeing

early episodes of The Housewives of Atlanta in Savannah.

- I like Chicago, Illinois and I would go back.
- I want to go back to Detroit, Michigan – to go inside the Motown Museum this time.
- Probably back to Memphis and Nashville, Tennessee – for the foodie in me.
- I am always ready to go to New Orleans, Louisiana for its scrumptious foods and beignets.
- I also want to spend time in the mountain areas of Colorado and Utah – for the fresh air, scenery, and spiritual energy that you feel like in Sedona, Arizona.
- I am always ready to revisit Sedona, Arizona.
- I would like to go back to Seattle, Washington, and would not mind another West Coast drive from Seattle to at least San Francisco again.
- I would not mind going cross-country to the northern United States again, probably with my grands because Jayla wants to see the big potato in Idaho. Because we went through Route 66 during COVID-19, and a lot of the places were either closed or we did not spend much time there I would do the return trip through Route 66. Which probably means spending the night in Iowa along the way.

- Ebony's Online Magazine post of 10 Black-Owned Hotels throughout the United States is on my list.
- My daughter wants to visit every Historical Black College, so that is also on my to-do list.
- I will (I will not say I want to) visit different countries as opportunities arise. Whatever catches my eye through my travel agent Marcia Morgan, through Reverend Edna Dismus' Englewood New Jersey #3666

AARP, even AAA or other travel groups I will visit other countries.

- I just mentioned to my husband that we should purchase a recreational vehicle at age 71 and travel around the United States and Canada. My concern with this is finding storage for the RV as my husband looks at me side eyed. This adventure will probably be documented in my third book.

In order to travel, I need to be healthy both physically and financially. I will continue to take care of my physical and mental health. Walking, God willing, walking will always be my most enjoyable form of exercise. I will continue with yoga. I will continue working out at the gym through classes and eventually get a trainer. I need to be conscientious about my foodiness (if that is a word). I cannot continue with the up-and-down seesaw weight gains and losses; it will eventually take a toll on my body and my health.

To be financially healthy, I need to be financially diligent with saving and also spending, with no unnecessary purchases or overspending. Jessica Nabongo said that she "always live below her means". I wonder if that is doable for me because I have always lived beyond my means. I will continue to balance and pay off my credit card traveling expenses with no interest fees. I also need to make sure that I am passing on the importance of generational wealth and not passing on the mindset of generational spending and debt.

To stay mentally acute by continuing with mindfulness techniques that I learned through Ramapo College, the Krame Center, and the Rodda Center. Also, continue with my jigsaw puzzles, read, and listen to Audible books, and stitching by continuing to make string-quilted pillows through my business #Her2ndStitch, as well as mental wellness checks by continuing with my therapist Lorna Hines-Cunningham as long as she will have me.

Caregiving is not easy. You do not realize how much someone else does until they are unable to do it anymore and you are doing it in addition to what you usually do. Me as a caregiver with my anal personality turns me into a bigger nag than normal. Being overly concerned while caregiving about medication, nutrition, and drinking water has me forgetting to take my own medication, eat right, drink water, relax, and take care of me too. I am such a scheduled-oriented person, even in retirement, that being off schedule throws my life completely off balance. It is so easy for caregivers not to take care of themselves. My prayers go up for all caregivers as well as those being cared for. With my next, I pray that Willie and I will always be able to care for ourselves. I also realized today after leaving the house after eleven days as a caregiver for my husband after his surgery that as an introvert, I have been forcing myself to leave the house and forcing myself to socialize in small doses. On Sunday mornings, I socialize before and after the church service, on Mondays, Tuesdays, and Fridays I have brief conversations at the gym and on Thursdays I have brief conversations at the Rodda Center. I realized that during these eleven days I was being overwhelmed with talking and texting (I do appreciate the well-wishes, prayers, and concerns for my husband) but I remember during my psychological testing many years ago in Massachusetts, I was told that too many interactions as an introvert will chip away at me. On Sunday, October 30, 2022, I spent six hours, from 9:30am to 3:30pm, in a silent mindfulness virtual retreat. After the retreat, surprisingly, I did not want to jump back into talking, I did not want to turn my phone back on to check for texts or social media posts, and I did not even want to turn on the television or listen to music on Alexa. I remember when we had one black and white television in our dining room when we were living in the projects on Madison Avenue in the Village of Harlem growing up my father used to call the television the idiot box because he thought that watching too much television would turn you into an idiot. I wonder what he would think about all this technology now. I usually have some type of noise all around me, but I unexpectedly appreciated the six hours of silence. Now on that Monday I realized that I was on both an emotional and social overload these last eleven days. I realize in my next that I have to keep a balance with my social interactions because it is so easy for me to go into social isolation when I got out of complete person-to-person social isolation after the 2020 pandemic. Even after a week, I feel no need to turn on the television in the morning as I am getting ready for the gym or turn on the radio on my way to the gym. My only concern is that I am missing out on current events. Even though I am practicing some mindful walking I still feel the need to listen to a book while I am walking and while I am soaking in the tub. I have not listened to music at bedtime in a while. I do not know how long this will last but I am enjoying quiet more now.

Putting God first will always be my priority. If I had 10,000 tongues, I could not thank God enough for what he has done, is doing, and will do in my life and the lives of my loved ones.

My Next is healthy mindful living and more traveling with a second book on my travels!

Loni Always Said

Before I get into what my mother always said as I prepare to travel, I am thinking about some of the things that my mother has passed on to me and that I have passed on to my daughter:

- Right now, I am cleaning my entire house and washing all of my clothes before leaving in the morning for a road trip because my mother taught us that you never know if you will be coming back home.
- A lot of us were taught that your entire home has to be clean and organized, as well as all clothes washed and put away, before the new year comes in. I have moved away from being consistent each New Years Eve with having peas; preferably hoppin' johns (that I have not learn how to make) and greens on the stove for money and luck.
- I am trying to move away from superstitions, but I tend to pick and choose what to keep and what to stop because I will not put a hat on the bed, and I am careful with sweeping near someone's feet.
- There is one thing that I am trying to unlearn, I tend to obsess with being prepared or overly prepared. I packed so many "what ifs" that I always end up over-packing and have things that I never get to wear or use. Even our car is overloaded for road trips with Trader Joe's water and Poland Springs water in addition to the "what ifs". Even though now forgotten or needed items are so accessible these days.
- I was taught to always wear clean and hole-free underwear because you never know if you will have an accident and end up in the hospital. Since retirement and

the pandemic, I have to make sure that I wear underwear when I leave the house.

- My mother has washed her floors on her knees as long as she was physically able. I do wash my bathroom floors on my knees, but I use a mop on my kitchen floor.

My mother, Alonzetta Casandra Moten Burns aka Loni, has so many sayings with some being mentioned in this book. These sayings have been passed down to her family therefore many might be Gullah-based sayings. These sayings are an intricate part of my life and memories, just like everything else in this book. For my mother's 89.5 birthday, we compiled all her almost daily words that we could think of to display at her party. Her birthday is January 14th, but we had the party on July 14, 2018.

My Mother Alonzetta's [ALMOST] Daily WORDS

- Good Better Best, Never Let It Rest, Until Your Good Gets Better, And Your Better Is Best.
- I'm From John's Island South Carolina!
- I grew up in Harlem! (Do not mess with me!).
- Do you know how I got my name?
- I am God's Favorite!
- I will talk to My Father Who Art In Heaven.
- I will talk to My Father Who Art In Heaven, He will Never Leave Me or Forsake Me!

- When I grow up, I am going to be a doctor because teaching did not work out (whenever someone is telling her what to do).
- You can be good but do not be 'good for nothing' (when she asks you how you're doing, and you answer good).
- Pray for me and I will pray for you (when she feels like you are being impatient with her).
- Keep me in your prayers (when she feels down or frustrated).
- Help Yourself and The Good Lord will Help Me (When you tell her you want to help her).
- Do not Start No SH there will not be no IT!
- I was born during the Depression (she will not waste food).
- Some of my friends only do snail mail (do not email).
- I check my email every day.
- I'm on a 'Seefood' Diet I See Food and Eat It.
- I'm Still Trucking (When you ask her how she is doing).
- I'm going to Chicago; Sorry I cannot take you.
- I'm going to Jamaica; Sorry I cannot take you.
- You look familiar…Are you Aunt Meilia?
- Can I get on your back? (When she does not want to walk).
- Is the elevator working? or Where's the elevator? (When she does not want to walk up steps).
- My son (Willie) makes sure I always have sodas.
- I do not think anyone makes red rice anymore.
- Did you join the club? (retirement) It's a good club to be in.
- Do you think I am R-A-T Fool? (She got that from her grandmother).
- Do you think senior citizens aren't wrapped too tight?

- Do you think I was born yesterday?
- No Speaka-De-Deutsch (when she's pretending, she does not understand you).
- Do not let me put you over my knees! (Like she can withstand any of our weight).
- I do not take any tea for the fever.
- Do not let the doorknob hit you where the good Lord split you (time to go).
- I am going to start locking my door (when Shelley wakes her for morning meds).
- There's one minister that called me Alanzetta (Mary Moragne would correct him), he would say "like I was saying Alanzetta. . ." (Reverend Mackey).
- Go to hell and freeze up.
- I'm fighting a headache and shortness of breath (when we try to get her to do something - like get out of bed or stopping her from going to bed).
- I'm a walker! (She was).
- I remember Julius used to say wait up, I am going your way (Because she used to walk so fast).
- Do not claim it! (When you are complaining about an ailment).
- Tell the devil he's A Liar!
- I know my body (when we try to get her to get up and do something).
- Listen to your body (Great advice!).
- Different Strokes For Different Folks.
- Give me 5 more minutes (do not want to get out of bed).
- Sprite no ice, Please (Ma's Drink of Choice).
- Do you have any Vodka and Orange Juice?
- After working with children all day, I had to have vodka and orange juice to deal with Julius' children.

- "We got our son, we got our son," Your father told me when Julius was born like I did not know.
- I'm not going back to Harlem Hospital after these first two.
- Is that my GG? (When she hears any child).
- Guess who's back? (As she pats your back).
- You have a great future behind you (As you walk away).
- Lordy Claudie Big and Forty She has enough for .
- When I was growing up there was a lady who used to say wait up – let me get a ride (Because she was skinny with a big behind).
- Do you want me to knock you down and tell you where to fall?
- I shop until I drop (That was on Be Good to Loni Days).
- To bed to bed said Sleepyhead...wait awhile said Slow...put on the pot said Greedy Gut - let sup before we go.
- Oh, say can you see there's a bedbug on you.
- Around the corner, and under a tree, a Sargent Major said to me, who will marry you, I would like to know because every time I look at your face it makes me want to go around the corner. . .

We (the entire family) will say Ma, Ma-ee, Grandma, GG, or Auntie would say. . . Her words are ingrained in us all!

My Travels

	2019	2020
New Jersey New York Maryland Virginia North Carolina		
January		18. New Orleans, Louisiana 18th -22nd Willie, J & Denetra 19. Mobile, Alabama 16th Willie 20. Biloxi, Mississippi 17th Willie
March	6. Indianapolis. Indiana 23rd -27th Shené	
April	7. Knoxville, Tennessee 18th -19th Willie, Dasaiah, Jayla & Darby 8. Mashantucket, Connecticut 29th Willie 9. Newport, Rhode Island 30th	
May		

2021	2022
	Panama Canal Cruise Holland American 16th -30th Ft. Lauderdale, Florida 14th -16th Willie, Shelley, Shamanie & J Cruise: 21st Panama 23rd Costa Rico 25th Huatulco, Mexico 27th Puerto Vallarta, Mexico Willie, Shelley & J San Diego, California 30th -1st Willie, Shelley & J
32. Seattle, Washington 16th -18th 33. Portland, Oregon 18th -20th Yreka, California 20th -21st San Francisco, California Willie 21st -23rd Los Angeles, California Willie, Shené & Dasaiah 23rd -29th	48. Bethany Beach, Delaware 7th -10th Shené

New Jersey New York Maryland Virginia North Carolina	2019	2020
June		
July	10. Massachusetts 15th -19th Willie (AARP) 11. Jeffersonville, Vermont 28th -4th 12. New Hampshire 31st 13. Booth Bay, Maine 31st -1st Willie, Dasaiah, Jayla & Darby	
August		

2021	2022
North Carolina 12th -22nd Willie 34. Charleston, West Virginia 23rd -24th 35. Central City, Kentucky 24th -25th 36. Hot Springs, Arkansas 25th -1st Willie, Jayla & Darby	
Nashville, Tennessee 1st -2nd Knoxville, Tennessee 2nd -3rd	Bangor, Maine 17th-19th Moncton New Brunswick Canada 19th-20th Margaree, Nova Scotia, Canada 20th-24th Willie, Jayla, Darby, Shelley, Soqui, Szymon, Shavon Jabari Fredericton New Brunswick 24h-25th Quebec, Canada 25th – 27th Montreal, Canada 27th-29th Toronto, Canada 29th – 31st Niagara Falls, Canada 31st – 2nd Willie, Jayla, Darby, Shelley, Soqui & Szymon
	49. Alaska 20th-27th Princess Cruise Line Royal Princess 20th Vancouver, Canada 22nd Ketchikan, Alaska 23rd Juneau, Alaska 24th Skagway, Alaska 27th Whittier, Alaska Willie

	2019	2020
New Jersey New York Maryland Virginia North Carolina		
September		Route 66 RV Trip September 23rd - October 7th 21. Chicago, Illinois 23rd -25th 22. Eureka, Missouri 25th 23. Oklahoma City, Oklahoma 26th 24. Canyon, Texas 27th 25. Tucumcari, New Mexico 28th 26. Holbrook, Arizona 29th 27. Encino, California 30th -1st 28. Verdi, Nevada 2nd 29. Salt Lake City, Utah 3rd 30. Cheyenne, Wyoming 4th 31. Gretna, Nebraska 5th Granger, Indiana 6th Willie, Shelley, Jayla, Darby& Szymon

2021	2022
Northern United States RV Trip September 14th -30th 37. Mercer, PA 14th -15th 38. Covert, Michigan 15th -16th 39. Milton, Wisconsin 16th -17th 40. Jackson, Minnesota 17th -18th 41. Jackson, South Dakota 18th -19th 42. Pine Ridge, South Dakota 19th -20th 43. Bismarck, North Dakota 20th -21st 44. Billings, Montana 21st -22nd 45. Pocatello, Idaho 22nd -23rd Fillmore, Utah 23rd -24th 46. Glenwood, Colorado 24th -25th Denver, Colorado 25th -26th 47. Salina. Kansas 26th -27th Oak Grove, Missouri 27th -28th Rock Island, Illinois 28th -29th Toledo, Ohio 29th -30th Willie	

New Jersey New York Maryland Virginia North Carolina	2019	2020
October	14. Xenia, Ohio 11th -13th Shené & Dasaiah	
November	15. South Carolina 16. Georgia 17. Kissimmee, Florida 26th -30th Willie, J, Denetra, Dasaiah, Jayla, Darby, Shelley, Soqui, Shavon, Shamanie & Szymon	

2021	2022

Acknowledgments

So many people need to be acknowledged for their contributions to this leg of my journey, so I will generalize some of my acknowledgments with the prayer that I do not forget anyone, and I pray that you know who you are:

I acknowledge and honor Jesus Christ my Lord and Savior for my daily blessings, as well as the blessings of my past, present, and future.

I am truly blessed with an amazing family. My family continues to encourage each other, where the word 'can't' cannot be a part of our vocabulary or thinking. Because of you, I know that everything is doable.

God has blessed me with a husband, Willie Curlee Owens, with 42 years of marriage, who is everything that I am not. We complete each other. Because of God and the village that God placed in our lives, we have two incredible young adult offsprings who are perfect examples of Philippians 4:13; "You can do all things through Christ which strengthens you." They have accomplished more than we can possibly ask or think: my son Willie J. Curlee Owens, whom we call J., and my daughter Shené Vivetta Owens. They have both gone beyond their parents' ceiling and have exceeded our high expectations.

I thank God and all of my family for their love, encouragement, and adjustments as I complete myself.

My sisters: Sharon, and Shelley, and my oldest sister Louise, not only tolerated me for as long as they have known me, but they support all my hair-brain ideas and plans. God has

337

also blessed me through my son with a wonderful daughter-in-law Denetra, and three amazing grandchildren: Dasaiah (20), Jayla (14), and Darby (9).

Marion Elizabeth Watkins (Rest in Power), whose conversation about her visiting 48 states sparked the possibility in me. She changed my life and the lives of those who took the treks with me

My Small Circles of Friends

My friend Rosemary Dunham planted the seed for me to write this book.

Gena Miller, my former neighbor. Because of Gena, there are pictures of my travels in this book.

Henri Bryan Stamps for being that free spirit that inspires me. Bryan is always that sounding board that helped to make my dreams, (some that I did not even know I had) a reality. Because of Bryan, there is no place that I cannot visit. Because of Bryan starting a business became doable.

I have to thank Shelley, Bryan, Willie J, Denetra, my niece Ashley, my nephew-in-law-to-be Gus, and even the rightful owner Shené for taking care of our grand dog, JerZey while we traveled.

I also need to thank those friends who transport us, no matter how early or how late, to and from airports and cruise ports; John and Winfield Mayo and now Anthony and (if needed) his brother Tyrone McKivor.

My church family, First Baptist Church of Teaneck who continues to be what I need when I need it

The Quilters at the Rodda Center

Janelle Malone Janelle of quiltsandmorebyjanelle was the first to suggest that I sell pillows.

Lisa Shepherd of Cultured Expressions in Rahway, New Jersey, who taught me how to do string quilting and is the small business consultant for my business #Her2ndStitch.

Gina Asante of African Heritage Fashions who sells #Her2ndStitch pillows and also was the second person to suggest the selling of pillows.

My gym buddies and instructors before and after 2020

Martin Bland, a Yogi and my Yoga Instructor

My forever Yoga Buddies

Black Authors Network encouraged me to get here.a

Candace Woods of "Prayer, Productivity & Intentional Writing" for your prayers, your ministry, and who got me to get up and write at 6:30 am on Tuesday mornings.

Shavon Evelyn for your assistance with my bio, being my sounding board and encourager

Tileah Alexander thank you for your constant "you got this Mom"

Writers On the Sound for our bimonthly meetings.

Sharon Mosley of Family Folk Tales and your monthly workshops

Tileah for the initial readings of chapters in my manuscript

Literary Consultant Marita Golden

Ashley Scarboro, for the initial editing of my proposal and your encouragement

Andrea Ceasar for your input on my proposal and connecting me with Peggy Hurley

Peggy Hurley for her encouragement as she edited my proposal.

Athena C. Shack, MDiv CEO/Publisher of Watersprings Media House, LLC

Viva Arte Fotografia in Natal, Brazil for the author bio photo.

Danielle Wilson make-up extraordinaire

Amazing Photographers Danielle Hadnott and Chad Houston of Noir Photography Studios for photo shoot and picture on the back cover

Last but definitely not least, my extraordinarily talented illustrator, Mayanthi Jayawardena of Serendib Creative in Durham, North Carolina, said yes when Completion was only a notion.

Those who took the time to read Completion before it became a book and those who are reading it now.

Author Bio

SHEILA R. BURNS-OWENS, since retiring, has been to all of 50 United States of America in the last three years with her travel companion, driver, and life partner, Willie C. Owens. Sheila is a wife, a mother, a grandmother, an ordained minister, and a retired educa- tor. She started a small busi-  ness after retirement in addition to traveling. Her travels included driving the Historic Route 66 expedition to fourteen states in an R.V. in September 2020, six months after the pandemic had been declared, with three adults and three children while doing virtual schooling. Sheila also tells how she strategized her visits to the 50 states.

Sheila was born in New York and spent the first 18 years of her life living in the Village of Harlem and the Bronx before attending Howard University in Washington, D.C. She reminisced about events in her childhood. She is honest throughout the book about her life, her weight loss journey, and her emotional and mental challenges. She has been a Teaneck, New Jersey resident for the last 35 years, a wife of 42 years, a mother of two now adult children, and a grandmother of three grandchildren. Sheila is also an associate minister of the First Baptist Church of Teaneck.

Sheila has been a retired educator of 31 years, since 2015, from two New York school systems: the New York City Board of Education from two Village of Harlem schools and a Southern Westchester County School District.

Since retiring, Sheila is now the creator and owner of #Her2ndStitch. Sheila is diligently working on improving her mental and physical lifestyle through therapy, mindfulness meditation, eating healthier, and exercising regularly, which has resulted in better self-awareness and the loss of 30 pounds. Now Sheila's work is working on Completion. Her completion includes being blessed to be able to travel to all 50 states and parts of eastern and western Canada, sometimes with her grandchildren. Sheila's Next is to travel to the other six continents, as she also includes workouts and improves her living a physically and mentally healthier lifestyle. Sheila is now the author of her first book, Completion, with the prayer that she can help someone along the way of her life journey.

Will we ever be complete on this side of the Jordan?